Born and raised in the Texas Panhandle, Dale A. Morgan moved to Wisconsin as a young woman and still makes it her home. For many years she filled notebooks with memories of her Texas childhood as she taught English to middle schoolers and raised three sons. During that time, she wrote poems for friends, plays for her students, and also taught creative writing to adults. In addition to writing, Dale enjoys spending time with friends and family, taking long walks with her dog, Charlie, and serving as housekeeper for her two cats. She holds a B.A. from Carroll University and an M.E.P.D. in the teaching of writing from the University of Wisconsin, Whitewater.

For J.R.M.W.
And to the THS Class of 1963
With apologies and abiding affection

DALE A. MORGAN

STRING TOO SHORT TO TIE

AUSTIN MACAULEY PUBLISHERS™

LONDON * CAMBRIDGE * NEW YORK * SHARJAH

Ordering Information
Quantity sales: Special discounts are available on quantity purchases by corporations, associations, and others. For details, contact the publisher at the address below.

Publisher's Cataloging-in-Publication data
Morgan, Dale A.
String Too Short to Tie

ISBN 9781649791023 (Paperback)
ISBN 9781649791030 (ePub e-book)

Library of Congress Control Number: 2021912400

www.austinmacauley.com/us

First Published (2021)
Austin Macauley Publishers LLC
40 Wall Street, 33rd Floor, Suite 3302
New York, NY 10005
USA

mail-usa@austinmacauley.com
+1 (646) 5125767

First of all, I want to express my deep appreciation to Kathie Giorgio and all the writers in her outstanding AllWriters' Workplace and Workshop in Waukesha, Wisconsin. Without their honest criticism and compliments, String Too Short to Tie would have died on the vine. I especially want to thank fellow writers and Tuesday night workshop attendees, Adelle Powers, Deb Tetzlaff, Nancy Jorgensen, Susan Martell Huebner, Amy Schneider, and Michael Giorgio. As excellent writers themselves, they shared their wealth of knowledge and experience. Without friend and fellow writer, Barb Geiger, I would never have found AllWriters to begin with. A big thank you for giving me the nudge I needed.

Also thank you to long-time friend, Kathryn Herman, for being my first reader. Her careful attention to detail and encouragement were invaluable. Also, thanks to Jean Bunke for noticing the forest rather than the trees, and to Patricia Reis for her artistic talent and ideas for the book cover design.

Most of all, a thank you to my wonderful family, Troy, Robin, Trey, Dre, Hazel, Michael, Shana, Dean and Avery. Your encouragement and suggestions made all the difference. Your "thumbs up" inspired me and your love sustains me.

Author's Note

String Too Short to Tie is a memoir. It is a true story, in so far as memories are true. Names of people and places are changed to protect privacy, including the name used for the author. And, like all good stories, certain parts may be slightly exaggerated for dramatic effect. Tumbleweed is a fictional name, yet the tumbleweed, or Russian thistle, did arrive on the Texas plains at about the same time as my great-grandparents, detaching from its roots and blowing freely across the plains until it was stopped by cattlemen's barbed wire. It is a fitting for a region that enjoyed giving towns names such as Muleshoe and Happy.

"There are two things that interest me: the relation of people to each other and the relation of people to land."

–Aldo Leopold

Chapter One

Tumbleweed and Prairie

I didn't want to be here. In fact, anywhere would have been better than standing at my mother's sink, looking out the cobwebbed windows. It was July 2013. I was in the farmhouse where I grew up, seven miles from my hometown, Tumbleweed, Texas. This was my fifth trip since January when my brother, Mack, was found dead. Even though I hadn't lived here for 50 years, I was executrix of his estate, and since his death, the trustee for all my family's property, including our farm covering four and one-half sections of land in the Texas Panhandle. My brother lived here for 13 years, and it now fell to me to clean out the house and care for his four dogs who were like his children. If I stood on my toes and peered out the grimy glass, I could see them stretched out in the sun, dozing on the yellowed grass.

I thought back to my first trip here after my brother died. That February day, I was standing in the exact same spot, when I heard the dogs bark as they always did when a truck rumbled into the yard. The dust-caked windows were defeating me as I scrubbed at the panes, so I dropped my cleaning cloth and headed to the backdoor. A big, white, Dodge Ram pickup was pulling in, surrounded by the excited dogs. The man in the driver's seat eased himself out and limped happily toward me. He was older now, more grizzled, with several, odd, assorted teeth in front that broke into a smile of delighted recognition.

"Well, if it isn't Jerry Bob Finch," I said as I met him halfway to the house. I pulled off my rubber gloves and he enfolded my damp hands into his large, rough ones. It was almost 50 years since I last saw him, yet I would have known him anywhere. He was still pudgy with a mischievous twinkle in his eye – the black sheep of the Finch family.

"Dalinda, I'v'a been meanin' to come up and say hello so thought I'd 'a do it while it looked like somebody was out here. So sorry about your brother.

Such a shock." He shook his head and took off his feed cap. "Yep, we heard the siren and then watched them lights a' goin' all night. We was havin' a couple of wedding receptions at the place, ya know, and I says to my wife, I says, 'I think somethin's wrong up to Mihlbauers.' I'll just bet Mack gone and had another seizure. That's what we all thought. Wasn't that what took him?"

"No, it wasn't a seizure. It was a ruptured aorta – right out of the blue. We had no idea there was anything wrong with his heart."

"Well, I'm mighty sorry. He was a good ol' guy. A little different, of course, but always friendly, kind to everyone. It's real sad…"

"We are going to miss him. Come on in, Jerry Bob. I've got fresh coffee in the pot."

"Well now, it's been a while since I seen you, hadn't it? Where is it you live? Up north somewheres, right? Is it Minnesota? Somewheres up there."

"Wisconsin. Near Milwaukee."

"Now, that's pretty near Chicago, right?"

"90 miles north," I said.

"Well, whatever caused you to stay up there in the cold?"

This was always what they asked me, bewildered that I would choose any place other than Hershwin County and shocked I chose any place north of Oklahoma. In fact, once you mentioned any state beyond that, their geography grew a bit hazy.

"Well, that's where my job is…and friends. My kids were born there, so it's home to them."

"My son's been up that direction before. You know he made a lawyer. Yup – started at W.T., then took hisself down to Tech for that law degree. Up in one of those tall office buildings in Amarillo now. Other than that, I got a daughter. My one little girl is cutting her some hair in town. I set her up in her own beauty parlor. Don't know if anybody come in or not. Already got two or three hair cuttin' places in town. Don't know if she'll make it or not. Now if she were to take herself up to Amarillo or down to Lubbock, she could get some real money at them places."

Jerry Bob and his family were among the few wealthy families in the county now. Most of my generation moved away, but the Finch family was solidly planted. In the '60s, Wyatt, Jerry Bob's father, invented an ingenious farm implement and started his own manufacturing company in his barn. Now the family was the largest employer in Hershwin County.

The family was what Mimi used to call 'Four-Square Gospel,' vaguely akin to Mennonite. It was a sect with a strong work ethic whose women of my mother's generation and older did not cut their hair, always wore practical lace-up shoes, and ankle-length dresses. Being a bit of a rebel, Jerry Bob married a short-haired woman from 'outside the faith.' They were good farmers and businesspeople, and now Jerry Bob and his nephew, Skeeter, rented our farmland.

When we were children, my sister and I were invited to spend the day with the Finch girls.

But the rule was that before we were allowed to play, we each had to wash a window. My mother wondered at the time whether washing windows was the reason we received the invitation. Then one year after Christmas, my sister went to play with the youngest daughter, Wynette. "Want to see what I got for Christmas?" Wynette asked my sister. "Look, I'll show you."

Susan, my sister, was led to the top floor of the house, which was built by Wyatt using blueprints for a pole barn. He added walls, bathrooms, miles of carpet, and a huge kitchen containing two of each appliance, plus a huge counter workspace. The upstairs room stretched for at least 20 yards. Standing proudly in the center of the room were five, identical, Hoover vacuum cleaners – one for each of the Finch children, adorned with a bright red Christmas bow.

Jerry Bob slurped his coffee and looked around the house. "Ya'll gonna have someone live here?"

"We have a long way to go before that." I replied. "I'm working on cleaning out four generations of stuff. Mother was a saver, wouldn't ever throw anything out. She even saved all the Christmas bows. We have a box labeled '1953 Xmas Bows,' one for '1954 Xmas Bows,' and so forth through 1990 when they moved to town. Wouldn't let us touch them, until, as she put it, 'She was dead and gone.' We even have things from the great-great grandparents and their relatives. Then there's the dust. It's awful."

"Oh yeah. Been mighty dusty for the past two-three years. No rain. No rain! Used to rain. When we was kids, it rained, remember? Why, I ain't had a decent wheat crop in five years. 'Course, the water's runnin' out too. Hopin' we all don't dry up and blow away."

"We're practically there already..." I murmured under my breath, looking up from my coffee at Joe. "Don't know exactly what we're doing with the house yet. May take years just to clean it out."

13

"Well," he drawled, "whatever you do, don't leave it empty. I got me a little house over there on 23 – have a lady I let live there for free just to keep people from comin' around and shootin' out the windows and all. Can't leave it vacant. It'll just turn to dust."

"About already is," I said, louder than intended.

"Well, I'll keep an eye on things for ya – sure will let you know if I see anything suspicious. How long ya stayin'? 'Course, I can't really see why you'd be a' goin' back up north to that cold."

On days like that, I understood his question. As I walked him back to his pickup, it was warm; even the slanting rays of the winter sun warmed you here. A hawk circled overhead and the dogs dozed again in the warm, dusty patches of grass. The sky was bigger here; the clouds whiter because that's all there was to notice. Skimpy little trees never grew past adolescence before the northeasterly leaning branches were choked dry with blowing dust. Each tree that grew to adulthood had to have been planted, watered regularly, and nurtured faithfully if it was to have a chance. So, you looked up and out. Here, you could imagine that you were the center of the world, the horizon stretching out in a perfect circle; the sky an inverted bowl atop a saucer, with you standing in the center of the dusty grass. A mourning dove cooed in the distance, and if you waited long enough, you could hear the cry of a meadowlark.

Yet, in the blink of an eye, it could all change. The wind would pick up from the north or southwest. With 50-mile per hour gusts could come snow or, more likely, blowing dust which left grit and grime in its wake and, with it, the peaceful day. Many were seduced by the serenity of the bright blue sky, and rotting buildings were a testament to their shattered dreams.

****

My memory of that February day was interrupted by a ringing phone, bringing me back to the present. It was my sister. "So, how ya rollin'?" she asked.

"Okay, I guess. When are you going to be out here?"

"I've got to pick up the kids, and I still haven't had my bath. Maybe this afternoon." As usual, Susan was putting it off.

"Okay," I said, dragging the sponge across the cabinet shelf. "I'm cleaning the kitchen."

"Oh, yuck. Bet you found mouse droppings, right?"

"It's not too bad…" I hesitated. "It's coming along."

I was hoping against hope my sister would offer to come earlier and help me clean, but she replied as usual, "Okay. I'll be out…whenever."

I sighed and looked around. The table was filled with assorted kitchenware: ancient, orphaned lids to pans which were now used to feed the dogs, broken pottery, and cracked glasses interspersed with delicate, cut-glass bowls belonging to my great-grandmother. Cheery red and yellow plastic salt and pepper shakers in the shape of Mexican sombreros stood next to an 'I Love You, Grandpa' coffee mug, or a feed-store cap. I hadn't even started on the pantry where there were jars of canned plums and grape jelly, decades old. Tupperware, old oven racks and flyswatters competed for space on shelves sticky with the residue of old cooking oil.

The bedrooms and living room were worse, packed with odd pieces of furniture, overstuffed chairs, and a trunk belonging to my grandfather's first cousin, a woman whom we called Cousin Jessie, our homeopathic, physician relative. Lovely lace doilies and fine porcelain china were side by side with ragged, smelly, stuffed animals once belonging to one of my niece's nine children.

The rooms and basement were full of books – childhood classics like Black Beauty and The Hardy Boys, plus agronomy textbooks from Iowa State, 1936. There were dozens of Reader's Digest Condensed Books from the 1960s, yearbooks from the 1930s, and seed catalogues from the '50s. My prom dress was there too – waiting for another young woman, safe in its plastic wrap.

I felt like Sisyphus, forever rolling the boulder up the mountain. There was no end to the work.

My sister finally arrived mid-afternoon. As usual, she had several of the grandchildren in tow. Since I couldn't face any more of the pantry cleaning, I started on the boxes stacked in the living room. I'd worked my way through to more glassware, trying to sort what needed to be donated or sold from what was worth saving. "So, what about these glasses?" I asked. "Do you want them?"

"They'll just get broken like everything else." She sniffed.

I persisted, "You could put them in the basement until you get a bigger place."

"And when will that be? Not ever if I have to pay for car insurance." Susan, my sister, slumped down into the only empty chair. Every other surface overflowed with boxes, books, blankets, and china from the dining room. The car insurance for her grandson was our latest disagreement. Susan was in the habit of insisting our family-trust money pay expenses for her daughter and nine grandchildren. I was cast in the role of stingy banker.

I ran a cloth around the inside of a water glass. "We can't afford to let him drive without it. Are you sure you don't want these glasses, because if you don't, I'll put them aside for the estate sale."

"What estate sale?" she snapped back.

"The one we have to have," I replied patiently.

"That's a waste of time. No one will come way out here. Why don't you take the glasses?" Susan put the emphasis on the YOU. She was already irritating me, and she just arrived.

I decided to ignore her tone. "Next time, maybe I'll drive down, then I can. It's just, I hate the long drive."

"This is depressing," she replied, looking around at all the disorder. "Let's go for a walk."

"I don't have much time," I complained, "This needs to be done."

"I don't see why. Let's just leave it," my sister persisted.

"Like this?" I replied with frustration. I was continually amazed that she seemed blind to what was right in front of our eyes.

It was a variation of the same argument we'd had for months now. I wanted to clean out the farmhouse, the home of our childhood, and sell or give away what we didn't want. We could then paint and fix-up the house and rent it out.

To my sister, it seemed to be a shrine to our parents, the grandparents, and the farm; also, to our hometown, and the heyday of The Golden Spread which is what T.V. announcers from Amarillo and Lubbock called it 40 years before. That was when water gushed from 10-inch wells, bringing prosperity to what was part of 'The Great American Desert.'

However, as I was quick to remind her, these shrines to our ancestors had a way of rotting away, collapsing, and weathering under the blistering sun until they faded to gray and gradually disappeared into the earth or blew away with the topsoil. You didn't have to drive very far in any direction to find an abandoned house sinking into the dust, just like Jerry Bob said.

"It will end up just like the McMurry house," I argued, "That's what Mack said to me the week before he died."

"What will?"

"This house. It will be empty, get its windows broken. The mice and rats will take up residence and pretty soon it will smell like death and decay. Its plumbing will be all yellow and pathetic. I can't stand the thought. It will be like Mimi's house. Look what happened to that." I tossed a wrapped glass figurine into the nearest box.

"It'll be fine." Susan started for the door. "The cattle got into Mimi's house; that's what happened to it."

"The cattle and lots of other creatures," I replied.

Susan turned back toward me. "And why would Mack say that?"

"Say what?"

"About this house. Why would he say that?"

I searched for the right word. "Prescience, I suppose."

"What's that?" she asked.

"You know, a premonition."

"Why didn't you just say that?"

"I did," I replied with irritation.

"I need to smoke. I'm going outside." She crawled over the crowded boxes and pushed open the screen door leading to the front porch. After wrapping and packing a few more cups and saucers, I gave up and followed her.

Outside, my sister's grandsons were throwing rocks at a pathetic old tree. They hummed with the unspent energy of adolescence, which erupted into scuffles and profanity. "Hey, when do we get to go into the barn? It's ours now, isn't it? There's a welder there and I want to practice."

The barn was padlocked a few months earlier, which made it even more attractive.

The oldest two boys were 21 and 19 but emotionally much younger. Both managed to graduate from high school, but now their lives seemed at a dead end. The other two, 17 and 15, only attended school when convenient. They all needed direction and jobs, but none had the skills necessary. All four had another chip stacked against them – a father in prison. Their mother, my niece, lived in a house my sister rented for her and some of her nine children. Despite this, Angie, my niece, using manipulation and temper tantrums, acquired both an iPad and a Mustang convertible yet had never held a job. Two of the boys lived with my sister; the other two supposedly lived with their mother, but they ate all their meals at my sister's.

Even Jerry Bob and his nephew who rented our land wouldn't hire them. They already had plenty of hired hands. Besides, according to them, "Those boys would be nothin' but trouble." Fact was that no one from around here would even give them a chance. They had a reputation – or at least their parents did. And in this part of the country, your reputation trumped everything else. It labeled you for life, even if it was an inherited label. On top of this, their father was Mexican, the term used in this part of the country for anyone Latino.

The barn they now wanted to explore was not Grandpa's barn of my childhood, filled with hay, milo, animals, and mysterious farm equipment we didn't understand. It wasn't filled with sweet-smelling hay which we could climb clear to the top where swallows built their nests. Instead, this was the modern pole barn my dad built when his brother inherited the homeplace with its barns and outhouses. It was built of steel and aluminum with a concrete floor.

I unbolted the door and they ran inside, hungry for the mysteries it might hold. But it was disappointing, mainly empty except for a small tractor and a 1938 Buick. There was a welder, some irrigation pipe, and lots of greasy, rusting tools lying about. The oldest went right to the welder standing in the corner.

"Look at this! I can pull it out, clean it up, and practice my welding. I can learn to get a bead on it, Aunt. I can practice so I can get a job."

The other three wandered toward the tractor, pulling themselves up like little boys pretending to drive.

Their grandmother, my sister, came up beside me and was watching them lovingly. "They could never come out here. Never get to see this. Mack wouldn't let them. This is what they want – the freedom to be here, that's all." Her bitterness toward our brother was showing.

"Guess I'll go back in and get to work." I said. "If you don't mind, I guess I'll take the glasses then. They were mother's good ones – the ones she used for company. I think she bought them in the '80s…"

She didn't look at me. "Go ahead. You always get what you want."

Chapter Two

Trust and Farmhouse

I watched as Susan heckled her grandsons back into the van, then sped off in a cloud of dust. I slammed back into the house and noticed a cheap souvenir glass teetering on the edge of the overflowing kitchen table. Instead of pushing it to safety, I picked it up and stomped back outside, intending to crash it down on the concrete steps.

I was so frustrated with my sister and the entire situation.

I wanted to be home on the deck of my condo, looking out over green trees and blooming flowers.

I wanted to put on my swimming suit, jump in the pool, and swim laps as fast and furiously as I could.

Why was it up to me to deal with all this mess?

I really did care for my sister and her grandchildren, but I had my own grandkids. I wanted to be in Oregon or New Jersey with them and my sons' families. Not here in this dusty, dirty, old house. I raised the glass over my head, letting out a string of expletives as the dogs watched with what seemed alarmed expressions. Just before I was ready to throw it to the ground, it occurred to me that I would also have to clean up the mess. With my luck, a shard of glass would land under a tire of the old pickup, then I would get a flat tire and be stranded without a spare on the seven-mile dirt road to town. It may have been my imagination, but it seemed the dogs looked at me with relieved expressions as I marched back into the house, the glass still gripped tightly in my hand. Teaching eighth grade for so many years taught me to redirect my anger rather than act on impulse. It was a good thing. Otherwise, lots of necks would have been wrung, severely limiting my career in education.

By now the late afternoon sun warmed the house to stifling. The ancient fan on the central air-conditioner my parents proudly installed in the 1960s was rumbling like a grain thresher – definitely in its death throes. I only resorted to turning it on when I couldn't take the heat any longer. Now was one of those times.

As it finally coughed into life and I wandered through the house, I thought of my brother, Mack. He didn't believe in air-conditioning, insisting it used way too much energy. Instead he tacked a heavy blanket over the door to his bedroom-den for insulation, turned on two, large, box fans, stripped to everything but his underwear, filled up a small tub with ice water, and placed his feet into the water. He would sit there quietly, smoking his self-rolled cigarettes and reading The Wall Street Journal. He honestly didn't understand why Susan and I refused to adopt his method.

Mack was the youngest of the three of us, and his premature death at 61 threw a wrench into everything. I insisted for a long time that we preplan what would happen after the family trust ended this coming September, which was now only two months away. I did my homework and decided it was best to keep the land in the family but divide ownership three ways, with each of us managing his/her part separately, or perhaps establish some kind of limited partnership.

My brother resisted. "Man plans; God laughs," was his mantra. Now, he and God were definitely getting the last laugh.

He was a man who believed in predictability. Every day was a clone of the day before. He arose at 7:00. Made eggs, toast, and bacon for himself, fed his four dogs, and read the paper. By 9:00, he was in the shower, and, by 10:00, he drove to town to pick up the mail at the post office. Noon found him at lunch with one of 'the misfits,' a group of men and women who knew each other in high school, and all wandered back to their hometown after divorces, business deals gone awry, or to care for aging parents. After lunch, he took a nap, then worked at the computer until it was time for his walk into the pasture with the dogs. He returned home to meditate, do yoga, and watch MacNeil/Lehrer. Supper was promptly at 7:00 p.m., then he either spent time on the computer or watched T.V. until after the local news and weather. By 10:30, he was in bed for the night. He resented any intrusion, including phone calls, especially those from his sisters. His friend, Lyle, always said you could set your clock by Mack's schedule rather than the other way around.

I noticed our old plug-in phone with the long accordion cord was still on his desk, now grimy after years of use. Whatever the afterlife offered, he was now free from those irritating phone calls.

Manila envelopes scrawled with large, unreadable Magic Marker were stacked in boxes – Mack's financial organization system. I picked one up and peeked inside. Bills and invoices were stuffed together in a big clump. There was no way I could face the task of untangling them right now. I shoved it all back in the box and turned to the other side of the room. The old recliner still showed the outline of my brother, with loose tobacco scattered over the old, plaid seat.

Years before, when the farm was prospering, our parents established an irrevocable family trust with Mack as the trustee. After the death of my mother, he made all decisions. Like our father and grandfather before him, Mack believed in keeping finances close to the chest. Despite the fact that Susan and I were equal beneficiaries with him, since he was trustee, he controlled the checkbook, believing we really didn't need to know much about the finances. Although insisting he believed in women's rights, that somehow didn't seem to include his sisters. Now the responsibility for the trust devolved to me. I was also the executrix of his estate, so I was in charge of settling his affairs.

I sunk into the old chair, overcome with the responsibility I faced. Since his death six months before, I traveled from my home in Wisconsin four different times in an attempt to bring some order to the chaos of bills, finances, and all the property. My only allies? Our devoted family lawyer and our accountant. This was now my fifth trip. I had three weeks to get everything done. Plus, I had taken on some responsibilities for my 50th high-school reunion which was soon to take place.

Why was I the one that had to do all this work?

Shane, Mack's oldest and sweetest dog, came over for a rub on the head. He was some combination of shepherd and collie and was kicked out of four homes before Mack adopted him. That was one thing my siblings and I shared – our love of animals. Otherwise, we were quite different.

Mack obviously inherited his frugality from our father. After both of his parents died and the original farm was split, our dad became both 'operator' and owner of his part of the farm. In High Plains lingo, an 'operator' was the person who did the actual farming, making all the decisions, deciding when and what to plant, and when to harvest or let the field go fallow. In this part of the country, the operator usually hired people to help drive tractors, oversee the irrigation, and help with other chores. No one person could manage three-thousand acres without help. Since our father owned the land, after deducting all costs for seed, fertilizer, irrigation, and all other expenses, he reaped the benefits at harvest. He also raised cattle which he grazed on pastureland and sold at market for whatever price the market allowed.

As long as Daddy was both the operator and the owner, he was able to put away money in savings, usually certificates of deposit. He kept the state of all finances well-guarded, so, as kids, we had no idea what was in the bank. We lived frugally but quite well for the mid-century High Plains.

From my saggy seat on the old recliner, I looked around the room. Memories bombarded me from all corners. On the built-in bookshelves across the room were photos of us as kids with our parents. If these weren't formal studio prints, they were Kodak snapshots that usually included an animal or two. My eyes settled on a picture of our mother sitting on the front porch with her apron and a pan of black-eyed peas, surrounded by a litter of puppies. This made her appear much more domestic than she actually was. In fact, she was a very independent woman with her own opinions plus her own bank account. As an only child, she inherited all her parents' assets. They were owners of a very successful Chevrolet-Oldsmobile dealership, two rental houses, a few city lots, and farmland of their own which was rented out to their own 'operator.' By almost any standards, my parents were financially secure for much of their lives. But since they were the exact opposite of ostentatious, it was obvious to no one, especially their children.

Another photo showed me with my newborn son, their first grandson. Obviously taken at a time I visited, there were dogs nuzzling up to examine this small stranger. It was about this time, in 1969, that our father suffered a life-changing stroke. He recovered enough to still operate the farm, but the part of his brain which controlled language was permanently damaged. Thereafter, he communicated in short, choppy phrases and wrote the same way. Once an avid reader, he now depended on the radio, T.V., and books on tape. The intensity of his type-A personality was gone for good, replaced by a warm, humorous gentleness combined with a wicked sense of humor which he communicated to all in shorthand phrases such as 'mighty right' or 'no foolin'?' and always referred to our mother as 'wife.' She capably took over as bookkeeper and the farm continued to prosper.

All that changed in 1990. Daddy was 72; Mother, 70. The slog to town over impassable muddy roads in springtime, plus the physical work, was getting to be too much. They decided to rent out the farm to a neighbor and move into town. Due to my father's frugality, there was plenty of money in the bank. They still owned the land, plus a couple of rental houses and the lots in town, and they were now collecting social security. They wouldn't have to worry – at least that's what everyone thought.

Now I sat in their farmhouse, my childhood home, with the job of shuffling through the debris. My parents' lives were packed away in the living room, basement, and two bedrooms, closed off from the rest of the house by Mack whose idea was 'out of sight; out of mind.' My brother's life was all in this bedroom-den with the four dog beds, boxes of manila folders, and the Tupperware tub he used as an air-conditioner.

I couldn't really face the daunting task of unscrambling it all right now, so I wandered outside to reflect on how it got to this point.

The farmhouse started life in the 1930s as a small bungalow for hired hands and cowboys. It wasn't exactly the kind of white frame, two-story farmhouse my Wisconsin friends would have imagined. For one thing, there was only one barn, steel-framed and practical. Beyond that, just a broad prairie where cattle grazed. My paternal grandparents, the Mihlbauers, lived a mile away at the actual 'farm.' There, the house was surrounded by traditional barns, bunkhouses, granaries, and other out-buildings. We called this 'Mimi's House,' since our grandmother was the heart and soul of the farm.

From the time of their marriage in the 1940s until 1990, my parents continued to live in the remodeled bungalow/farmhouse. By then, Mack was in Austin, and I was in Wisconsin. Only my sister and her family were nearby. It was actually my mother's decision to move from the farm to the house in town. She started as a 'town girl,' and her parents' house, where she grew up, was where she wanted to end up. My father reluctantly agreed. There was one caveat – he was not willing to live in town all the time. Except for the years away in college and a stint in Alaska with the army during World War II, he lived all 70-plus years on the farm, and town life seemed too confining to him.

Mother insisted; Daddy resisted.

This standoff resulted in Mother taking a few items that fit into her parents' house and leaving the rest behind. This was the perfect solution. Daddy would eat supper and sleep in town and then go to the farm during the day for peace and quiet and few hours away from my mother's futile attempts to turn him into a 'town kid,' as he put it. Gradually, Mother added items to their 'townhouse,' and now, more than 20 years later, there were two houses full of furniture, household items, and memorabilia from not only my parents but both sets of grandparents.

I was drawn back to the present when a mockingbird dived in front of me, searching for lunch. I looked up the cloudless sky, relishing the quiet of the late afternoon.

There really was no doubt about it. I had to do as my friend, Ginger, advised, "Put on my big girl pants and deal with it." But it wasn't just the cleaning out. There were so many decisions to be made in the next two months before the family trust ended. As per our parents' will, five years after the death of whichever one survived the other, the trust would end, and all the assets be divided between the three of us. However, Mack's death meant that now it was only Susan and I who would inherit what was left of our parents' estate. Since my sister seldom seemed to have time to help with all the sorting, much less time to have a decent conversation about the trust, I decided to make it easier. I would go to her and insist we talk.

It's not that I didn't understand that her life was complicated. I did. She was essentially raising her daughter's nine children. On any given day, at least four or five of the children would be at her house. She was constantly feeding them, driving them somewhere, or intervening in a quarrel. If their mother showed up, it was usually to drop off another child or ask for money. I didn't blame the children, but I did blame my niece, and I was becoming increasingly frustrated and angry with my sister whose whole world revolved around meeting the needs of so many. Why couldn't she just learn to say no?

The next morning, she was smoking in the backyard when I arrived. Several grandchildren greeted me at the door while keeping their hands on the videogame controls.

"Hi, guys. What've you been doing?" I pushed aside a bowl of soggy cereal on the couch and sank down into the stained cushions.

"Hi, Aunt. We're good, mighty good," Marty, the oldest, replied. The others grinned and turned back to the screen.

"How was school today?"

"Huh?"

"I said, how was school today?" For them, summer school was still in session.

The nine-year-old girl sidled over beside me and smiled shyly. "Did you know that I have a dollar?"

"Really? Where did you get that?"

"I found it under the bed."

"Did you tell your grandmother about it?"

"It's fine with her. She's outside, I guess."

"Okay, I'll go talk to her outside." I gave her a quick hug and went to find my sister. Remains of last night's supper were still on the dining-room table – tortilla chips, pieces of pizza, and a half-empty can of Dr. Pepper, plus the emptied contents of the rest of the box of cereal in a warm bowl of milk. I tried to ignore the kitchen as I passed through. There were two days' dirty dishes standing in cold, greasy water, half-eaten oranges with smears of peanut butter and jelly, plus a rotting can of tuna fish next to the pan of simmering water she called her humidifier. Susan met me on the way out the door.

"We need to talk," she said, not meeting my eyes.

"Right. Where shall we go? How about we go out to eat and talk then."

"No. You know what this town is like. I'm not talking about anything that might be overheard." She put her glass of iced tea down on top of the phonebook she kept outside, which was where she made all calls on her cordless phone.

"Seems to me that everyone is too busy with their own lives to care much about ours," I insisted. Conversation in my sister's kitchen was not appealing.

"You'd be surprised," she replied. "Let's just sit in the car. I don't want the kids to hear."

I rolled my eyes and followed her back through the house to her van. She yanked open the creaky door, pulled out a generic package of cigarettes, and rolled down the window. "I know you don't understand. You haven't had to live with this like I have." She exhaled, coughed, and turned to me. "I want to give Mack's pickup to the boys."

"We've been over this before." I got in, rolled down my own window, and glanced her way. "I can't give anything away. We have to bank every penny to pay for expenses. We can get about five thousand for the new one, and the old one really isn't safe to drive."

"D.J. needs a boost right now, and I'd like to do this for him."

"And how does this help D.J.?"

"Well, you know. It gets him started."

"Started?" I replied.

"Yeah, then he can get an apartment in Lubbock and get a job."

"How can he afford an apartment and a car without a job?"

"Well, the farm will pay for it at first. You said."

"I said? Not that the farm will pay for his gas, his insurance, his registration, his license, and his apartment. You know this is money coming out of the trust, right?"

"It will be fine," she said, reverting to the fairytale world of our childhood.

I was incredulous. "What?"

"Fine. It will be fine."

"So, you want me to give him a five-thousand-dollar pickup, which means that you and I will have five-thousand less to use for the farm and expenses?"

She did not look at me. "It will be okay."

"Sounds like a problem to me."

"It will be okay." She drowned her cigarette in another of the cups she used for iced tea. "I need money. I don't have enough money. Can you write me a check? I don't have enough to live on."

It was true. She didn't have enough money to live on. For the 13 years before, it was our brother who dealt with her constant requests for money. Now she turned to me.

"You just said you wanted to give away a five-thousand-dollar pickup instead of selling it. And this rented-out farm cannot support ten people!" By now, my voice was rising. This was an old conversation.

Her voice rose to meet mine. "It doesn't matter to you. You have a pension. Money should go to the people that need it."

I bit my tongue, struggling to keep from screaming at her. Didn't she remember I raised three sons single-handed on a teacher's salary?

I paused to regain my composure. "Susan, we have been over this a thousand times. I have to follow what is set down in the trust that Mother and Daddy decided on. I can't just willy-nilly hand out money. And I have to follow what Mack specified in his will. Besides that, Angie and Hilario need to be supporting their own children."

She reached for the car door. "You always think you're right, don't you? I hate the trust. I think Stu is on your side. That probably isn't even what's in the trust."

"What?" I could feel my blood pressure rising. "Stu has been the family attorney for years. He is one of the most respected men in town. He's just translating the legalese for us."

She started to get up but turned back to me. "He's on your side. Before that, he was on Mack's side. No one understands that I have all these kids to raise."

Ever since our mother's death five years before, we had been having bi-annual family meetings with our attorney and accountant. Before that, it was at least yearly. No matter when we met, it always played out the same. As soon as we would get to the financial details, which included how much Mother gave to the church and her family, my sister would suddenly remember an appointment or errand and leave the meeting. She didn't want to face the fact that most of Mother's money was going to my niece, Angie, plus her children and Susan. One year alone, it was 90-thousand dollars, dribbled out weekly as Angie took advantage of my mother's deteriorating memory to request money for 'necessities.' Before my brother moved from his beloved Texas hill country home to take over the finances, only Susan was there to notice when the above-ground swimming pool showed up in Angie's backyard or the fancy bentwood crib appeared for baby number five. Except for a few veiled references from Susan about all the money Mother was spending, Mack and I remained largely oblivious, still trusting the judgment of who we still thought of as our wise and frugal mother.

Now everything was gone. All the C.D.s containing our dad's carefully saved money, all the savings accounts. Even Mother's credit cards had been maxed out, with 20% interest credit-card checks written to benefit my niece who insisted the money was for food, clothes, or medical procedures. Later, the 'emergency medical procedure' in Dallas would turn out to be a trip to Six Flags Great America.

I now had the controlling interest in the trust, due to the amount of money Susan and her daughter requested from Mother through the years. In this trust were all my parents' assets, including the farm and other properties. I was the trustee in charge of the bank accounts. Not only that, but because I was in charge of settling my brother's estate, I had the checkbook for his account. This meant that I was the mean banker standing guard at the vault.

I resorted to my teacher voice: "I have a fiduciary responsibility here. Don't you get it?"

"Sure, I get it. You want to throw around big words just to belittle me. That's what you always do. So, my opinion doesn't matter. It never has. I have to go feed the kids." She slammed the car door behind her, leaving me staring at the dashboard, up again against another brick wall.

Chapter Three

Mimi's House

It was better to do the sorting and tossing at the farm by myself without the expectation that Susan would help. If she wasn't willing to even tell me what she wanted to keep, I would separate out the few things I wanted, throw away items that deserved that fate, and give away the rest. I needed to get this done in three weeks' time, plus there was my 50th reunion to help plan.

I turned back to the boxes just as my cellphone rang. It was Joyce, a friend from home.

"So, how is all the work progressing?" She knew the whole story and it was good to have a lifeline to sanity.

"You wouldn't believe it. I need an army. Wish you were here to help me."

"No thanks, I don't do Texas in July. Isn't it hot there?"

"Funny, but I hadn't even thought that much about the heat. That is the least of my worries... Yeah, I guess it is. Yes. It is hot, and dusty, and difficult."

"So, have you decided what you're going to do with the farm?" Joyce was eagerly awaiting the next chapter of my life.

I settled back with a glass of ice water, tossing my mother's old, nylon half-slips into the throw-away pile. "No. I haven't decided what to do."

Joyce spoke with confidence, "Well, I'd just sell it and be done with it. I know how hard this has been on you for months now... No, how hard it's been for years! It's a no-brainer. Sell and be done with it."

"I know you feel that way, Joyce," I said. "But it's not that simple. And it's real hard to explain, especially if you never grew up here or have never even been here."

"Well, most people I know who have been in that predicament have been lots better off after they sold. Think about it. How is the situation with your sister? Oh, and when is that big class reunion? Bet some of your old boyfriends will be there." Joyce was a good friend but also something of a busybody. For her, the lives of her friends picked up where soap operas left off. I qualified as the latest mini-series.

I wasn't ready to get into any of that and the boxes were a good excuse. "I would really love to talk to you, Joyce, but right now, I'm in the middle of some clothes sorting I have to get done. But hey, thanks for checking in. You really are a lifesaver. I've practically forgotten what normal people sound like."

"Ha, now I get to be normal! That's a laugh." Joyce wasn't ready to end the conversation.

"I'll give you a call in a few days and fill you in, how about that?"

The decisions before me were not easily explained to anyone. It wasn't just the farm; the legacy of my parents encompassed so much more. Explaining it was like assembling a complicated jigsaw puzzle with its pieces scattered all over the floor. There was my mother's family and my father's family. And then there were the other families.

My water glass was resting on top of Noona's marble-topped table; she was my mother's mother. Next to my glass was the filigreed, silver, service set which belonged to Mimi; she was my father's mother. It was impossible to understand the claim the farm had on our lives without understanding the stories behind all that surrounded me.

As I looked through the box I was trying to sort, artifacts from that house kept reminding me of a happier time with my sister. Grandpa's cracked, crockery, shaving cup appeared alongside the dainty silver as I relived those days in Mimi's rambling old farmhouse. That house was gone now, bulldozed over after years of neglect. It used to stand a mile away from the farmhouse where I grew up – the one I was now cleaning out. After Mimi and Grandpa died, my uncle inherited the part of the farm where Mimi's house stood. To my father's dismay and alarm, Uncle Lawton became an absentee landlord, more concerned with his other investments than with his part of my grandparents' land. The harsh southwesterly wind and dust pounded the frame house endlessly, birds nested in the rafters, generations of mice raised families, and eventually grazing cattle tramped through the rooms, seeking shelter.

On a whim, I decided to go see what remained of the place I remembered. I jumped into the older pickup I began to call Trusty Rusty and bumped through the pasture trail, heading for the scraggly trees a mile away. As I drove up the long driveway, I was overcome with sadness. All the Chinese Elm trees Grandpa planted by hand were now jagged sticks rising out of the barren landscape. At one time, they stretched for hundreds of yards, lining the driveway and outlining the house and farmyard. I rolled slowly up to a pile of concrete and stones which was all that remained of the two-story frame house, blueprints and lumber ordered from Sears-Roebuck where I spent so much of my childhood. Also, there was the sidewalk that at one time veered off in different directions, leading to the barn, horse corral, and Mimi's garden. Now it was hard to imagine that the small foundation was really the outline for what I remembered as a large home. Only the ancient lilac bush that stood beside the backdoor showed signs of life.

It would be a small house by today's standards, but to a child, it was fascinating. There were the steep open stairs to the attic – rafters soaring to a high peak. At the bottom of the stairs on the ground floor, you stepped across a small hall to the cellar. If you opened the door, your senses were bombarded with the loamy odor of damp earth and pickling spices. Here you saw an open stairway leading into a dark, earthen cave lined with homemade shelving units where Mimi lined up the canned black-eyed peas, green beans, pickled peaches, and plums.

No one ever entered the farmhouse from the front door, though that opened into what Mimi called 'the parlor.' Instead, everyone came in through the door at the back of the house, which led to a sloping, screened-in porch. A huge table took up most of the space, so there was just a narrow passageway from the backdoor through the porch to the tiny kitchen. Mimi herself took up most of the space as she flung her flour and beat the eggs to high heaven, preparing pies for the hired hands and whoever else happened to stop by. It was an ordinary day when she turned out five pies at a time, all with tender crusts and mouthwatering fillings.

However small, her kitchen, as I remembered from childhood, was very modern by 1950 standards. There was a well-used electric mixer, a pasteurizer for ol' Jerse's milk, and even a dishwasher. Usually these would be whirring and groaning at the same time. I could still picture her as she cooked and simultaneously held the phone under her chin, talking to her friend, Esther Barker, the phone cord curling around mixing bowls and steaming pots. A narrow hall led to one door of the bathroom. The other bathroom door could be entered from Grandpa's bedroom/office. The problem was that only one door locked, which led to much underwear pulling and gasps of surprise.

Grandpa had his own room, filled almost completely by a massive roll-top desk, plus stacks of books, newspapers, and magazines. A small bed was pushed into the corner. Now that same roll-top desk was a bone of contention between Susan and me, just like so many household items that now took on symbolic meaning. Our cousin, Uncle Law's daughter, offered to buy it to give to her grandson who was named after Grandpa. I was all in favor. Susan was not, insisting it was ours and she would use it herself.

I sighed, visualizing the house layout in my memory.

Opening into both the kitchen and Grandpa's room was the dining room with the big mahogany table and sideboard. A huge oil painting of a vase of lilacs always hung above the buffet. On top sat the silver, tea-service set that now collected dust in in a box at the farmhouse. It had belonged to Grandmother Lawton, as Mimi always reminded us, and was probably 'worth a fortune.' Our grandpa could have cared less. Fortune, for him, was in land and one's education. His overflow of books and magazines dribbled into the dining room where he had his easy chair and reading light.

Next came the parlor – with its velvet-covered davenport, as my grandmother called it. There were also faded velvet-covered chairs, one with a bright ribbon stretching from arm to arm like a museum piece. It was to remind us that forever and all times it belonged to Mimi's grandfather, Russell Lawton. Under no circumstances was it to be sat upon. Now, it too resided at the farmhouse, covered in dust and old plastic.

Best of all, there was the piano and the large cabinet that housed the Victrola. Here, Mimi would listen to Enrico Caruso, and we would sing along when Mimi played 'Come with me, Lucille, in my Merry Oldsmobile,' or 'How Great Thou Art,' with Grandpa joining in to provide the bass to her wavy soprano.

Off the parlor was Mimi's room with her high bed and overflowing bookcases filled with Winnie the Pooh, Mary Poppins, and lots of racy, dime, store novels with naughty women on the cover. Her bedroom smelled of camphor and unknown ointments, which she piled on the bedside table, along with her box of Kleenex and nail scissors.

The best part of the house, though, was the closet that connected Mimi's room to Grandpa's. We kids used this as our favorite hiding place, covering ourselves with sacheted dresses and gravy-stained ties to avoid being found. It was a bona fide secret passageway.

I walked around the rough concrete, searching for some hint of what I knew as a child. Sticking out of the ground was a dirty piece of faded, yellow cloth. It looked vaguely familiar. I reached down and pulled it up, watching with fascination as a faded calico sunbonnet emerged from the earth. It was ragged and moldy but still recognizable as belonging to my beloved grandmother. I picked it up and brushed off the dirt, slowly walking back toward the pickup.

I saw as much as I needed to see. I would save the sunbonnet to remind me of those childhood years and Mimi's house.

Returning to the farmhouse, I spotted a vehicle parked in front. The dogs were dancing around my sister's van. Had she changed her mind and decided to help me after all?

Susan met me at the door with four, empty, plastic, milk jugs dangling from her fingers. "I came to get some country water. I can't stand the water in town. It even smells bad."

"Oh, I thought you came out to help me," I said. "I did give you the check you wanted yesterday."

She ignored my comment, turning her back and flipping on the kitchen faucet. "Where have you been, and what are you doing now? Don't throw anything away before I get a chance to look at it."

"I'm working my way through some of Mimi and Grandpa's stuff. Mostly pictures of all these people I don't know. But I just found one of Mimi's house with no trees, standing all by itself on the prairie. It must have been taken in the '20s." I rummaged through the box sitting on a nearby chair. "Here, look at the car." She finished filling the bottles and took the picture from me. The car was a Model T, and the woman beside it was dressed for travel.

"Is that Mimi standing by the car?"

I looked at the photo again. "Probably. It's so strange to see the house without all the trees, standing alone like that. Just a house and windmill, no barns or anything."

"It's practically like that now. Uncle Law never watered," Susan sounded wistful.

"No, he didn't," I agreed with her. "All those trees are just jagged gray skeletons, and Mimi and Grandpa's house has rotted away. I was always so proud of that long tree line. Isn't that silly? I think it was the longest in the county."

"I guess Uncle Law decided it cost too much to water them." Memories of the farm in its prime seemed to come back to us both.

"Yeah," I said. "I think one of the first things Grandpa did, after he broke the sod and planted crops, was to plant trees. Mimi said he ordered them from a catalogue and planted them by hand."

"When was it they came from Michigan? I mean Mimi and Grandpa, not the trees."

"It was when Uncle Law was a baby, in 1916. They came on a train and lived in the hotel until Grandpa got the house built, remember?"

"Well, Daddy hated it that he let the trees die and everything else just fall apart. He didn't feel it was fair that Uncle Law inherited the homeplace as he was the one who worked for Grandpa all those years."

Recounting all this, Susan was perfectly calm and rational, and I appreciated this short thaw in our relationship. I decided to pick up the thread and continue, "No. Daddy would have tried to keep it up. But I wonder...wonder if he could have afforded to? The buildings and equipment were getting old, and the water table was falling, so it cost more to irrigate."

"Oh, he would have figured out a way. He loved the farm." Susan was quick to defend all our father ever did. And there was no doubt she was his favorite. Our mother, on the other hand, seemed to bring out the worst in my sister. At least that was the way it was until she died, then Mack was the target of her anger. Now it was me. I pulled a photo album out of another box just as her phone rang.

She ran across the room to retrieve it. "So, what do you need? Okay, wait a minute." She held her phone over her breasts and turned to me. "Sorry, I need to take care of something. I'm going outside to talk, okay?"

I nodded, knowing this was probably one of those phone calls from Angie or the kids that involved money. It would probably involve screaming and yelling and take some time. My expectations for help from Susan were low. I shoved a box off the nearest chair and sat down to look at an album. Most of the pictures were black and white prints, showing the early days of the farm when it was a luxury to own a camera and take your own photographs. The photographer was obviously trying to capture the scale of the farm, but if you didn't know how it looked already, you'd be hard pressed to appreciate the perspective. It was difficult to photograph such a large, empty expanse.

All the fields were laid out in one-mile squares, or sections, and most were enclosed with barbed wire. If you stood stock-still in the middle of Grandpa and Mimi's property and looked up, you would find yourself enclosed in a sphere – a blue bowl, sometimes lightly sprinkled with a few white clouds. The land itself stretched to the horizon, an endless sea of prairie grass. Around the rim of the bowl were darkened stretches that I could identify as other farms, composed of houses, barns, and planted trees nestled against the earth. The longer your dark streak of trees against the sky, the more prosperous your farm. Grandpa and Mimi's was a testament to their Yankee persistence and hard work. Though using the word 'Yankee' to describe their work ethic was not appreciated by the Texas neighbors.

The vast sections of wheat, cotton, and milo were the cash crops that paid the bills, but there was also a picture of Grandpa's lovely little orchard with his well-pruned rows of apple, peach, pear, plum, and cherry trees. In the heydays of the '40s and '50s, the Ogallala aquifer was producing vast amounts of water, and these flowering fruit trees brought a little bit of their Michigan childhoods into the heart of the dry Texas plains thanks to gas-powered, irrigation wells. Those were the days when everything bloomed and flourished.

Besides the orchard and the vegetable gardens, there were also two huge barns, a silo, chicken coop, corral, bunkhouse, and two houses. One was the farmhouse built by my grandpa in 1916, the other a bungalow, built for my uncle, aunt, and cousins. Later, when my uncle left to become a farm/ranch manager downstate, it housed the 'hired man,' Cotton, along with Ruby and her son, Alton. Cotton was our main farmhand, and Ruby worked in town and helped out with the cooking and cleaning when Mimi needed it. Sometimes I heard my aunt and mother whispering about Ruby and her trips to town, but she was always there when they needed her.

A summer day at the farm usually started the same way. By 5:30 a.m., Mimi had worked at least an hour in her huge vegetable garden, fed the chickens, gathered eggs, and made breakfast for various friends, relatives, and hired hands. The rest of the morning was devoted to baking pies, cakes, breads, and preparing the large noon meal. On special days, she would select a fat chicken which she raised from a fuzzy chick, grab it by the feet and feathers, and plop its neck on the stump of a tree that served as a chopping block. With a quick flick of the wrist, her hatchet sent one half of the bird flopping around the yard while the surprised head looked up at us from the tree stump. All this flopping and flying sent my cousins and me screaming toward the house while Mimi calmly placed another unfortunate bird on the block.

The next step was an assault on the olfactory lobes. Holding the headless chicken by the feet, she dipped each one into a huge vat of boiling water several times and began plucking feathers. The odor of scalding flesh and feathers was bad enough, but even worse was the sight when she used the sharp knife to deftly gut the carcass and pull out the steamy 'innards' with her bare hands.

When everything was carefully washed, neatly cut, and sectioned, she dipped each piece into an egg-and-flour mixture and placed it into a large frying pan full of Crisco. Within minutes, the green beans were boiled to perfection with a meaty slice of salt pork. Then with a flourish of flour, butter, baking powder, and buttermilk, she threw dough onto a board and began cutting out biscuits with an upended drinking glass. Rich gravy came from the frying-pan drippings, and cantaloupes and fresh tomatoes were sliced into neat sections and added to an enormous platter to complement the midday meal. One bite of the fried chicken and we forgot all about the messy process that produced it. The ends justified the means.

All the men viewed the food with a reverence reserved for weddings and funerals, diving in ravenously after waiting politely for Grandpa to offer table grace. Usually not one word was spoken until after the last bite of apple pie, served with aged cheddar cheese and frosty glasses of iced tea, were devoured. The wages were not what they worked for; it was Mimi's cooking.

My reverie was rudely interrupted when I heard the door slam and Susan stormed back into the house. "I have to go. The kids don't have anything to eat."

"I thought you said they just got their food stamps."

"You obviously don't know what it's like to feed nine kids. Food stamps don't cover it."

This was so predictable. Our time of reminiscing was gone for this day. I tried not to show my irritation. "Well, okay, but just take a minute to look at some of these, otherwise I'm going to toss them."

"You aren't sentimental at all, are you? Can't you just wait until I have time? Right now, I can only stay a minute." She impatiently shuffled through the piles of photos in another box until she came to one, she recognized. "Do you remember this? It's Grandpa and us kids, but I don't remember it."

I looked over her shoulder. "Remember? That was the day he took us to town to the photography studio to have our pictures made and he let us sit in the back bed of the truck with the dogs?"

"He did? I don't remember that. I think you make up most of this stuff you tell me. I can't imagine Mother letting us do that. She would have had a fit."

"She did. We'd all been playing outside, and Mack had on a muddy shirt, plus his face was dirty. All us girls had on sundresses, see that? Mother must have given us fresh perms, just look at our hair! It's all fuzzy and sticks out at the sides. See?"

"Oh, I remember now," Susan replied, glancing at the photo. "But Grandpa loved having his picture made. Mimi hated people taking pictures of her. I'm like Mimi. I don't like pictures of me either. But I gotta go. Here." She shoved the photo at me and headed for the door.

I looked around at all the scattered memories. Why was I bothering to even do this? Maybe I should take my sons' advice and just burn the whole house down and collect the insurance money.

Despite my frustration, the photos churned up memories of my Mihlbauer grandparents. Mimi and Grandpa were different in so many ways. The original farmland was Mimi's inheritance. After the Civil War, her great-grandfather, who lived in Illinois, was one of the men chosen by the U.S. Government to survey the land that became the Texas Panhandle. In return, he received 17 square miles of land still occupied by the Comanches. But within a few years, Quanah Parker surrendered, and ranchers began moving in. Once farmers realized they could pump water out of the aquifer with windmills, they also began to arrive. My Mihlbauer grandparents were relative latecomers, but Grandpa had a shiny new degree in horticulture and knew a good thing when he saw it. Mimi always reminded him that it belonged to her, even though Grandpa adopted it as his own. In all ways, their relationship was unique.

Whenever Mimi wanted Grandpa for anything, she would stomp out the backdoor and, with the vocal cords of a mezzo soprano, cup her hands and scream into the wind, "Jaaaccoob! Jaaacccobb!!!"

After waiting a sufficient length of time, just long enough to aggravate his wife, he would appear, ambling slowly toward the house, intentionally delaying for as long as possible.

He was a rather short man compared to Mimi who stretched to almost six feet. With red hair and freckles, he was as quiet and silent as she was loquacious. When he made up his mind about something, he was as unmovable as a block of stone – but it was a quiet stubbornness. They made a strange but very successful pair. Both loved music and sang in the choir of the First Presbyterian Church for over 40 years, yet they never drove the seven miles to town together. Grandpa plodded along in his old Ford pickup, while Mimi sped around corners with abandon in her zippy '57 Chevy, furiously swerving from ditch to ditch. She lived just like she drove, with a fierce and enthusiastic exuberance.

****

At least Susan and I shared some happy memories of not only Mimi and Grandpa but other people and experiences of our childhood. The events of the last 20 years, however, opened up a permanent rift in our relationship. I wished it were not so, but it was not a time for magical thinking. A decision about the farm needed to be made soon. The water was running out – all the fracking in the Dakotas and Oklahoma dimmed the prospect of wind power becoming a source of income, even as transmission lines were being constructed across some counties by optimistic power companies. The drought was in its third year.

Before my brother died, the plan had been to keep the farm intact, rent to the same farmers, and divide up any expenses and profits three ways, each of us managing our share. The problem was, there was much more than the farm to manage. In addition to the farmhouse, our mother owned four rental houses in town, plus several vacant lots. All were now in the trust, and we had to divide them up or sell them. Then there was the furniture, the books, and the remains of all that came before. Mack enjoyed managing everything, though both Susan and I agreed that his management style left something to be desired. Since the last thing he wanted was useful suggestions from his sisters, this resulted in lots of conflict, especially between Susan and Mack. Selling most of what we had and dividing it up was more manageable, but not what either my brother or sister wanted. Now Mack was dead, and the trust was ending in two months. Susan wanted to keep everything; I wanted to keep the land and sell everything else. At least, that was what I wanted before Mack died.

I was surprised when Susan appeared again the next day. She explained it this way: "You said you are going to throw everything away, and I want most of everything for when I get a new house. So, I came out to tell you that."

"Well, you already told me that, but I'd like to know where you want to put all of this?" I pointed to the stacked tables, chairs, trunks, and boxes. I hadn't even started on the stuffed closets.

Susan ignored me, sitting down and shuffling through a large box of photos that contained heavily framed portraits of somber, long-lost relatives as well as fading, Brownie camera snapshots from the 1950s.

"You're just going to sit there and not answer me?" I was irate. "You could at least tell me what to do with all of this."

Instead, she acted as though she hadn't heard me and leisurely studied each picture, trying to figure out who the people were. "So, who do you think this is with Mimi?"

I swallowed the anger arising in my throat and roughly stuffed a wad of newsprint inside a large vase. Snatching the photo from her, my voice dripped with sarcasm, "Gee, I don't know. The whole box is full of people we don't know. There must be 15 pictures of young men with slicked-back hair, each in its own little folio."

"The date on this one says 1938," Susan informed me as she pulled another photo out of the box.

"Yep," I replied. "That's the year Mother graduated from high school. Those are probably her old boyfriends."

"All of them?"

I sighed and sank down on the nearest box. "I have no idea and it doesn't matter. We just need to toss them. We have no way to figure out who they were or why they were kept."

"You just want to throw it all away, don't you?" was my sister's helpful reply.

"No. Quit saying those things. I just want to have you help me get this done. If you want all of those photos, just take them right now and get them out of my sight."

"Well, I just might. You know how much I love family history."

I rolled my eyes and stuffed the vase into the box marked 'Throw Away.'

"Okay," Susan replied. "If you're going to be like that, I'm going to leave. I thought we could enjoy working on all this together and talk about everything like we used to. You're always so serious."

"Maybe that's because I'm exhausted from working at this all day." I heard myself whine.

"Oh really? You don't know what real work is. You should try taking care of six or seven kids all the time. But you really don't care about that." She stood up, dumping the pictures from her lap to the floor. "I'm going home, okay?"

I stared speechlessly at her as she walked out, leaving what seemed like hundreds of old photos lying all over the floor. Kicking away the nearest ones, I left the others lying there. My sister could just deal with them the next time she decided to honor me with her presence.

There was a time when Susan and I were very close. We each married young. I moved away; she stayed. I finished college and taught school, then gave birth to three sons in five years; she adopted a girl, then a boy, and finished her degree later. We both married men very much alike. Both were salesmen who played golf and had mothers who doted on them. Both were very different from our father who was a sun-up to sundown farmer who poo-pooed golf or any leisure activity that didn't involve getting your hands dirty. We both divorced our husbands. For me, it was early on; for her, it was later. At one time, as young wives and mothers, we chose the same skirts and blouses to wear, even though we lived more than a thousand miles apart. There were times when she picked me up at the airport and we realized we purchased the exact same purse or suitcase, yet we had no knowledge of the other's choice.

All my sister ever wanted was a husband, children, and a happy home. She was a talented artist and a caring teacher of small children, and later adults. Staying close to the farm and our parents was important to her. In high school, she was surrounded by wonderful girlfriends who were still supportive of her years later. She was the apple of our daddy's eye; he appreciated her sensitive side and understood when she was easily frustrated or anxious. She had an 'I Love Lucy' sense of humor she shared with both friends and family. We never knew when she might burst into a room, impersonating a member of the family, complete with props and clothes. She was rewarded with enthusiastic laughter and applause.

As she grew into adulthood, her shiny, dark hair was perfect for the long, straight styles of the early '70s, and she attracted young men wherever she went. After high school, she attended three different colleges for three consecutive semesters but dropped out each time. To be fair, it was a restless time – the world, as we knew it, was undergoing changes that we were not prepared for. Like many others in our country, she longed for security, and the man she married seemed most likely to provide that.

Their late March wedding day dawned bright and sunny, but by 3:00 p.m., there were tornado warnings, and by the time of the wedding, snow was blowing out of the north at 40mph. The few guests who were able to get into the church were stranded there until nearby neighbors offered them a bed for the night. The bride and groom were eager to get out of town, no matter what the weather. They struck out for Lubbock. A few miles out of town, they slid into a ditch and were stuck. Along came a car – the groom's boss and his wife, still trying to make his way to the wedding. They stopped and gave the bride and groom a ride back to the Lariat Motel where the two couples shared the last room available.

This should have been an omen. Yet, even the tornado that struck their Lubbock apartment building later that year was not seen as a sign of trouble ahead. They got a puppy, and my sister was hoping to soon be pregnant like many of her friends. Despite their best efforts, the longed-for babies did not arrive, and after raising an especially easygoing German shepherd pup, they decided to adopt a baby girl.

None of us had any idea how that would affect all our lives.

After working into the afternoon, trying to decide, among other things, which of my mother's sets of embroidered napkins to keep, if any, I was interrupted by the whining Patch who was ready for his walk. He arrived at Mack's several years before on a windy winter day with a ragged rope around his neck, walking right in through the doggy door. The other dogs sniffed him over and decided he could stay. Mack deferred to their decision, and Patch joined the pack.

Shane and the other dogs were waiting for us at the door. Fizzy was a nervous little terrier Mack stole from the previous owner who kept him locked in a cage for the first few years of his life. Jack was an elegant German shepherd who once belonged to a local cop who had to get rid of him when he kept jumping the backyard fence. The cop decided he belonged on a farm. Mack obliged, and Jack happily adapted to his new home.

As we headed out, all four dogs sniffed around the two white pickups, perhaps still hoping for some scent of Mack, especially around the newer of the two vehicles. Trusty Rusty, the elder truck, was probably 20 years old, always caked with mud or dirt and bruised with dents and scratches. Next to it was a shinier, newer version with doors that opened easily and upholstery that was not pocked with tobacco burns. Right after Mack's death, I arrived to make arrangements and, to avoid paying for a rental car, decided I would use the newer pickup. However, the battery was dead, with no jumper cables in sight. Besides that, the right front tire was flat. Resigned to my fate, I tried the older truck. Even though the door wouldn't close properly, and the windshield was cracked, it started right up. After I had time to think it over and understand the finances, I decided the best thing to do was sell the newer truck. It wasn't exactly brand new either, but we could still get at least five-thousand dollars for it, and we needed the money. Leaving the battery dead and the tire flat discouraged certain young thieves from taking it for a joy ride, so it still sat as Mack left it.

This was the pickup Susan wanted to give to her grandson.

Once when visiting before his death, I asked Mack about the newer truck he seemed proud to own and why he sometimes drove the old one. "Why don't you sell the old one? There are farmers around here that need old pickups for their workers. They'd be happy to give you a couple of hundred for it."

Mack gave me the look he reserved for his clueless sisters: "What do you mean?" he asked. "That's my toolbox."

"Your toolbox?"

"I have my toolbox in that one."

"So, why don't you just put your toolbox in the new truck?"

"Nope. I like it the way it is."

And that was that.

The dogs finally followed me as I walked out into the pasture, happy to get away from the house for a while.

Chapter Four

Old Friends and Babies

I pulled against the seatbelt which was stuck again. Dust. It got into every joint, every crack and crevice. I finally got it latched, started the engine, shifted into reverse, and waited for the familiar clank as the glove-compartment door fell to the floor. I was driving Trusty Rusty to town to meet an old friend. How many times in my life had I traveled this road to town? Seven miles one way and seven another. Five miles of pavement; two miles of dirt road that became sticky clay in the unlikely chance there was a thunderstorm. I thought of my dad and the stories he told about traveling to town in the Model T and having to open and close seven gates on the way. That was before the Farm-to-Market roads split everything into neat, geometric patterns, with a road every mile. Daddy's drive to town had been cross-country, provided you were on good terms with the neighbors whose land you had to cross.

For me, it meant driving past more than 60 years of memories. That was one thing that made it hard for me to be here. In town, practically the only thing that remained the same were the wide brick streets constructed by F.D.R.'s C.C.C. during the Depression. They were so empty now. I remembered the streets as they had been when I was a teenager in the '60s, filled with slow-moving cars with windows rolled down. Girls with teased hair at the wheel, sipping their Cokes from a straw as they trolled for boys on Dip Street. We tuned our car radios to KOMA and listened to Lubbock native, Buddy Holly, belt out, 'That'll be the Day.' By my senior year, 'Puff the Magic Dragon' was at #1 on The Hit Parade, and 'The Sound of Music' and 'Mary Poppins' were lighting up the movie marquees.

The wide, wine-red brick streets had been laid by hand. At the end of every block was a deep, wide 'dip' in the street to provide runoff in case of rain. That meant that we learned to take these dips at an angle. It was the perfect street for cruising because we had to go slow or we would bottom-out the family car. There was also a wide, paved boulevard in the middle, perfect for pulling up beside a carload of boys. All teenagers yearned to borrow the family car on Sunday afternoon and 'cruise Dip.' Every other lap, we would round 'the Monument,' a marker designating a side path of some old cattle trail, and head out Mineral Street, turning left at Noona and Granddaddy's house and heading west on 6th until we pulled into the Dairy Queen drive-in. Out again down the highway for a few blocks, then a left turn onto Dip. That was the pattern.

I was meeting an old, high-school friend for lunch. She wouldn't be able to attend the reunion – they were just driving through on their way from Austin to Wyoming. Her absence was probably intentional. Just like my family, hers went from one of impeccable respectability in her parent's day to one now marred by gossip and innuendo. I hadn't seen her in many years, yet we stayed in touch via infrequent emails and the occasional phone call. Like me, she married and moved away from Texas, becoming a nurse and making her home near Kansas City. Only recently had she and her husband taken over the family lake house near Austin where they now spent the winter.

As kids, our families were best friends; her mother one of the women I admired most. Like mine, her family's roots went deep, yet now only a divorced sister-in-law remained in the area. When I thought of her, images of church-family picnics in the canyons and homemade ice-cream parties always came to mind. I remembered the dark, wooden, church pews where we gathered around, holding hands, singing 'Bless be the Tie that Binds'; and the wavy, purple, stained-glass windows which I was sure was like the Sea of Galilee. There were other times too when, in our teens, we sought each other out for serious philosophic discussions. Unlike many of our classmates, we appreciated discussing politics and religion but never let our other friends know. We would be laughed out of the small circle that made up the girls in our class. Yet sometimes at night, when I stayed at her house, we snuck out the window and sat on the roof, awed by the sight of the Milky Way in that still-dark sky of the 1960s.

I spotted her coming from across the parking lot. Her hair was graying and curly, but her generous smile was the same. "Emily! I am so glad to see you!"

"And you! You look just the same."

"Liar!" I laughed.

She embraced me warmly, and we looked around for someone to seat us. We chose El Sombrero, one of the four restaurants in town now that Dairy Queen closed. We were seated by an older woman who looked vaguely familiar. After a waiter brought us water, Emily took a sip and looked at me with kind eyes. If anyone knew what I was experiencing, she did. "So, tell me about your family. The grandkids? Susan? I was so very sorry to hear of Mack's death. You know we lost Joe last year. It is really hard to lose a brother, isn't it?"

"Oh, it is. Mack was so health conscious. Never did we think he might have heart problems. A seizure would not have been a surprise. He had been on phenobarbital since his accident 40 years ago, but a ruptured aorta was a total surprise."

She looked at me with concern. "Is everything here going, okay?"

"Well, how much time do you have? It's a long story."

"Go ahead," she said. "I have until 1:30. That's when I need to meet Doug at the ranch. He inherited that after Mother died, you know. I got the Georgetown house, and Chuck the cabin in Taos."

"I have such great memories of going up to the cabin with you and your grandmother," I replied. "Does it look the same?"

"Well, I haven't been there for a while now," she said.

"Remember when we you and I and Betsy went there? How old were we?"

"Oh gosh, I don't know, maybe nine or ten?"

"There was a lovely little stream at the bottom of the mountain where we got to wade and play with sticks and leaves, we made into boats. It was so green and so different from our lives on the dry plains. I was enchanted by that little bridge where we played hide and seek. Remember?"

"Yes, I do. I'm so glad we had that time there when we were kids." Emily sighed and fidgeted with tableware. "But you know what happened, don't you?"

I shook my head. The details of both of our lives were lost in the busyness of demanding jobs and raising children. Time and distance left huge gaps in recent family history.

"Well, we had an awful time dividing everything up. In the end, I just gave in to my brothers. There were hard feelings, so I may never see the cabin in Taos again." She looked wistful as she returned the fork to its place and met my gaze. "But what about you and your situation? Tell me about Susan.

45

Remember? She used to always say that we were all raised on guilt and red Jell-O."

"Yes, I think about that a lot these days." I smiled.

"I get bits and pieces of the hometown gossip from Dora, you know, my ex-sister-in-law? But I have to admit that most of the time I don't pay much attention to it. Since Mom and Dad died, I find few reasons to return here, but I was fond of Susan. She was several years younger than we were, but our families were together so much when we were kids that I'd love to hear about her life too."

"Susan isn't dealing very well with things right now," I said, hesitating to go into all the details even though Emily seemed genuine in her concern. "Well, for one thing, she depended too much on Mother and Daddy and always thought the farm would provide plenty of money. But then there is this other little matter – her daughter, good-for-nothing son-in-law, and their nine children."

"They have nine children? What do they do for a living?" Emily was as surprised by this news of so many kids as everyone else and barely noticed as the young waitress came up to take our order. "Oh, sorry. Let me take a minute to look at the menu."

The young woman, who spoke quietly in flowing syllables, looked about 14. "Yez, ma'am. No probleem," she replied, "I'll give you a few minutes." Her black hair was pulled back into a long braid that swung gracefully down her back as she walked toward another table.

"Sorry," Emily replied. "What did you say about their jobs?"

"Well, that is the problem. They don't work at all."

"What?" Emily looked up from the plastic menu.

"They depended on Mother before she died, and since then, it's been Susan and the farm. Mack was trustee, you know. He did his best, but after a while, he couldn't stand the harassment and would give in and write a check. I often wonder if that stress contributed to his death."

"Oh, this sounds so familiar," Emily replied. "Joe was our trustee, and we ran into a similar problem with Doug, but at least he didn't have a daughter with nine children. What's the story there? Why did they have so many children?"

"Well, now we know that it was partially because of food-stamp fraud. Hilario, Angie's husband, perfected the system: the more kids, the more food stamps. All he had to do was trade the food stamps for cash. It's sad. Instead of working hard like the rest of his family, he decided to use the old barter system, just an off-the-records new economy version." I paused for a sip of water. "But that's only part of the story."

"I'm here to listen," said Emily. "Anything is better than worrying about my own family issues."

I gathered my thoughts as the young waitress took our order. Then, I began. "It all started almost 40 years ago when Susan and Hugh adopted Angie. They dearly loved the little girl, but she proved to be colicky and asthmatic, and Susan was anxious and hovering. Soon, a pattern developed. Her normal two-year-old temper tantrums were placated by giving in to her every whim. As she grew, and her needs became greater, so did the tantrums. The louder the screams, the more she was indulged. Susan gave up her teaching job so she could be at home with Angie, but the teeth-rattling meltdowns continued. By the time she was a teenager, she added manipulation to her repertoire, followed by lying and stealing. The household revolved around keeping her pacified."

Emily chimed in, "So they just had the one child?"

"No, their son, Will, was adopted two years after Angie. Thankfully, he was a cheerful, compliant child. He learned to adapt, like his parents, to his sister's tantrums. He and his family are now living in South Dakota, away from the chaos."

Our food arrived, and I continued the story between bites of taco salad, more taco than salad. "After a while, Hugh, Susan's husband, you remember him? Anyway, he was spending his time at work, his basement office, or at the golf course. He was running the car dealership that had been Granddaddy's. It was Mother's dream to continue his legacy." I glanced at Emily. "You know how she was. Anyway, she finally convinced Daddy to help her buy the dealership back from the Samuels. They were the ones who bought it after Granddaddy died. Once it was back in family hands, Mother decided that Hugh was the perfect person to manage it, especially since he recently lost his job as a veterinarian supply salesman. It was not a good choice."

Emily was eating slowly as she took all this in. "Hugh? I vaguely remember him. Wasn't he pretty successful? Dora used to talk about him."

"He had a lot of people fooled, including Mother and Daddy. After a few years, it became obvious that he was not only an incompetent manager but also a bit east of honest. You probably didn't know this," I said, looking across the table, "but Daddy had to mortgage the farm to bail him out of trouble."

"I guess that I did hear something like that, but you know how the gossip is. I just took it all with a grain of salt," Emily replied.

"Well, they lost the dealership," I continued. "But before it closed, he gave Angie her own car. That was a big mistake. She was only 16. Several years later, I found out that my mother – my very conventional mother – let Angie and a friend live in the duplex she owned. Susan and Hugh got so tired of her screaming tantrums they gave in to her. It wasn't long after that she dropped out of high school and announced she was pregnant."

"Oh no," Emily said, shaking her head.

"Oh yeah, I'm afraid so. Anyway, after the baby was born, both sets of parents convinced Angie and Hilario, the baby's father, to get married. His family insisted they have the ceremony in their home and agreed to provide the bridal lunch of tamales, beans, and rice. Susan brought Mimi's Jell-O Cool Whip salad with fruit cocktail."

"So far, this sounds like so many other stories I've heard." Emily was examining a tortilla chip at close range.

"Well, there's lots more. Are you sure you want to hear all this?"

"Go ahead, I have until 1:30."

"Okay. It's quite a story." I paused to scoop up the runny salsa with a salt-heavy tortilla strip. "It was after my divorce, and I had my own three kids to raise and support. But anyway, another baby boy followed 18 months after the first. Mother bought the kids a mobile home in the trailer park. Then when another baby boy came along 11 months after that, she moved them into an old house she bought for them on Darnell Street. It was her plan that Hilario would get a job and pay her rent to cover the mortgage."

The server arrived with our food and we took a minute to rearrange the small table to make room for the plastic plates covered with a large tostado, beans, lettuce, and a few pieces of pale-pink tomato.

"Go ahead," Emily prompted, sampling her wilted lettuce.

"So, by the time Nate, the fourth baby, arrived, there was still no job." I paused, watching as Emily tossed the oversized pieces of lettuce around, searching for a piece without brown edges. "Anyway, about that time, Daddy was diagnosed with Parkinson's and Mother took over the checkbook for the farm. Angie helped out by loudly lobbying for a larger house," my tone morphed into sarcasm as I paused to take a sip of my iced tea. "Mother was so tired and vulnerable; Angie was loud and demanding. It wasn't long before Mother let us know that she was buying that big brick house on Bradford Street where the bank president used to live."

"The one that got run out of town?" Emily asked. "I remember my mother talking about that."

"Yep, that's the one," I continued. "So, then she rented out the first house and they moved into the bigger one. For a while, Hilario worked for a neighbor, pouring poison down prairie dog holes, but when he stopped showing up for work, he was let go. He went back to playing videogames."

"Wait. Wait!" Emily put down her fork and shook her head. "I'm getting confused. How many houses? How many babies? I can't keep all this in my head."

"Oh. Sorry, I forget how confusing this all is to others. Do you need to take notes?"

"Lord, I hope not," Emily replied.

"Okay, I'll slow down. By this time, there were five houses. There was the farmhouse where we used to live. Then there was what you knew as my grandparents' house in town. Mother inherited that, and that's where Mother and Daddy lived after they left the farm. We called that the townhouse. Then there was this old duplex which Mother also inherited. After that was the house across the street from the church which was the first house Mother bought for Angie and Hilario. Susan lives there now. We call that the Darnell Street house. That's the one Mother bought for them after they had baby number four. Next was the house on Bradford Street where the banker used to live."

"I hope there won't be a test." Emily tentatively forked a piece of tomato. "What's next?"

"Do you want the whole story?"

"Sure, you can't stop now."

"I know it sounds pretty unbelievable."

"Oh, just wait until I tell you what you've missed about my crazy family." Instead of starting in on her own family, Emily gave the salad a disgusted look. "Get a load of this lettuce. This would end up on the compost pile in Austin. Sorry, go ahead."

"Yeah, you'd think someone would grow commercial lettuce around here. Anyway…their next baby was a beautiful little girl. They named her Heather, baby number five. Since it was the first girl, Angie talked Tutu – that's what the kids called Mother – into buying a new crib at a cost of $1200.00. By now, Mack and I were really concerned. The farm was rented out because Daddy couldn't manage it any longer. The renter was Ray Stevens. Remember him? He was quite a bit younger than us, more like Mack's age. Anyway, he was young and had new equipment, and Daddy trusted him because he was a neighbor boy."

Emily stared at me. "This just gets worse and worse."

"I'm not done yet," I replied. "Their sixth baby was another little boy. For a while, Hilario worked at the lumberyard. You know, the one that used to belong to the Nixons? It was open until a few years ago. By this time, my niece realized that cute little babies grow into demanding children who could not be controlled except by physical means. So, she decided she needed her husband at home to help with the kids. Besides that, he hurt his back at work, and if they could sue the lumberyard, well, maybe they could make a killing."

"Did that work?" Emily asked.

"No," I said, "but they were discovering that six children were expensive. And you know Mother. She was always a compassionate person. If you needed it, she would give you the coat off her back. Now here was a need. She had the checkbook. The needs were met."

"Could she afford this?"

"No. But she thought she could. I guess that's the tragedy," I replied.

"Wasn't there something you could do about it?" Emily asked.

"You'd think so. My excuse was that I was 1200 miles away. Mack was 600. Most of this, we didn't learn about until later. But even Mother had her limits. After baby number six, she did confide in me. She told me she talked seriously with my niece about birth control. Angie was never reliable about taking pills for birth control, or maybe just didn't bother, and of course, she was afraid of anesthesia, so a tubal ligation was out. Besides that, by now, Hilario was drinking heavily and needed the extra food stamps to trade in for booze." I paused to take a few bites of my lunch. "Of course, there were other options."

Emily reached for another tortilla chip, all but abandoning her salad, and looked at me. "And what was that?"

"Pretty soon, Angie was back in Mother's living room, pleading for a vasectomy to get Hilario fixed. I really think Mother thought that would be the solution, so she got out the checkbook."

"Okay, I'm getting confused." Emily was looking puzzled. "I thought they had nine children?"

I gave a short, bitter laugh. "Just wait. By summer, there was a large, above-ground swimming pool in their fenced-in backyard. After avoiding Mother for several weeks, Angie visited her grandmother to break the news – baby number seven was on the way. It was another little girl."

Emily looked at me, wide-eyed. "What happened to the vasectomy?"

"Well, according to Angie, it failed," I said. "Of course, to Mack and me, it was obvious they used the money to buy the swimming pool. Susan seemed to be oblivious to all this. Her focus was helping to care for all the babies."

I stopped for a moment to collect my thoughts. Relating this story was exhausting. But then, I always remembered what that time was like for my mother. The stress of running the farm and taking care of my dad was taking its toll. He was more and more dependent on her. Years before, he suffered a life-changing stroke at age 50. He was able to overcome so much of his disability, but that, plus Parkinson's, was creating conditions that made it more and more difficult for my mother to care for him and also manage the farming business and the other property she owned. Finally, he agreed to go live in the custodial wing of the local hospital, which was at least better than the nursing home on the edge of town.

Emily was watching me expectantly. "So, what happened?"

"Mother gave her the money for another vasectomy."

Emily's mouth dropped open. "She did?"

"Yep, and before long, a late-model van appeared in their driveway, and Angie announced that the next baby, number eight, was on the way."

"Oh my God!" Emily gave me a horrified look.

"By now, Mack and I were really alarmed. He was driving up from Austin every month to help Mother and visit Daddy. One time, Daddy grabbed his hand, struggling to talk. You remember how he always talked in shorthand after the stroke?"

"Oh yes. It was just part of his sweet personality. I always visited your dad when I came home." Emily had been one of my dad's favorites.

"Well, he finally made it obvious to Mack that he had to do something. Mother was showing serious signs of forgetfulness and was not using good judgment. So even though he loved the area where he lived and had a girlfriend he would be leaving, Mack saw the handwriting on the wall. He began a slow transition to the Panhandle and the farmhouse."

"Oh, your poor mother. And Mack." Emily could identify.

I continued, "But before he made that decision, Angie went to Mother again with her hat in hand. This time, she tried a new tactic. She told Mother that Hilario had drug and alcohol problems and needed treatment. Could Tutu please write a check and make it out to her? The drug and alcohol problems were very real, but this was just her latest scam."

Emily stared at me incredulously. "Couldn't you stop this?"

"I know this is hard to believe, but you knew Mother. She was a very bright but stubborn lady, and she had been managing the farm for several years. Also, she only told us what she wanted us to know. Most of the conversations I had with her were about Daddy's condition. When I'd bring up my concerns about Angie and the money, she would change the subject. By now, Mack and I were definitely aware of the problem but still not the extent of it." I paused. "Also, both Mother and Daddy were always so close to the chest about their finances. They did not believe in sharing the details at all. Finally, by insisting on the family meetings once a year, we began to get a sense of the problem. But I still had my head in the sand."

"I don't think I want to hear anymore. This is just awful... No," Emily hesitated, "I do want to hear about this, but if you'll excuse me a minute, I'm going to run to the ladies' room."

"Sure. Go ahead. I'll just wait here, wishing this wasn't a dry county."

I watched as she was stopped by a table of elderly ladies who recognized her. She would be gone for a while. I really couldn't tell her about the next part anyway. It included a confidence I didn't feel free to violate. It happened one week when Mack was still going back and forth to Austin.

Chapter Five

The Townhouse

Not long after Mack moved back to Tumbleweed, he got a call from Jim, a former classmate, who was now the local postmaster. "Mack, I could get in real trouble for telling you this, but I can't sleep at night, knowing what I know."

The postmaster hesitated. Mack realized this was not just a friendly welcome-back-to-Tumbleweed call. "What's up?"

"For the past several months, one of our mail carriers has been delivering bills to your niece's home, but the bills have your mother's name on them with your niece's address. I been worrin' about it, and I just thought you should know."

It took Mack a few moments for this to sink in. "So, what time does the mail carrier deliver to the Bradford Street house?"

"I'd be there by 11:00 a.m."

Angie had been able to find Mother's social-security number, opened a credit card in her name, and charged it to its limit. The bills delivered to Angie's house went right into the trash. Our mother's credit rating was shot. Mack and I told Mother. She was surprised and upset but refused to press charges.

A couple of years before, when the eighth baby was on the way, Angie convinced her grandmother to convert the two-car garage into another room, insisting they needed more space for their growing family. For reasons that only became clear in retrospect, Mother decided this was a great idea, even though she would have to cash-in almost all the remaining C.D.s where my dad squirreled away savings. Instead of seeing the futility of pouring money into this house, she was excited about the prospect of 'adding to her investment.'

The aphasia which took away much of my father's speech after his stroke had not affected his clarity of mind. When Mack told him about the state of their finances, he was devastated.

On one of my biannual visits, he grabbed my hand from his hospital bed. "Not right in the head, Sissy, not right in the head. Tutu not right in the head. Number-one problem – Angie. Angie – number one, number-one problem!"

The stroke made it impossible to access our given names, but the more affectionate names were always there.

All this was running through my mind as I waited for Emily. How could I explain it all? There was too much and it was too complicated. By now, I was emotionally drained, and she would soon have to leave. "You know," I said when she returned, "I don't think I have time to finish this – it's a long, long story. I'm so sorry."

"That's okay," she replied. "I just realized what time it is. I have to leave anyway. How about this, I'll give you my cell number, and we can talk after the reunion. I'll want to hear all about that too."

"Oh yes, the reunion," I replied. "I don't know whether I'm dreading it or looking forward to it." Emily was one of only a small handful of my high-school classmates who was on my wavelength. She got up to leave and I rose to hug her.

"I'll miss you, old friend," I said. "I'm so sorry I didn't get to hear all about you and your family. I've dominated the conversation. Let's talk soon."

There were tears in her eyes. "You too, old friend."

My conversation with Emily dredged up memories of my childhood, and I decided to drive past the 'townhouse.' It had been the home of my maternal grandparents whom we called Noona and Granddaddy – pet names obviously being a part of our family culture. Soon after our mother's death, we sold the house, but what happened before that was still very difficult for me to think about. This was the house I lived in for the first few years of my life. It had been built in 1929, right before the crash on Wall Street. At one time, it had been the nicest house in town with its beautiful brick work, soaring peaked roof, and two-car garage. During the Depression, my maternal grandparents rented out the spare bedroom to teachers who needed a place to live; the money also helped pay the bills. Mother inherited the house after my grandparents died and always intended to make it a retirement home for herself and Daddy. It was rented out for a number of years until they finally moved to town.

When I was a child, I came here on sweaty, hot, summer afternoons and collapsed in the central air-conditioning. The only other place in town that had such luxury was the First National Bank. Here, it was always cool and quiet. The living and dining rooms were carpeted in soft, pink wool and there was always a lace tablecloth covering the mahogany dining table. If Noona wasn't out visiting shut-ins, she would be sitting in her chair, humming a hymn with embroidery on her lap and her onion-skin King James Bible beside her on the table. She always made sure my shoes were shined and insisted that I memorized the 23rd Psalm. Her home was as neat, quiet, and orderly as Mimi's was loud and rambunctious. And like my paternal grandparents, Granddaddy and Noona left a deep imprint on my life.

Her given name was Loona, but to her grandchildren, she was always Noona. Everyone loved and admired her kind and compassionate nature. Many even called her saintly because of her giving nature. She visited all the shut-ins in town and even took food to those who weren't Baptists. But it was the Burgess girls, Louise and Charlene, who became her mission project.

They lived on the edge of town in a trailer house with a disheveled mother and alcoholic father, several siblings, and various mangy cats and dogs. Noona picked them up for church each Sunday and would send them out to our house to help Mother when housework got the best of her. Noona loved giving teas for the Missionary Society and would hire the girls to help her make dainty little sandwiches and her special spiced tea. It was Louise, the older Burgess girl, rather than my mother, who told me the facts of life while picking up toys and clothes in my bedroom while I plied her with questions. She showed me her pointy bra and also told me matter-of-factly, "World's comin' to an end. That's why your grandmother built her a bomb shelter in the backyard. I figure the nuclur war will be here any day. We'll all be blown to smithereens and the Communists will take over."

I lived with this reassuring thought until well into my teen years.

Indeed, there was a bomb shelter in my grandparents' backyard. But for some reason the concrete never dried properly, and it always smelled like wet cement. But that did not deter Noona. She stocked it with peanut butter, raisins, powdered milk, and water. There were flashlights and blankets and later a transistor radio that failed to pick up a signal. Granddaddy harrumphed at this expense but indulged her whims, probably believing, like most in my town, that we might not be able to count on nuclear disaster, but we could be sure there would someday be a tornado.

True to her religious convictions, Noona did not give up on Louise. She provided funds for her to complete a two-year degree at the nearby Baptist College where she met and married a young man studying for the ministry. This was Noona's dream-come-true. That and the fact that, some 60 years later, I can still recite the 23rd Psalm.

Since Granddaddy owned the Chevrolet-Oldsmobile-Frigidaire dealership, he could acquire appliances at cost. So, when they remodeled their kitchen, Noona got a brand-new pink stove, refrigerator, and dishwasher, all custom-ordered. It was Noona's pride and joy. Then, to complement this, they installed lime-green linoleum and countertops. Since the house sat on a prominent corner, it became something of a landmark. Granddaddy, at Noona's insistence, hired men to keep the lawn mowed and hedges trimmed, just so. When I was older, I would sit on the big front porch behind the trumpet vine in a niche of brickwork designed as an open window. There, I could hide and watch as the older kids cruised by on dates, the girl nuzzled up right next to her date, and the boy with one elbow sticking out the window.

****

As my mother neared the end of her life, she made sure to let us know that she wanted each of her children to be left with a house. So even though everything was supposed to go into the trust on her death, she corralled our attorney and accountant to let them know this was her wish. Mack was to get the farmhouse; Susan the Darnell Street house, originally purchased for Angie and family, but where Susan now lived. I was to receive the townhouse where Noona and Granddaddy had lived. I tried to tell her that I already had a house in Wisconsin, but she was adamant, hoping, I'm sure, that I would finally come to my senses and move back to my hometown.

What happened between the time she made her wishes known and her death was what haunted me now.

Once, when I was working with a counselor, I asked him about my recurrent dreams which always featured houses. In the dreams, I was always wandering through a house, though seldom the same one from dream to dream. They would usually be framed-in but incomplete, and there were always many,

many confusing hallways and rooms. I was the only one in each house, and I was always searching for something but was never sure what I was looking for. Sometimes the houses would be spectacular mansions with spacious rooms, beautifully decorated. At other times, they would be a maze of confusing hallways and doors. Sometimes the houses would open up to outdoors leading down to a beach or beautiful vista of rolling hills; other times there would be a confusing convergence of roads and trails leading to unknown places.

When I told my counselor about these house dreams, the wise man I was working with smiled at me patiently. "Those houses, my friend, represent your soul."

The houses in my life right now, unlike those of my dreams, overflowed with the lives of others. They were all too real, definitely not empty, and were sorely testing whatever soul I had left.

****

I pulled off the road into the driveway of the townhouse as all these memories ran through my mind. Tumbleweed didn't exactly have lots of traffic, but the house was on the corner of a state farm-to-market road and one of the two main streets in town. It didn't look like anyone was home, but I really wanted to see the house now that the new owners remodeled. On the outside, it looked the same as it did when it was built in 1929, the beautiful brick work rising to a high peak at the front, and a deep, covered porch where I used to sit on the wide swing between my grandparents.

Just as I got out of the car to ring the doorbell, I was startled by a loud car honk in the street behind me. It was Carla, one of the town's unique characters, and a long-time family friend. She was beeping away on the horn in what she called her 'feeding-the-calves pickup.' Traffic on the street lined up behind her as she rolled down the window.

"Well, there you are," she hollered out the window. "Why haven't you been by to see me? I heard you been here almost a week and I haven't heard a word, not a word. Forgetting your old friends?"

I rushed down the driveway toward her. "Carla, you're backing up traffic! Get out of the street. Just pull in behind me, okay?"

With a sudden shift into reverse, followed by a squeal of tires suddenly accelerating forward, she pulled off the street, almost hitting the old pickup. She came to a sudden stop inches away from me. "I don't have much time right now, but we really need to visit and I've been tryin' to reach you I still guess you have that same phone number at the farmhouse? Anyway, I can't talk much right now. What's ya doin' here, anyway?" Carla talked in one, long, run-on sentence.

"I wanted to see Noona's house now that the new owners have remodeled. I was thinking about asking if I could go in for a look around."

"Well, I can tell you for sure certain they're not there. They both work in Plainfield and drive back and forth because you know how those houses have just doubled in price compared to here in Tumbleweed, or maybe you don't bein' as how you live way up yonder. When ya goin' to come over for a real visit, that's what I want to know."

Stifling a laugh, I shook my head in disbelief. Carla was one of a kind, and her kind heart was only superseded by her persistence and running commentary. "How about we try for lunch next week?"

"You're waitin' 'til then? Whatcha doin' with your time anyway?"

"I'm cleaning out the farmhouse, remember?"

There was a momentary pause as Carla recalculated. "Oh, I sure do know that; your sister been pestering me all week about you throwing away all her stuff, but you know I don't pay much attention to what she says and I plum forgot about that house you're working on and that's a big job, I bet."

"You can say that again."

"I'll catch ya later, okay? Those calves out near Broadview need feeding and I gotta go."

And with another screech of her tires, she backed up into traffic, completely ignoring the drivers who swerved and honked as she sped into the street.

"Bless her heart," I heard myself whisper, surprising myself by using the local lingo. I'd known Carla all my life, and if there was one thing I could count on, it was that Carla would always be Carla, marching to her own drummer, not caring a whit what other people thought.

Despite what Carla told me, I rang the doorbell and waited. All was quiet. On either side of the porch steps behind me was a curved brickwork that practically begged to be sat upon. So, I sat down for a minute, thinking of all the stories this house could tell – the history contained in its walls.

After moving from the farm, my mom and dad lived here together until my father's Parkinson's became too much for Mother to handle. Then, at the end of 1999, my uncle died, and I flew down for the funeral. I stayed to visit my parents, especially my father who continued to deteriorate. It was right before Christmas and carolers from the churches came through the hospital corridors. As I sat with my father, the sweet sounds of 'Away in a Manger' floated into his room. With enormous effort, he tried to sing with them… A few minutes later, he turned to me. "Love me? Do you love me?"

I could only nod, tears rolling down both of our faces. Three weeks later, he fell when trying to get out of bed during the night. No one responded to his cries, and he wasn't found until the next morning. Unconscious but still alive, he was moved to Amarillo, only gaining consciousness at the end when he called out to my brother: "Don't leave me, Macky, don't leave me." He died later that night.

I returned to Texas with my sons as everyone gathered for the funeral, then stayed to be with my mother for a few days, despite the fact that I needed to return to my classroom. By now, she entered another world, one filled with grief and regret. A month later, she suffered a heart attack, and I came again for a long weekend. My brother, sister, and I began to talk to her about moving to assisted living and renting out the townhouse. We needed the money, and she needed the care.

That was when Mack sold everything and moved permanently from Austin into the farmhouse. Mother, despite her insistence that she 'would not desert Tumbleweed,' finally agreed to move to assisted living in a nearby town. Fortunately, years before, someone talked her into a long-term care insurance policy. She would be taken care of. Mack began the long process of untangling the finances and paying down the debt, but Tutu insisted on staying in control, only agreeing to a joint account with Mack.

We hoped that by being 25 miles away, my niece's visits would stop, yet she continued to visit her grandmother, extorting money. After each visit, Tutu would beg Mack to write a check, convinced the lives of Angie's children depended on her help. She was adamant, insisting it was her money and that this was what she had to do. It was her Christian responsibility… My brother had low tolerance for her pleadings. Checks were written, but he realized something had to change. Finally, after falling in a hallway, Mother consented to completely turn over the checkbook and power-of-attorney. Mack began the process of forcing my niece and her family out of the sprawling Bradford Street house. We could not pay the electric bill anymore because it was built like a barn with large, open spaces and no insulation. And since Angie and Hilario never made the promised monthly payments on the mortgage, that was another liability. We needed to rent it out. To his credit, my brother endured my niece's screaming profanity and constant harassment. He stood strong. They had to leave.

Susan was beside herself. If her daughter and family left the Bradford house, where would they live? No one would rent to them.

There was an empty house in the country, Susan told Mack. It was in foreclosure. The family could move in there for $8000.00, or what it would cost to pay the back taxes. Susan cried and pleaded. Couldn't we find the money to keep them off the street? The wheat had just been harvested, and rather than using our portion of the profits to pay down debts, Mack wrote the check.

Finally, the family moved, taking with them huge boxes of old clothes and half-broken toys. There were hundreds of secondhand household goods Angie acquired at rummage sales intending to resell at a profit. They moved cats, dogs, and three parrots in cages, as well as eight children.

That was the year it finally rained. Water poured in through the leaky roof of the foreclosed house. After that ended, the septic system failed, and mold ran up and down the walls. The cats and dogs multiplied, and Jessie, their ten-year-old son, ran away. The sheriff considered draining the contaminated pond next to the municipal dump a mile away before they found him. He walked three miles to town, climbed in through my sister's attic window and was found hiding in her closet.

My sister insisted they could not remain there…another baby was on the way.

I guess Mack tried to resist the pleadings, but despite his concern about finances, he inherited some of Mother's soft heart. The Bradford Street house was now rented out to someone else. There was nowhere else for Angie's family to live.

Angie and family moved into the townhouse. I didn't find this out until several weeks later. By that time, the house was cleared of my parents' possessions. It happened on one frenzied weekend when almost everything in Mother's well-ordered house was piled onto pickups and cars and transported to the farmhouse bedrooms for storage. Angie's family, with all their boxes, dogs, cats, kids, and parrots, moved into the townhouse – the house Mother wanted to leave to me.

A few months later, Mother fell again, breaking her hip. She wanted to be back in the town she loved, so Mack moved her into the nursing home on the edge of Tumbleweed. The cleanliness and care left something to be desired, but she loved the location. It was only a few yards away from where her grandparents built their dugout when they first arrived in their covered wagon in 1887, the first citizens of what would become Tumbleweed.

When I came down to see her, I was finally told about the new residents of what had once been my grandparents' home. I remember asking my sister if we could visit.

"Why do you want to go over there?" she replied.

"Well, for one thing, I'd like to see the kids, and since Mother wants me to have the house when she's gone, I'd like to see that too."

"I don't see why. You know what it looks like. The kids will be coming over here anyway. You can see them here." She obviously was not eager for me to see the house.

I considered this, then replied, "I don't want to intrude, but I'd really like to see if it's being taken care of."

She gave me a hard look. "You are always so critical. Do you know that every time you come down here, I hire someone to help me clean just so I won't have to listen to your bellyaching?"

This left me wordless. If what I saw was after the cleaning lady, I couldn't imagine what it was like before. For now, I let the subject drop. I would prevail on my brother for help. Legally, this was now a 'rent house,' as he called it, even though Angie and family never paid rent nor was there ever an indication they intended to.

Mack needed to check on it too, so, finally, at the end of the week, we stopped by. If they wouldn't come to the door, he had the key.

Angie opened the door, holding a new baby.

"Oh my," I said, looking first at the new little one. "Let me see."

Angie, dressed in a faded Mickey Mouse T-shirt, pulled back the blanket and I took a peek. Baby number nine was another little girl, and this one looked a lot like her mother, with light skin and blue eyes in contrast to the dark hair and eyes of the others. Despite all her other problems, when her babies were infants, Angie was a devoted mother, holding them and attending to their every need while the others ran wild through the house. She loved babies, but once her children could talk back, she lost interest.

"Hilario's asleep in there," she said, pointing to what had been my mother and grandmother's formal living room. A blanket was now tacked across the wide opening that led from the dining room, but the sound of the blaring T.V. was easily heard. All the windows were covered with dark-out shades, and lights blazed throughout the house although it was a beautiful sunny day outside. When I peeked into the kitchen, all I saw were scattered toys and a stove piled high with pans and dishes. Long gone were the well-scrubbed pink appliances of my childhood. Huge piles of dirty laundry blocked the door that led from the kitchen into the laundry area.

"Okay, well, we don't want to bother him, I guess. I just thought I'd stop by to see how everything is."

"Oh," she spoke with confidence, "we'll be doing lots of work in here. Hilario's brothers can help. We really need a new shower. Mack, did I tell you about that?"

Mack answered in a resigned voice, "Yes. Many times." He turned to me. "Come on, let's go have a look."

Angie shifted the baby to the other arm. "One of the boys is probably in there now."

"Well, let's go check." Mack gestured for me to follow. My grandmother's beloved rose-colored wool carpet was gone and scarred, stained wood, pocked with nails, covered all the floors, except the bathroom. In here was black-and-white tile popular in the '20s, now coming up from the floor. Lavender Kohler fixtures of unique design still stood proudly, although all the faucets were gone, replaced by pliers clamped to the fastenings. Most of the bath tile was gone too, and water dripped ominously from the bathroom faucet.

"Mack, this is awful!" I hissed to my brother.

"I know, but what could I do?"

Angie followed behind us, the two-year-old pulling at her shirt. "Oh, that's not what I meant. It's the other bathroom."

The other one was part of 'the addition' that Granddaddy added in the '50s. It was off the master bedroom and had a shower instead of a tub. If I thought the first bathroom was bad, this one practically reduced me to tears. All the blue ceramic tile was pulled away from the shower stall, and a black substance oozed from the walls. The residue of many overflowing toilets was evident by the damp wood poking through the linoleum flooring. I really didn't want to see any more.

"Okay. I guess this needs to be repaired, Mack," I began, my voice dripping sarcasm.

Ignoring by tone, Angie chimed in, "Yes. It's awful. We really need more room too. We can't even get our cars in the garage because it's the only place we have to put our stuff."

"That's gonna cost a lot more than we have right now." Mack's disgust showed on his face.

Once we were safely out the door and back in the pickup, I turned to Mack. "I can't believe you let them move in and wreck Mother's house. What were you thinking? And you didn't even tell me?"

"Settle down. So, what was I supposed to do? They couldn't live in the horrible house in the country. Nobody will rent to them. I can't just let them live on the street!"

I couldn't argue with that. "We really are over a barrel, aren't we? But this is horrible. We can't just let it go on. It gets worse all the time. We already lost eight-thousand dollars on a house that needs condemning and will just revert back to the county."

"Well, what do you think we should do?"

I thought about this a lot. Honestly, I didn't know either. We were taught compassion since childhood. We helped other people; we didn't cause them misery. We believed people should be given a hand up, especially those who had not been as fortunate as we. In a way, what Mack and I now faced was diametrically opposed to everything we believed and held dear. For Pete's sake, we were Democrats!

"All I know, Mack, is that we have run out of money, and nothing can change that fact. It isn't a matter of choice anymore. Even if we sold all the lots and property in town, we'd only clear a few thousand dollars. The only way we could meet all their needs would be to sell the farm."

"And that," he replied firmly, "is not an option."

What finally happened was that the renters moved out of the Bradford Street house after discovering how difficult it was to heat or air-condition. It was empty at a convenient time. Mack told Angie they had to get out of the townhouse because it needed to be sold. Our money was gone. Since there was no place else for them to go, he agreed they could go back to the Bradford Street house for now, even though that meant we received no money for rent. This, of course, did not really solve the problem. Like everything else, it was a temporary solution to an unsolvable dilemma.

Now, it was almost five years later. After our mother's death, the townhouse was sold at a deep discount to a young couple who had the expertise and willingness to repair all the damage. Angie's family lived in the Bradford Street house until the door frames started falling off, and the cockroaches got so bad, they had to move. They were again out in the country in a small house paid for by farm money. Most of the kids actually lived with Susan, yet their parents continued to collect the food stamps.

As I walked back to the pickup, away from the townhouse that held so many happy memories for me, I was relieved to see that the new owners were keeping their word. From what I saw from peeking in the windows, it looked like someone cared.

Chapter Six

Hattie's Dress

I was feeling the pressure of all I had to do. This week was filled with commitments. There was a luncheon meeting with my class-reunion committee and another with the lawyer and accountant. Also, the Bradford Street house needed to be put on the market. Time was running out to clear out the farmhouse and I really didn't want to make all the decisions about everything by myself. Susan said she did not want me to throw anything away unless she agreed, but she was never here. Since I wrote the check she wanted, there were a couple of days of a fragile peace where she didn't bring up giving the pickup to the boys, and I didn't try to discuss the future of the farm. Now, she insisted she was coming out to help, however, it was late in the afternoon when she arrived.

I had just found a few empty plastic crates in the basement and labeled them 'Give-away,' 'Keep-Susan,' 'Keep-DA,' and 'Trash.' I was just getting ready to scoop all the photographs Susan dumped on the floor the last time she was here into the trash container when I finally heard her van.

"I lost my phone," she said, sounding frazzled as she burst through the door, tramping through the photos. "Either that or one of the kids took it. Sorry I'm late. What are you doing?"

"What does it look like?" I snapped.

She hadn't even heard me. "Can I borrow your phone to call the kids?"

"Okay," I said, resigned to today's crisis. "But first, I think you need to help me do something with Mother's old, high-school photos."

For the first time, she looked down, noticing all the photo folders. "Why are they all over the floor like this?"

"That's where you left them!" I practically shouted.

"Oh. I don't remember that. I'll just stick them back in this box. I want to look at them sometime."

I bit down hard on my lower lip, trying to refocus, then pulled out my phone and handed it over. She made a few frantic calls to the grandkids, trying to locate her phone, then gave it back with a resigned look. "Okay. Nobody will answer, so I'll work a minute, but I've got to get back and see who has it."

"You'll work a minute? I've been working hours and you want to look at everything before I get rid of it. I want to get this done," my voice was rising in proportion to my frustration. Susan ignored me, looking down at my phone as she punched in numbers again.

"What?" She hadn't heard a word I said.

"Okay, I give up," I said, resigned to the situation. "I've worked my way through several of the boxes. The stuff you may want to look through is over there." I pointed to the 'Keep-Susan' container. "I was just getting ready to look through the trunks." Three large trunks plus a smaller footlocker had not yet been opened. "These old trunks fascinate me," I said. "I think at one time, they were all used for distance traveling, especially when they went by railroad. All of these are rounded on the top, indicated that our great-grandparents considered themselves well-off."

"Huh?"

"Yeah, the more well-to-do bought rounded-top trunks so nothing would be stacked on top of them. They didn't want to be stuck on the bottom. Isn't that interesting?"

"Well," she sniffed, "I didn't ask for a lesson on trunks. You don't have to go into detail. All I want to know is what's inside."

Ignoring her attitude, I opened the trunk. "It looks like all this belonged to Mother's side of the family, the Conroys. Oh my God, there is so much here! Look at this." I pulled out an ancient leather wallet still containing Granddaddy's driver's license from 1968, the year he died.

Susan reached in and pulled out a stained, brown, three-inch tube squashed at one end. "What's this?" She held it up for me to see.

"Oh! That's Granddaddy's cigarette holder. Remember? He always used it when he smoked."

"No," she replied. "I don't remember."

"People used to think it made him look like FDR."

"Who?" she asked.

"Franklin Roosevelt. You know, the president?" I said. "He always used one."

"You really are old, aren't you?" she said, only half-kidding.

"Very funny," I replied, sounding more defensive than I intended. "What else is here?"

"I'm surprised you're interested," she replied. "I thought you just wanted to sell everything and be done with it."

"Why would you say that?" I replied indignantly. "History matters to me. Remember, I work at Old World Wisconsin? That's a museum."

"I'm not stupid. I know that," she said, jerking out a pair of monogramed cufflinks. "But you don't act like you care."

"Well, I do. Come on, let's see what's in the other trunk. Remember this one?"

After a few minutes, we were deep into our maternal history, pulling out lovely embroidered pillowcases, handkerchiefs, and tablecloths. There were also old clothes, handmade and fragile. We were both being careful. We didn't want to further damage the old garments which were just as frayed as our fragile sisterhood.

We turned to another larger, rounded-top, steamer trunk. For years, it was in Noona's attic but was moved to the farmhouse when Angie and family moved into the townhouse. When I was a child, the attic itself held countless mysteries for me, and whenever I got chance, I snuck up the steep stairs into the narrow space which was the 'finished part.' The trunk itself was inaccessible, piled precariously with old blankets, hat boxes, and picture frames. Since I was forbidden to go there, the lure of the unknown fed my imagination.

Later, as a teenager, the unfinished part of the attic was even more enticing. It was a huge space of rafters and windows, with two by fours offering a hopscotch design of danger above ancient, dusty, fiberglass insulation. It was there I found an old pack of Lucky Strikes, probably left there a generation before by my mother. It also contained the furnace and air-conditioners, plus a few sparrows and their nests, so it made a wonderful refuge for a sulky teen who was always warned to beware of the floor. I remembered my mother calling to me from downstairs, "Get down here this minute! You could fall through! Right now, get down. You could land spank dab on top of my grandmother's dining table! Do you want me to get out the paddle?"

I was afraid of the consequences, so I just spent time imagining. Fed by mystery books and romantic novels, I could create scenarios of treasure maps, stacks of 100-dollar bills, and beautiful jewelry. Maybe old letters that told of a secret love or forgotten adventure.

It wasn't until 50 years later that I was finally able to open the trunk. Instead of valuables, it was filled with clothes – beautiful, beaded, black dresses, satin nightgowns, and tiny, cotton, baby bonnets. The dress at the bottom was a rough muslin, turned yellow with age. Actually, it was a chemise – designed to be worn under a corset. On the inside of the collar, penned in ancient ink, the name Hattie Conroy.

"Susan, look at this!" My sister was examining a pair of lacy black sleeves, meant to attach to a bodice. She turned to see what I found.

"Oh wow, that's really old," she said, taking the chemise from me. "The name inside the collar says Hattie, but I never heard of anyone by that name. Who was she?" For a minute, she forgot about the kids and her missing phone.

"Hang on. I think the family Bible is here somewhere and it lists all the Conroys." I was glad to finally have her attention. Searching through a pile of books stacked on a nearby table, I pulled out the heavy hard-covered book with its faded yellow pages. I remembered that for many years it occupied a place of honor was on Noona's formal living-room coffee table. I hadn't really looked at it for years.

Susan looked over my shoulder and I stood up and handed it to her. "Be careful, it's really heavy."

She gave me a dirty look, then dumped it on a side table and opened it. "Oh yeah. I tried to read the names and dates in there lots of times when I was younger, but now I can't see it well enough. You know I need cataract surgery, don't you?"

"Yes, you've told me many times," I said.

"Well, that's a tacky way to put it," she replied, opening the heavy cover.

"Sorry," I responded. "What do you want me to look at?"

"I think all the family history is here, right at the front, all the births and deaths and marriages. You read them out to me, and I'll write them down, okay?" Suddenly, my sister was more animated than I'd seen her in a long time. Together, we began to piece together the story of Hattie Conroy. Not only was the writing faded, it was also in the script of the 19th century, before the Palmer Method, so a 'T' could look like an 'F,' or a 'B' could be mistaken for an 'S.' Besides that, the ink was faded and hard to see. Strangely, however, the section that told of Hattie's death was much easier to read than the rest.

Born in 1855, Cooper County, Missouri, the daughter of Mary Ann Bousfield and James Frederick Conroy; sister to William Green Conroy, my great-grandfather. According to the fading ink, she died in 1876 of spinal meningitis while attending Normal School. She was 21. Her mother, Mary Ann, died 13 years earlier in 1863 when Hattie was only eight years old. Three of her young brothers died before their mother, in 1860, 1861, and 1862. Then her ten-year-old brother died right before her mother in 1963. To make matter worse, Missouri was embroiled in the question of slavery and soon the family would be caught up in the anguish of the Civil War. A few years before Hattie died, her older sister, Elizabeth, married and went home to attend to her three, surviving, older brothers.

I stood up and looked at Susan. "Can you imagine Hattie's mother? Losing four children and then dying so young? Our great-great-grandmother was only 37 years of age when she died."

"Maybe," replied my sister, "she died of grief."

"Yes," I nodded, "and hard work."

Life for women was difficult on the frontier. Family lore told us that James Frederick, Hattie's father and our great-great-grandfather, emigrated as a young boy from Kentucky to Missouri. Later, he owned a prosperous mill which furnished ground grain to the wagon trains headed west. He perfected a way of milling wheat that made the flour a favorite of the gold prospectors and families looking to homestead. There is no reliable record about what happened during the war years, but that area of Missouri had families fighting both for the North and for the South, as small, local, militia units. When war arrived, it tore apart the state, and the mill and family home were burned to the ground. We were never sure which side they were on.

Susan pulled out a thick, velvet-covered photo album lying on the bottom of the trunk. "Look at this." She held it out to me.

"Oh my gosh. Who are these people?" Staring back at me on each page were well-dressed men and children with the serious expressions typical of mid-19th century photography. Most were young men. A few were African American. "Mother never told us about this."

Susan agreed. "There were lots of things she never told us."

"I hate to think this, but I wonder if they were the family's slaves?"

"Oh, that's awful. No, I don't think so. Look at how they're dressed. It's not like slaves. Besides that, they're having their pictures taken."

"I don't know," I replied. "From what I've read, that part of Missouri was known as 'Little Dixie' because so many of the Scotch-Irish residents traveled there from eastern Kentucky. Many of them owned a family of slaves, maybe six or seven adults and kids. Maybe our great-great-grandparents were just what were called 'good slave-owners,' as awful as that sounds."

Susan gave me a scornful look. "You don't know that. You aren't right about everything, you know."

"No," I said, "I'm certainly not right about everything."

After a long, uncomfortable pause, I turned back to the Hattie's dress. Unlike all the other clothes we found with 18-inch waists and tiny, lacy sleeves, the heavy muslin chemise with Hattie's name was designed to fit a larger woman.

"Hattie may not have been built like the other women in her family, but she obviously had their determination, since she was able to convince her father to send her away to Normal School at a time when that was not typical of a woman."

"I wonder why she decided to do that." Susan examined the dress as I thought about what might have happened.

"Well, I'd guess that the years after her sister left would have been really difficult."

"So," Susan replied, "what makes you think that?"

"Well, her older sister was gone, and she was the only woman taking care of her father and brothers." I hesitated. "Really, I don't know. Maybe it's just how I would feel if I were in her place."

"Or" my sister suggested, "maybe ol' James Frederick hoped that if she left home, Hattie would find a man to marry."

"Could be," I replied. "All we know for sure is that Hattie was on the way home from school when she died."

"That's awful. All those losses. Her brothers died, then her mother died, and, after that, her sister left. Poor Hattie, she never had much of a chance for happiness." My sister gently folded the old, yellowed chemise and lay it on the dining table. "Maybe she really died of a broken heart because she missed her sister who was so far away."

This seemed a strange comment for my sister to make.

I looked up quickly to catch her expression. Was she just talking about Hattie or was she thinking of someone else? Nothing in her facial expressions or body language gave me a clue. "Well," I said, "one thing is sure. The family loved Hattie enough to preserve something that reminded them of her. We have the dress to prove it."

"Maybe we'll find some letters or something and find out more about her." Susan suddenly stood up. "Oh, my gosh, I've got to go. I've got to figure out what happened to my phone."

There was alarm in her voice as she again shouldered the responsibility of her grandchildren and all that went with it.

"We're almost finished with this trunk," I said. "Can't you wait until then?" If this was the first time Susan's phone was missing, I might have been concerned, but this happened all the time. One of the grandkids would take the phone to call or text their friends, then keep it until the battery ran down. In the meantime, Susan was left playing the guessing game of which grandchild had it this time.

My sister was already headed for the door. "Nope. Gotta go."

"Hey, wait! Remember, we need to talk about having the farm appraised." My plea was drowned out by the screen banging behind her, awakening the dogs from their naps.

I sighed and turned back to the task at hand. It troubled me that Susan had no time in her life for anything except reacting to her daughter and her grandchildren. At some time or other, my sister's sense of self disappeared, leaving someone else behind. Possibly that was the trade-off many women used to make – sacrificing selfhood for the greater good of the family. I was still thinking about my mother's grandparents. Was this a pattern that ran in our family?

It didn't sound like that was the case with Hattie. According to the records in the bible, a year after Hattie's death, her older brother, my great-grandfather, William, married a feisty, young schoolteacher who moved with her family to Missouri from Cadmus County, Ohio. Her name was Lucy Canary, and had she known what her future held, I'm not so sure she would have hitched her wagon to his star.

I was always fascinated by the romantic story my mother told about her family, the Conroys. Unlike my father's side of the family who arrived from

Michigan in 1916 by train, my mother's family arrived 30 years earlier via covered wagon and horseback.

Shortly after my great-grandfather's marriage to Lucy Canary, my great-great-grandfather and his sons, William and Lincoln, decided that life in post-war Missouri held no future, since wagon trains headed west were being replaced by the railroad. After selling their land, they joined Elizabeth and her family in Texas, following glowing reports of the rich pastures of North Central Texas where enterprising young cattlemen could fatten up their herds, then drive them to market in Kansas City.

A year after their move, in 1886, our great-great-grandfather died, and soon his two sons, their wives, and families decided to pull up stakes again. They loaded up their families and possessions and followed the cattle northwest from Clay County to the Llano Estacado, and what came to be known as the Texas Panhandle, a land of endless grass and mesquite that had until recently been Comanche territory. Here were huge ranches that stretched into the horizon, the longest shadow cast for miles being that of a scrawny cactus.

Lucy brought her piano, her gilded gold picture frames, the family bible, and huge trunks filled with necessities – delicate kerosene lamps, lacy corsets, precious china dishes, fine-cut crystal, plus heavy cookware. Hand-carved furniture was loaded into the wagons. Within the space of a few years, Lucy moved from Ohio to Missouri, taught school, married William, bore a daughter and son, moved with her young family to north Texas, then into what was, until recently, Indian territory where she had four more children, including my grandfather.

As my mother told it, unlike many years, the spring of 1887 was one of incredible beauty on the high plains. The rain arrived at the right time. The grasses rippled into endless waves punctuated by brilliant wildflowers. Land was cheap, and the railroad and U.S. government were eager to sell. Here was land to make one rich overnight – the prairie had not been plowed, and under the root mat of thousands of years, the soil was rich, fertile, and for the taking.

As I looked through the old trunk in front of me, I wondered about their lives. Had these eager young men scouted out the land beforehand? Did the women know they would be living with their young children in a spider-filled dugout for the first few years? Had W.C., as my great-grandfather came to be known, told his wife about the hardships they would face? What had Lucy Canary given up of herself to become the faithful wife? Or was it her independence and resilience that provided the determination to insist that the land they homesteaded be listed in her name as well as her husband's?

When my mother told us the story of our family history years later, her voice took on an ethereal quality – there was a reverence toward these brave pioneers: "They stopped at the most beautiful place on earth – green grass as far as the eye could see...then close to a narrow branch of the Prairie Dog Branch of the Red River, they dug a hole into the side of a small incline, and they were home." For the rest of her life, my mother would continue to see the land as she saw it in her imagination – beautiful and brimming with life. My sister still wanted to see it that way. I was the realist, shattering that lifelong illusion.

By the time I was old enough to hear the stories, all I heard was the Texas part. Seldom mentioned were the stops along the way: my ancestors left Scotland, Ulster/Ireland, Virginia, Ohio, Kentucky, Missouri, and Central Texas. Within a few generations, they emigrated a third of the way around the world. Left behind at each stop were brothers, sisters, cousins, aunts, uncles, and tiny graves of children. Also left behind was their precious land, representing status and hard work, plus people they loved.

They named their little settlement Tumbleweed after the invasive Russian thistle that took root on the plains at about the same time as they arrived. Starting life as a bush, it peppered the land with greenery until late in the summer when it would dry up, turn brown, and detach from its root, blowing across the prairie into the small towns and against the new barbed-wire fences. Like my ancestors, they didn't stay put. Rolling and tumbling until stopped by an obstacle beyond their control. There they dropped their seeds, propagating new generations to roll toward the horizon.

I could identify with these people who bequeathed me more than their DNA. They put down roots, growing to love the rough land, hoping to defy the tumbleweeds and stay put, putting up windmills to pump up precious water. Now it was up to me to decide the fate of a piece of the earth dearly beloved by people I loved.

I wrapped up the bible in an old wool shawl and placed it tenderly next to the other old books piled on the table.

Chapter Seven
Reunion Lunch

The next day was filled with meetings and errands in town. I stopped at Susan's to pick up my class yearbook. Somehow, our yearbooks were switched years before. Ever since she misplaced her phone, I had not been able to reach her. When I walked in, she was lying on the couch with her arm thrown over her head. "Oh, sorry to bother you," I began. "I'm off to Taco Tienda to meet with Penny and the others about the reunion."

"So, I thought we were going to talk doing an appraisal on the farm...and the pickup," she replied from under her elbow.

Now she wanted to talk! "I have to do this first, since I already promised. Could we do it later?" I asked, pulling my yearbook from her stuffed bookcase.

"Sure," she sniffed. "We'll go with what you want to do."

"Do you have a conflict in the morning?" I replied as I turned toward the door.

"I never know what I'll need to do for the kids. You know I can't plan my life like you can."

"Okay. We'll hope tomorrow works out. Sorry." No matter what I did, it seemed to be wrong for Susan. Now I wished I never agreed to help with the reunion, but I couldn't back out now.

I was halfway out the door when she sat up and said, "I can't believe you are actually helping with your reunion since you hate this town so much."

"What?" I asked.

"You hate this town. You don't like anything about it. You're always complaining about the stores and the schools and everything." She rose and moved toward the kitchen.

"Look," I said, "I don't hate this town, I just don't think it is the same place it was when I was a child, but that's not unusual. It's where I grew up, how could I hate it?" As I turned to come back in and have it out with her, I realized that Susan already walked into the next room, my reply disappearing into thin air.

****

Taco Tienda was built in the '70s when windows were out of favor. No natural light entered the restaurant for over 40 years. The dark paneling added to the gloom, yet it was known for good Mexican food and attracted out-of-towners. Penny arrived early – bright and freshly washed. The others dribbled in, including Cindy who was the star athlete of our winning 1963 girls' basketball team and was married to a prominent rancher. She still exuded the same confidence and privilege as she did in high school. Even though she wasn't on the official reunion committee, her opinion was always worth 51%.

Marcia arrived with a fanfare, removing her jewel-studded sunglasses and depositing a large bag on the chair next to me. "Well, I hope no one minds if I make a memory book." Marcia, once our head cheerleader, looked pointedly at Cindy. She was on safe ground here; all of us were just glad our pictures and obituaries weren't in the book yet. Our class of 100 was dwindling rapidly. Quite a few still lived nearby and ascribed to various sects of fundamentalist religions that morphed, in the last few years, into a kind of southwestern Tea-party-populism. They were honest, hardworking, salt-of-the-earth, and hooked on Fox News. By comparison, I looked very 'blue,' so I tried to fit in by changing my order from a salad, which raised eight pairs of eyebrows, to the Taco Tienda special – a chili relleno with beans.

Johnetta sat across from me, warm, plush, and pink, smelling of lily-of-the-valley. She was the picture of serene, her years falling into soft folds below her cocker, spaniel, brown eyes. She always accepted with equanimity her place in the hierarchy of our class.

Van, Al, and Gene were seated at the end of the table. These men came into their own after high school. Van was a farmer, Al owned the Ford dealership, and Gene managed the feedlot. They all reached that age when they had solid marriages and satisfactory careers behind them. As we waited for our food, Van spoke up.

"Well, ladies, I got the float all figured out. Got the trailer and the hay bales, and I'll have the tractor there on Saturday morning."

"You got the foldin' chairs?" Johnetta piped up from our end of the table. "And, ya know, I think you better get a stool or ladder, 'cause some of us'll have trouble gettin' up there."

"You know, I hadn't thought 'a that. I'll get us something to use." Van was always friendly and agreeable, and this time was no exception.

Tumbleweed's annual summer celebration was called Picnic. Of course, there was a parade and it was tradition to have each high-school class celebrating a special reunion ride in a flatbed trailer. Sitting on our high perch of hay bales and folding chairs, we would throw wrapped candy down for the kids to catch. Each class was recognized with a banner on the side, recognizing the year of graduation. It was the town's biggest celebration of the year, and every church, business, and organization sponsored a float. The high-school band, sweating along in their maroon wool uniforms, played the school fight-song, and Miss Tumbleweed, in her formal gown, waved and smiled. All the Junior Miss Tumbleweeds in their rhinestone tiaras circled around her dais of hay bales, giddy with their first taste of celebrity.

"It'll probably take a ramp to get me up there," laughed Penny, diving into the sea of cheese covering her chili relleno. "There's lots of us who can't get up a ladder anymore."

I added my two cents, remembering the last reunion I attended, "We have to think about the heat too. That sun will be beating down on us several hours."

"Oh, for Pete's sake, just put on a hat and bring along your water," Cindy added helpfully, "What do you think we are anyway – old?"

Actually, that was all that was running through our minds as we stared down at our cholesterol-filled plates. The runny, yellow cheese always reminded me of the pimento cheese and Velveeta sandwiches my mother would make using soft, white Wonder Bread.

"You know, don't you, that Betty has dementia," Penny offered.

"Wasn't she, our Valedictorian?" This came from Al at the end of the table.

"No. She was Salutatorian. Greg was the top one. You know, she even needs help pulling down her underwear to go to the bathroom. At least, that's what her sister told me last week at the beauty parlor. But now, don't go talkin' about it. They don't want people to know." Penny was the picture of decorum when it came to gossip.

Nobody said anything as we contemplated this ominous news and chewed on our nacho chips.

"Yeah," Gene added, "And Bill Howe is in assisted living down yonder near Kerrville."

"What's wrong with ol' Bill?" asked Van.

"Don't know. Just know that's just where he's at."

"Well," continued Penny briskly, "then there's 15 or so we can't locate at all – wonder where they are and what happened to them. Used to be we'd contact their folks, but practically all our folks are long gone now, and if there aren't any relatives around, well—"

"Now speak for yourself, Penny," Cindy interrupted. "My parents are in their 90s and still drive to Amarillo to see my great-nieces' basketball games. They tell everybody they have to stay healthy, so they can take the old folks to the doctors. Used to be they'd just take the Methodists, but now they pretty much take everybody, since it seems the Baptists are all worn out."

Quiet settled on us again as we crunched.

"So," continued Penny, "anything else? If nobody else does, I think it's time to decide on money and what this all's gonna cost. My vote is to use Mz. Cruz over at Senior Citizens. She does a real good plate, plus drink and dessert for $15.00. Otherwise, it's gonna get pricey real fast."

"What are our other options?" I asked, even though I already knew I was outvoted.

"Well, it's Picnic," continued Penny. "So, all the places with good barbecue are already booked solid."

"I thought we could maybe look at something else," I added.

"Well," Johnetta spoke up, "using Mz. Cruz sounds fine to me. You get the price up more'n that, people just stay away."

"What kind of plate does Mrs. Cruz do?" I asked.

"Oh, the usual. Barbecue, slaw, and beans – that kind of thing – plus iced tea and a sheet cake." Penny was anxious to get this pinned down.

By now, the men tuned out, and everyone seemed ready to get the details behind us. The conversation was turning to the weather and grandkids when Al spoke up again.

"Ya'll know the other classes are doin' a collection for Sonny's grave, don't you?"

"Oh, that's right," chimed in Penny. "We don't want to be the only class that doesn't chip in."

"What?" I asked, confused. "Fill me in?"

"Oh, that's right, you probably don't know," Al replied. "Well, you know ol' Sonny got plum run-over a few months ago, and some of us got together and decided we needed to buy a marker for his grave. That's what I'm a talkin' about."

"Sonny? Who are you talking about? You mean Sonny Simons?" He was the only Sonny I could think of. "What happened?"

"Well, if you got a few minutes, I'll fill you in. The rest of ya'll don' need to stay. I know you got places to be and this reunion's gonna come off just fine."

"Well, okay," said Penny, picking up her purse. "We'll see ya'll down at the Memorial Building on Wednesday, right? That way, we can look things over and make sure we have everything we need. Now ya'll don't forget. Let's make it 10:30 on Wednesday."

Al gave me a little wink. "Now you sit yourself down and wait right here while I make a stopover yonder at the little boys' room. I'll be back in a jiffy and tell you all about it."

I sank into a nearby folding chair and thought about the Simons family:

Behind my grandfather's Chevy-Olds dealership was a little railroad-car of a house that our family rented to the Simons for many years. Several years before she died, my mother gave the property to the city with the understanding that the brothers could stay there for as long as they lived. At one time, the Simons family were prominent citizens of the town – present in the photos showing a groundbreaking or cornerstone laying. But by the time I knew them, the Simons fell on hard times. There were rumors about desertion and incest, but all most of us knew for sure was that Dickie and Sonny were both in 'special classes.' As they aged out of school, any responsible older relatives seemed to be out of the picture, and the two 'boys' were on their own.

If there was a wedding, funeral, or anniversary event, both men showed up for refreshments, stuffing their pockets with what wouldn't fit onto their plates. They wandered from store to store, library to post office, usually walking one behind the other down the middle of the street. Sporting identical, felt Stetsons with the sides furled up, and Lee Rider jeans with pant legs turned up at least six inches, the lighter-sided denim almost reaching their knees, they marched along, oblivious to the astonished glances of strangers to town who honked and swerved as they rounded a corner, nearly missing running down one of the brothers.

Of course, everyone in town knew them and always drove accordingly, aware that at any minute, one of the brothers could materialize right in front of their vehicles. These were 'our boys' and, as such, were cared for by the entire community. As a rule, they attended Donnie Granger's church, the Gospel Tabernacle, but they could also show up at any of the churches, depending on the weather. Mostly they were non-verbal, though Dickie would make eye contact and mumble more to himself than others. Sonny just followed Dickie, usually shuffling along at least three paces behind.

As children, they represented to us all that we did not want to be. Associating a girl's name romantically with one of the brothers was the worst insult that could be thrown at another, and one long remembered. As older teenagers, we began to realize that these men were people to be cared for rather than pitied and made fun of, and we too began to watch out for them as we passed our driving tests and acquired the coveted license.

Returning from the little boys' room, Al took off his seed cap and smoothed back his thinning hair before putting it back on over his bald spot. "It's mighty sad what happened to poor ol' Sonny," he began. "Started out on one of those drizzly gray mornings, I guess. There's this little ol' gal, 'bout 15 years old or so, and she was late to school and ended up jumpin' into her brother's pickup and taking off for school. Gossip says she was a lookin' in the rearview mirror, puttin' on makeup or somethin' or h'other, and she hit what she thought was a big bump. Turned out, wasn't a bump at all."

"Oh no," I said as my hand flew to my mouth. "Don't tell me that it was Sonny?"

"Yep. Sure 'nuff. 'At little gal got out and realized that she had run right over a body. Well, what does she do but panic. Rather than callin' the sheriff or somebody, she just got right back into that pickup and headed up to the high school. Nobody figured it out 'til that afternoon. I guess her brother was lookin' for his pickup, and he went up there to the high school and hauled her outta that school. 'Bout that time, she broke down and told him what all had happened…"

"And Sonny?" I was almost afraid to ask.

"Well, he was dead. I s'pose he was a walkin' down the middle of the street and didn't even see what hit him. You know how he and Dickie used to do, don't ya?"

"Oh yes. They were still doing that, huh?"

"Yep. But funniest thing. Nobody could find Dickie. Looked high and low and nobody could find him for nothin'." Al was folding up a paper napkin as he talked.

"So, what happened?" I asked.

"After a few days, somebody decided they better just go ahead and bury Sonny, and just as the refreshments come out, here comes Dickie, lookin' all foggy and lost but helping hisself to a pile of cookies and crackers. Never would say a word…'course he never did, just kinda grunted and groaned. Now it just got worse."

"Oh, Al," I said. "I feel so sorry for that poor man."

"Well, we all do. That's why we decided to take a collection and buy a marker for Sonny's grave. Also, lots of the churches 'round here are makin' sure ol' Dickie has food and clothes and takes a bath and shaves every now and then. He's still alivin' in that little ol' house with all his National Geographics. Guess he's doin' okay." Al glanced at his watch. "Well, I gotta get goin', I'll be seein' you in a few days up to the Memorial building, right?"

On the way back to the farm, I stopped at the post office to pick up the mail which was still being delivered to my brother's box. As I turned the steering wheel to pull out into the street, it turned freely in a perfect circle. After a few tries, however, it seemed to reengage and I drove directly to the auto-repair place that once housed my grandfather's Chevrolet dealership. Fortunately, it was only a couple of blocks away, and after he looked it over, the young man who worked there advised me not to drive it any distance. Repairs would be several hundred dollars. I limped the vehicle toward my sister's house to deliver the news.

"Well," I began, "it looks like the old white pickup has hit the dust. Cy at the Auto Repair just told me it needs lots of work."

Susan was resting on the couch again. "What does it need?"

"Looks like there are several things, but right now, it's the steering," I replied.

"Well, then," she said, "We probably can't sell it, so we might as well give that one to the boys."

I looked at her with disbelief. "No, you don't understand. It really isn't safe to drive. We don't want them to get in an accident. Besides, not one of them has a driver's license."

"They need a vehicle to drive," Susan persisted. "We got to drive a car when we were their age."

"We got to drive Mother's car when she agreed we could borrow it for an hour on Sunday afternoon, but that was after we got our driver's licenses! And I didn't have a car of my own until after I graduated from college and had a job," my voice was rising.

Susan avoided looking at me. "You always have a good answer, don't you?"

"Susan," I continued, refusing to rise to her bait. "We need to sell it for whatever we can get for it. Don't you realize that we don't even have enough money to pay the bills as it is? What about that don't you understand?"

"Well, whoop-de-do, you have the checkbook, so you have all the answers." She was in no mood to negotiate.

"Look," I said, "I'm going back out to the farm and hope and pray I make it out and back before it conks out on me for good. I have an appointment to get it fixed tomorrow. I'll still be here for a couple of weeks, and I might as well pay to at least have the steering repaired instead of renting a car. In the meantime, I'm going to see if the guy down at the used car lot will still buy it." Susan turned over on the couch with her back to me as I walked out the door.

As I pulled out into the street that led to the Farm-to-Market road, a familiar figure appeared in front of me. It was Dickie, still walking down the middle of the street.

Chapter Eight
Silver, Gold, and Guns

Back at the farm, Mack's dogs pranced to greet me, with tails wagging. These had been his kids, and both Susan and I agreed we needed to keep them until we decided what would happen to the farmhouse. When I was here, I took care of them; otherwise, it was up to Susan. I was glad they were with me. I didn't remember feeling apprehensive about being so far out of town when I was a kid, but then, Mimi and Grandpa were a mile away, and we had other neighbors a mile down the road in all other directions. Later, when the older generation died, their children sold or rented out the farmland. Most of the places that used to house lively families were deserted and decaying. Now, our closest neighbors were the Finches, Jerry Bob's extended family. It seemed lonely and desolate, especially at night when the coyotes howled. I was glad to have the dogs letting me know if anyone came near.

I fed them and we headed out to the pasture, just like Mack used to do. Soon they were scaring up jack rabbits and racing toward the runoff pond half a mile away. Everything was dry, and dust sprang up from the course prairie grass. Yet under the bright sunshine of day, there was an eternal sense of peace in this place, no background noise except the call of a mockingbird. Prairie-walking was like meditation, calming the mind. It was always where I went to think and clear my head when I was a kid. I felt at home here, in my father's pasture. There were so many decisions to make, both small and large. It was all so overwhelming and exhausting. As much as I loved the wide-open spaces where I grew up, I was deeply troubled about sharing this land with my sister, even from a distance, and despite the fact that the farming operation was rented out.

We did agree on having everything appraised. At least that was decided. Maybe after that we could at least have a conversation about dividing it up rather than trying to manage it as a partnership. I didn't see how we could successfully work together when our ways of thinking and doing things were so different.

The dogs finally gave up on the jackrabbit and turned around, panting and exhausted, as we headed back to the house and into the chaos of the real world. I turned on the radio and tackled clearing out more of the kitchen cabinets. Mack's computer and T.V. were still here, but there was no internet connection or antenna anymore. On a good day, I could pick up a snowy and unreliable A.B.C. affiliate, but, otherwise, the radio was my only form of diversion. The radio stations were all Christian talk-shows or Country and Western. Right now, Eric Church was letting me know that somebody loved him like Jesus does. For now, I would have to settle for that.

I decided that I would sell the pickups, no matter what Susan wanted me to do. We could get $5000.00 for the newer truck and Irv, down at the used car lot, offered $1500.00 for the old truck before the steering went out, insisting that the engine was good and that, "Most ol' boys 'round here could fix 'er up, since they're mostly lookin' for a field pickup for their hands." I could try to get Irv out here to change the tire on the newer pickup and get it started, but knowing how things worked around here, it probably would be weeks before he made time for that. I'd talk to him about it before I dropped off Trusty Rusty for repair tomorrow, but in the meantime, I needed a vehicle.

I pondered this as I pulled down the old, faded, Pyrex bowls, red, blue, yellow, and green. Abruptly, I was jarred out of my reverie by the old rotary phone in the hall. It rang with the same loud shrill as 40 years before. It was Lyle. He and Mack had been good friends since childhood, and he was the one who called me that night in January after he found Mack. I called him before I left home, but I hadn't had time to see him yet.

"How are you doin'?" he asked.

"I'm hanging in there," I replied. "How about you."

"I'm okay. Don't you worry about me. I'm returning your call about the guns. Is there a time we could get together to figure it out?"

I hesitated, thinking of everything on my plate. With everything else going on, I completely forgot that I asked him to help me with the guns and gold. "Hmm, why don't I meet you for lunch tomorrow, would that work?"

"All right. Let's meet at Delores's. That way, won't be many people to bother with."

"Delores's?"

"Yeah. Remember Delores? She was cook up at the school cafeteria. Decided to open her own place and recreate those cafeteria meals. Just opened up over to where the Fowler Jewelry store used to be? Over to the north side of the square."

"Okay, sounds good," I replied, imagining the starchy fried food of my childhood. The food really wouldn't matter though, since talking to Lyle always brought back that night more than six months before.

****

It was January, six months before. I just returned home from our annual, family, business meeting with Andy and Stu, the accountant and attorney. The trust my parents set up years before to avoid probate would sunset in September. My sister, brother, and I had decisions to make. The meeting was tense. Mack wanted to continue managing everything for us, with little input from either Susan or me. I was grateful for his help in getting on top of most of the debt but not so sure he should continue as sole manager. He was very protective of the finances, probably due to his eccentric bookkeeping system which involved envelopes and boxes. Despite all his talk about women needing equal rights, he insisted that keeping the books was really a man's work. Fortunately, once a year, he loaded all the boxes into the pickup and took them into the accountant's office where he dumped them in Evelyn's office. She gave him his yearly scolding and then got to work, organizing it all into tidy rows and columns of numbers. However, Evelyn was aging and wouldn't be around forever to do the unscrambling. It was time for a change. I felt each of us should at least manage our own share once the trust ended. Susan agreed. However, both Stu and Andy advised us that there was much work to be done if we were going to form a partnership.

Mack did not want to have to deal with meddling sisters and made it clear he did not think a partnership would work.

Our accountant and lawyer first suggested we sell the farm and split the proceeds. Both Mack and Susan were adamant – that was not what they wanted to do. The next option they suggested was that we jointly own the farm, dividing any income, after expenses, three ways. But there was a problem; the elephant in the room we tiptoed around. My sister had already taken twice as much money out of the trust as my brother and me. Now would come the accounting, and it was not pretty, neat, or tidy. Angry words were slung and feelings bruised. Andy and Stu intervened, giving advice, providing financial figures, explaining legal obligations, reminding us of our parents' final wishes at the time the irrevocable trust was established.

After a long, exhausting meeting, a tentative settlement was hammered out. We would each manage our share of the farmland and sell as much of the other property as possible. Susan would be given the Darnell Street house where she lived; Mack would get the farmhouse. The townhouse, which Mother intended for me to have, was already sold, and I would receive proceeds from that as my share. Mack reluctantly agreed to the plan. Susan was silently seething. Her share was less than ours. All three of us realized the arrangement was far from perfect; we would still be yoked together, each pulling in a different direction. We were all emotionally drained. I was looking forward to leaving for home the next day.

We left the office and I said my goodbyes to Mack on the corner across the street from Hartley and James, the drugstore where he used to buy Emeraude perfume for our mother on special occasions and then charge it to her. He planned to take me to the airport the next day, but for some unknown reason, Susan insisted she drive me. Not itching for another conflict, I agreed.

I gave Mack a final hug and got into Susan's old van to drive back to the chaos of her house where I was staying. We passed the afternoon and evening in frosty politeness. The 50-mile trip to the airport the next morning was long, and I breathed a sigh of relief when I cleared security and was safely buckled into my seat. Next stop, Denver International, then on to Milwaukee and home.

Later that evening, a devastated Lyle told me what happened: he and Mack planned to meet for lunch that day. When Mack failed to show up and didn't respond to phone calls or emails, Lyle was worried.

While Lyle was worrying over the no-show lunch date, I arrived home to find everything covered with snow. The frostiness of a deep, dark, January evening felt refreshing after the tense, tight quarters at my sister's. I breathed in the cold air through my fleece scarf, watching my little dog, Lexie, pick just the right spot to yellow the snow. Minutes ticked by as I looked up at the stars, then down at an amazing sight in front of me. The moonlight hitting the snow seemed to be alive with flickering lights, unlike anything I ever saw. For a moment, I wondered if someone placed a string of white Christmas lights on the lawn because the snow was blinking, alive like fireflies. Mesmerized, I stood watching for long moments until Lexie tugged me toward the door. I was pulling off my coat and boots when the phone rang. My world tilted.

Lyle was on the line. He just found Mack dead on the floor of his bedroom office, his head on top of a dented trashcan. He had probably been there since shortly after I said goodbye to him the day before.

A few foggy hours later, I was back in the Denver Airport, on my way again to Amarillo and the responsibility of assuming stewardship of my parents' estate which included 2500 acres of farmland. On top of that, I was dealing with the shock of my brother's death. Lyle met me at the airport, still suspended in a state of disbelief. "He seemed fine when I saw him last. The day of that meeting, after you left, we had lunch, and then he headed to the farm for his afternoon nap."

He shoved a ring of keys into my hand. "Your sister is furious at me because there are some things at the farmhouse, he didn't want her to know about. You're the only one he trusted. I'm pretty sure you're his executor."

"Me? He never told me…"

"He never thought this would really happen, but he did plan ahead. Can you believe it, he planned ahead?"

I thought of all my nagging lectures about durable power of attorney. "But I just asked him. Last week, I asked him and he wouldn't say…"

"You're going to be surprised."

"What do you mean?"

"He had a locked file – I just gave you the key. Also, there's extra keys to the pickups, the house and the barn, and a lockbox at Stan's Safe Storage."

I looked at the devastated man who stood in front of me. Together, he and Mack survived divorces, alcohol, drugs, and tragedy. Always, they supported each other. This man had been my brother's rock – his shelter after a car accident many years before almost ended Mack's life and took the life of a friend. Lyle was drawn, pale, exhausted, and still in shock.

"I'm so glad you are here," he said. "I can't keep your sister away for any longer. She says the farmhouse is hers, not mine, and that I have no legal standing…"

"Does she know that I do?"

"She doesn't really believe that either, but she can't deny that you are part-owner too."

"So, what's in the file?"

"His will and papers from the attorney…also guns, gold, and silver."

"Guns? Gold and silver?"

"Lots. We went together and bought bullion, government issued. Not all of it is there though. Some is locked in a safe vault in Amarillo. You know that life-insurance policy your mom had that paid out after she died? Well, he cashed it out, bought the precious metals and some gemstones. Didn't trust the market all the way, I guess."

"How much?"

"You'll have to count it. I'll help you. I invested in it too."

"So, he had guns too?"

"Yep, a couple of 'em are really old. I figure they might have been your daddy's or granddaddy's. There's a shotgun and a rifle."

"In the file cabinet? How could that be?"

"No, those ones are way back on that wide shelf in the closet. It's the revolvers that are in the file. You know that big, ol', heavy, four-drawer one? It's got those long drawers and I'll betcha it weighs 500 pounds."

"So, how many revolvers are you talking about? And why did he need them?"

"Protection, I figure."

"I'm surprised. Mack was always such a pacifist. What did he have to protect?"

Lyle gave me a sidelong glance from the driver's seat. "All that silver and gold, I figure. Plus, this country's fillin' up with druggies who'd do most anything to get money for dope. But that's one reason I didn't give your sister the keys. I was afraid those grandkids of hers might figure out a way to get to those guns and the other stuff, and then who knows what would happen… I tell you what, though, I'll take 'em and keep 'em safe for you for now, if you're worrying about 'em."

"I think that might be a good idea, Lyle. Wow, is there ever lots to think about…?" Exhaustion was already setting in and I hadn't even begun to face all there was in front of me.

"I'll drop you at Susan's. That's where you'll be staying for now, isn't it? I mean, until you have a chance to get out to the farmhouse and set up things for yourself?"

"Yes. Thanks, Lyle. I can't face staying at the farmhouse right now. Funny how death affects you…"

I expected tearful, loving hugs from my sister when I arrived at her house. Instead, there was a perfunctory greeting as she turned away from my outstretched arms. She was furious. "I can't get into my own house. Yes! I am furious. My own house and he won't give me the keys. Mack would never give me a set and now neither will Lyle. Can you ask him for them? Maybe he'll give them to you. It's my house. Not his! He won't let me go into my own house!" I followed her as she walked toward the backyard and the sanctuary of her smoking corner littered with cigarette butts and stained cups of half-frozen coffee. "We have to talk."

"So, just let me set down my bags and go to the bathroom, okay?" I said. She was clearly agitated, and probably beyond reason, but that didn't keep me from trying. "I need to talk to you too, but not here, okay?"

"Why not? What's wrong with right here?"

"It's just that this needs to be a private conversation." Her oldest grandson appeared, greeting me as he always did.

"Hello, Aunt. How's it going? How's it going?"

"Good. Good. How are you?"

"Good, Aunt. Good. I'm real good. I'm reading up on my math and praying every day – helping my gram. Yes, ma'am. Yes, ma'am."

Two of the other grandsons wandered out too, greeting me with quick, embarrassed hugs. They were age-wise, in order of appearance, 20, 19, and 18. Recently, the youngest two were released from a child-protection shelter and were trying to reintegrate back into the family. Their childhood had been tragic, and now they were adults in name only.

My sister blew smoke away from us and glanced at them. "They don't care about what we say; most of the time, they don't even listen to adults."

By now, of course, they were all ears.

"Look, I've been on a plane for the better part of two days, plus I'm dealing with the shock of our brother's death. Could you just let me catch my breath? Then we could just head out to the farm and take a walk, okay?" That was always our way of dealing with stress.

"You know I have to go pick up the girls from school."

"Can't their mother do it?" I asked.

"No gas."

"Okay, I'll wait. Where do you want me to sleep? Where should I put my things?"

"Probably in the downstairs room with the boys. I'm not kicking them out again for you. I know you want your own room and all. This time, it's just not going to happen, okay?"

I understood that my sister's feelings were hurt. Our brother shared nothing with her. But the Mihlbauer men were like that – private people. Since Mark's divorce many years before, Lyle was his only confidant.

This was only the beginning of what proved to be a very difficult time on many different levels. It was the guns I worried most about. The kids' father was in prison, doing time for child abuse – his own kids, his victims. Their mother was seriously emotionally unstable. We didn't need the boys getting their hands on the guns. Next, I worried about the gold and silver. Everything had to be inventoried, a value determined and all secured.

But first, I realized, I needed to go to the funeral home. On our drive from the airport to my sister's, Lyle told me that Mack wanted to be cremated and have his ashes sprinkled in the wheat field. My brother mentioned that to me only once, laughing about fertilizing the fields. There was no doubt, however, that this was his wish. I was sure there would be a battle; however, I was not prepared for the intensity of my sister's feelings. Susan was a traditionalist who believed in having the casket open, plus all the usual rituals of a small-town burial.

At the last minute, Susan decided to go with me. As we waited on the faded, floral-patterned, funeral-home chairs for Kent, the funeral director, I told her that Mack wanted cremation. She looked at me directly for the first time that day. "What? Why would he want to be cremated? He never told me that."

"He talked to Lyle about it, and he mentioned to me he wanted to just be thrown in with the wheat seed at planting time," I explained.

"Just because he told Lyle doesn't mean we have to do it that way. Lyle's not family, or haven't you noticed?"

"I don't think Mack would want us spending money on a fancy coffin and casket," I replied.

Susan hesitated, seeming to think this over. "Well, that's what we did for Mother and Daddy."

"Yes," I replied, "but they both made it clear that's what they wanted."

Susan's hands shook as she picked up her Peaceful Rest coffee cup. "Maybe that's what Mack would want too. You really don't know."

"Yes, I do, Susan," I said with impatience. "Mack liked simple, and he certainly would confide in Lyle before you or me. I feel strongly that being cremated and scattered in the wheat field would be what he wanted."

"I can't go visit him in a wheat field! I need a place to go, like for Mother and Daddy. Besides, I need to see him in the casket, so I know it's real."

"But you saw him right after Lyle found him. You got there before the ambulance," I insisted.

"I don't want any new-age burial ceremony, okay?" she replied tearfully.

I decided not to argue. "Why don't we do this? We can rent a casket and have his body at the funeral home for the visitation. After that, we could have him cremated. We could bury part of the ashes near Mother and Daddy, and, the rest, we could scatter in the field."

Susan seemed thoughtful, staring into her empty coffee cup. Finally, she replied, "I never heard of renting a coffin. Where did you get a crazy idea like that? I want it to be just a regular funeral. Why do you just want to burn him up?"

I took a deep breath. "Ashes to ashes, dust to dust. I think, for him, that made sense. And just so you know, that's what I would want done with my remains too."

"You do?" My sister was incredulous. "I think that's awful. I don't want anybody to do that to me."

"Okay. Make sure you write that down so your kids and grandkids know for sure what your wishes are. I wish Mack put in writing what he wanted. Then we wouldn't even have to have this conversation."

"Please," she replied with quiet fury, looking as if she would burst into tears any minute, "don't tell me what to do."

"It was just a suggestion," I said, my anger beginning to match hers. "We have to let the funeral home know what we want."

"I'm going to call Mary Rose and see if he ever talked to her about it, okay?"

"Go ahead," I said. "But I doubt he confided in her either." Mary Rose was Mack's ex-wife who remarried and now lived in Fort Worth. We needed to let her know about Mack's death, and maybe talking to her would help resolve this for Susan.

My brother was the only Mihlbauer grandson; the one carrying the Mihlbauer name. Family stories told that Grandpa cried with joy the day my mother gave birth to a son because the old European tradition of the sons carrying on the family name would continue. My brother had no children. Now there was no one continue my grandfather's name, legacy, or the traditions. My brother was dead.

Two of my three sons, Matt and Pete, plus Susan's son, Will, all flew in for the traditional church funeral three days later. A saddened Mary Rose agreed with Lyle and me. Mack would not want a traditional service. Even though they were divorced many years before, they shared their early years together and always remained friends. So, to pacify my sister, a rented casket was open for the service, and as executrix, I made the decision, over my sister's wishes, that the body be cremated afterward. Right after the funeral, when we still had help from our sons, we did our best to clean Mack's things out of the farmhouse. All of his possessions were in the large, back bedroom/office. Racks of old clothes were taken to the church Clothing Closet, the few pieces of old furniture dropped off at the second-hand store. Under the bed, the grandchildren found Mason jars of coins that Lyle insisted be examined. Some might be rare and valuable. For now, the guns were in Lyle's custody, and the gold and silver locked away.

"Oh, and I wouldn't let the kids get into that computer either," Lyle warned. So, again with the help of my sons and Susan's, important information about the farm and finances were moved to a flash drive while the rest was scrubbed and the computer put away. It was becoming apparent that Mack had more secrets than we realized but probably not uncommon for grown single men who lived alone.

Several months later, with the help of my third son, Chris, who had been abroad for the funeral, we buried a small box of ashes next to our parents. The rest, we scattered with the wheat, watching them blow away with the southwest wind.

Chapter Nine
Delores's and the Boys

It was now six months since Mack's death. July heat-wave mirages shimmered above the horizon as I yanked open the door to the old pickup, fervently praying it would get me to town. I crept along, holding my breath that the steering would hold out until I got there. Lyle knew to come find me if I didn't arrive by noon. It was with a great sigh of relief that I pulled into Cy's Auto Repair. Lyle picked me up and soon we were sitting in the store-front restaurant that was Delores's. Her customers were remnants of the kids she served during her years as school-cafeteria cook. All the other places to eat served only Mexican food – one burrito closely resembling another.

Lyle introduced me to Delores, the elderly lady behind the cash register. She took the job of head cook after I graduated, so I never had the pleasure of her cooking.

"Well, I'll be," she greeted me. "Sure didn't know Mack had another sister. What can I get you two today? I got the usual, the chicken-fried or the meatloaf. 'Course that comes with a trip to the salad bar, and a drink for $6.95." This was the only place in town where you could still get the 1960s Panhandle special, chicken-fried steak, mashed potatoes and gravy, with a side of canned, green beans.

We both ordered the chicken-fried and turned to the salad bar. There was a huge bowl of iceberg lettuce, sad pieces of under-ripe, pinkish tomatoes, and a small container of grated carrots to choose from. For dressing, it was ranch or spicy ranch. We helped ourselves and sat down to talk. This was a good place for a private conversation since most of Delores's customers, including Delores herself, were hard of hearing and more interested in their own aches and pains than what we might be discussing. After glancing with interest at me, assuming I might be Lyle's new girlfriend, they turned back to their meatloaf. We selected a table in the corner and spent the first few minutes eating and discussing what you always started with around here – crops and weather – before I got down to business.

"Lyle," I began, "I thank you so much for taking the guns and keeping them for me. I really want you to have them. If you don't want to keep them, then they're yours to sell."

"Are you sure about that? I think one of them, the shotgun, belonged to your grandpa. You might want to keep it in the family." Lyle sawed off a piece of meat.

"I'll talk to Will," I replied. "If anyone should get it, it should be him." Susan's son was the only hunter in the family. "But, please, I don't want to keep them out at the farm or anywhere around the kids. If Will doesn't want them, just sell them. Please."

Lyle nodded solemnly. "So, what about all the gold and silver? Do you need help with that? You know Mack and I both bought in at the same time, and I know quite a bit about what everything's worth."

"Okay," I said. "Everything is still in that heavy, old, filing cabinet where Mack kept it. I have the key you gave me, and I've been guarding it with my life. We need to inventory everything and make sure we have a good idea what it's worth. Susan needs to be there too. The will stipulated that his assets be split 50/50. Half of it will be hers, and I don't want her to think we are doing anything behind her back."

Lyle looked up from his plate and put down his fork. "You know, lots of it is up at Stan's Safe Storage. The other half is what's locked up in the file. I gave you that Stan's key too, remember?"

"I have it, plus the others. After the funeral, I waited until Susan settled down and could be with me and we opened the file together. That's where I found the guns. We also looked at the gold and silver, but, right away, we locked it up again. Neither of us had any idea how to figure out what it was worth. I've had the key with me ever since. Now I'm ready to move it all to someplace away from the farm. Probably Stan's, if you think that's a good place."

"Yep. That's what I'd recommend." Lyle picked up his fork and took another bite of the droopy salad. "That place is like trying to get into the U.S. Mint. Those people are real careful and they know their stuff. Tell you what

I'll do. You find a time Susan can join us and I'll help you figure out what it's all worth, if you trust my judgment."

"Well," I replied, "I know nothing about it, and there is no one I'd trust more than you right now."

Lyle looked up. "That, though, is not how your sister feels about me. I'm not too sure she'll let me in the door. She's never forgiven me for keeping the keys until you came. It's just that I was too afraid they would fall into the wrong hands."

"And you were so right," I said. "Do you know how many times the kids have stolen Susan's keys and taken her car for a joyride in the middle of the night? I'll try to set up a time next week, if that's okay with you. I have reunion stuff to get done this week." Despite the animosity Susan felt toward Lyle, I was quite sure she would want to be with us for the inventory. Now it was just finding a time when we could be there without Angie or any of the grandkids.

"So, what's happening with those kids of Angie's?" Lyle pushed his plate away and took a sip of iced tea.

"Well, as you know, Heather, the 15-year-old, is at Boys' Ranch. Of course, now they take both girls and boys. Anyway, she'll be there until she's 18. That was so hard for Susan, but the structure seems to be what that girl needs."

"Now fill me in; all I hear is the gossip. What exactly happened?"

Talking about all the turmoil made me tired, but I owed Lyle the truth. "She and a girlfriend stole a debit card that belonged to the friend's grandmother. Anyway, they snuck out of Susan's house in the middle of the night and got a bunch of boys to pick them up and take them to Walmart. They had the grandmother's PIN number and they withdrew $2000.00 and went on a spending spree."

"Well," Lyle chuckled, "this time, I guess the gossip is true."

"Sadly so," I replied, crumbling my napkin into small pellets. "The kids never thought about the camera on the ATM, and, of course, when the police looked at the video, it showed it was Heather who withdrew the money. Rather than send her to the juvenile center, the judge pulled some strings and got her into Boys' Ranch."

"So at least she is safe for now, and Susan doesn't have to worry where she is or what she's doing, right?"

"Right. That just leaves the boys, since the younger girls usually stay with their mother and are too intimidated by Angie to cause problems. Anyway, the boys periodically take Susan's car and any cash they can find. But she won't press charges, so it just continues. It's beyond sad."

Delores ambled over to our table. "Can I get you folks some pie today? I got apple or peach, so which one ya want?"

"All this is mighty good, Delores," Lyle began, "but we are plum full up. Thank you, though."

"You sure?" Delores was clearly disappointed. "It comes with the meal. I'll even throw in a scoop of ice cream on top."

"I tell you what, Delores." I smiled up at her. "I'll come in another day and order a piece of each kind of pie when I can really appreciate it. How's that?"

Delores sighed with resignation. Lyle handed over a $20.00 bill. "This one's on me and you keep the change now."

"Well now, you don't need to hurry off." By now, her other customers cleared out and Delores looked lonely. "Seems like it would be nice to get to know you a bit. I just thought the world of that brother of yours. So sad he had to leave us so soon."

I was anxious to finish my conversation with Lyle and get on with the day, but my 'Panhandle Polite' kicked in. "Yes, he was a fine man," I said. "He was always talking about how much he enjoyed your cooking, Delores. But, you know, I've got to get going right now, so I promise to come back later for that pie."

"Now you have yourself a nice day, Delores," Lyle said, pushing back from the table.

We headed back to his pickup. "So now, you want me to drop you off at Susan's since you don't have a car?"

This was one day I wanted a break from my sister and all the conflict and chaos. "No, drop me off at Carla's," I said. "She's letting me borrow her old Oldsmobile for a few days."

I talked to Carla on the phone but hadn't seen her since the day she almost ran into my car when I tried to visit the townhouse that used to belong to my grandparents. Everyone in town knew Carla, but she was always especially close to our family. She was always there with a car, a casserole, or a shoulder to cry on whenever it was needed. Her 1978 Oldsmobile station wagon was always available to anyone in a jam. She'd purchased it from the elderly widow of the Baptist preacher who only drove it to church and back, so it was the kind of deal you couldn't pass up. It came complete with a bumper sticker from a Billy Graham crusade, so Carla promptly christened it the Billy Graham Mobile. There were definitely some benefits to small-town living.

Lyle gave me a hand-up into his pickup. "You mind if we drive around a minute? I been meaning to ask you about those boys of Angie's."

"Sure. Carla told me where she hides the key and to just come help myself, so no need to hurry. I wanted to ask you about Mack's computer too. You know, after my sons erased all the questionable websites, we put everything we thought we might need on a flash drive. Problem is we can't open those files. Do you have any idea what his password might be?"

"Nope, can't say that I do. Mack was always real private like that. All he told me was that he was always afraid those boys would get in there and be able to figure it out. Couple of 'em are pretty tech-savvy, you know."

We pulled out and headed around the square. The town was a ghost of what it had been in my childhood when small businesses circled the square. During my growing-up years, Ted Crawley owned the men's store that was in the middle of the block. He always reminded me of pictures I'd seen of Harry Truman. And, like Harry, Ted at one time sold hats. He was an open-faced, cheerful man who presided behind counters of crisp white shirts, sedate 1950s' neckties, and men's felt Stetsons.

Down the street was the lumberyard owned by J.D. Nickerson, like Ted, another great friend of my dad's. He smoked Pall Malls and told jokes that made Daddy spit out his pipe and slap his knee. His wife was Wanda, my mother's good friend. She had been a home eco major in college and cooked exotic food like homemade lasagna. After the meal, she'd pack the leftovers in a special plastic container that she bought at a special party. It was the envy of all the women and made a little burp if you opened it to steal a cupcake.

Ray and Veda Holtz owned the jewelry store on the other side of the square. This was where high-school seniors went to order their class rings, and clumsy young farmers came in to look at engagement rings for the girl down the road. Foreman Jewelry was the second jewelry store in town. They stocked my clarinet reeds and everything else needed by the band kids. Amazingly there was also a third jewelry store – Glower Jewelry stocked the china and crystal that every young bride needed to select prior to her wedding shower.

Diagonal to each other across the square were our two drug stores, Hartley and James, and City Drug. Both had wonderful pea-green soda fountains with high stools. As a child, I have vivid memories of going with Granddaddy to City Drug. He would proudly squire me to the soda fountain and lift me up on a red, leather-covered, bar stool. I got to order my very own chocolate ice-cream cone which cost five cents. The lady that worked there and waited on us seemed to know Granddaddy quite well. She wore bright, red lipstick and had long, black eyelashes that left little marks on her cheeks when she blinked. She smelled just like the perfume counter where you could find her if she wasn't behind the soda fountain.

The other drug store was where we could 'charge it.' I didn't exactly understand the concept, but I knew that if the ladies that worked there recognized me, I could just say 'charge it,' and I didn't have to have money. This was Hartley and James. It was right around the corner from our doctor's office and we went there when we needed medicine or magazines. For years, my boyfriend's mother worked behind the cash register. She would always smile at me in a special way, like we both had a little private secret.

Our town had three stores that only sold clothes, shoes, and bolts of assorted fabrics but were, nonetheless, what we called our department stores. There was Huxleys, Fay-Dee's, and Anthony's. We had two dime stores which were my brother's favorites. Across the street from Hartley and James was my granddaddy's Chevrolet-Oldsmobile dealership. The Ford House was on the Amarillo highway, and the Pontiac place was on the farm-to-market road.

As we circled the square, Lyle seemed to read my thoughts. "Not exactly the same as when we were kids, is it?"

"No," I said, looking down the side streets. "It's pretty sad if you ask me."

Lyle seemed to bristle a bit at this. "Well now, I don't know... Some like to live in a little town like this with no traffic jams or whatever..." Lyle was stopped respectfully at the red light on the corner of 6th Street and Mason. No other vehicle was in sight, but I remembered the great excitement when our traffic light was first installed in the early '60s. Now nobody from Levelland or Muleshoe could tease us about not even being big enough for a stoplight.

I decided to drop the subject, but I couldn't help thinking about other problems, like the drug bust a few years back that made national news. It was a sore subject here, so I turned my attention to the rest of the downtown, deciding to keep my thoughts to myself and remember what the town was like in its heyday.

In those days, the brown, sandstone courthouse with its high dome stood proudly at the center of the square. I was never sure what the purpose was for this high structure, but I definitely knew about the first floor. That was where we had the public library. It became my favorite place each Saturday when my mother would drop me off to choose books while she did the shopping. I would check out sequential volumes of Nancy Drew, Beverly Gray, and Cherry Ames, devouring several a week. The aroma of the musty books beckoned to me. I knew just which aisles to go down and what ladder to climb to reach the next edition, for the library ceiling seemed to stretch into the sky. As far as I knew, the plain, gray lady who sat behind the high desk, stamping books, lived there. To me, she seemed a storybook character with her ink-stained fingers and the wadded handkerchiefs she used to wipe behind her round, little glasses. I don't remember her name. Her identify was interwoven into the fabric of the library and the town itself.

All these memories went through my mind as Lyle headed out toward Carla's. Growing up, this place was as familiar to me as the house where I lived. Now, the only thing the same were the broad brick streets which city fathers optimistically designed decades before.

The courthouse dome was gone now – demolished during a period of enthusiastic 'modernization' in the 1970s when the city remodeled, making it into a box-shaped rectangle stripped of patina and character. Second-hand furniture stores, resale shops, and the Good Shepherd Center, run by the town's churches, now took up a few of the stores on the square. All the rest stared at us with vacant eyes. The busiest store in town was Dollar General, located on the old highway.

"So, help me remember about those boys, Susan's grandkids," Lyle said, interrupting my rumination. "I never can seem to keep them straight. And I have to admit, I'm a little bit afraid of those big ones." This surprised me. As well as Lyle knew Mack, he really didn't know Angie's kids at all. But Lyle, like some others in the town, was deeply suspicious of any brown-skinned person whom they referred to as 'Mexcans' no matter what their nationality.

"Okay," I began. "I'll do my best, and you have to know you don't really have anything to be afraid of. They're the ones most afraid. That bravado you see is a cover-up for their fear."

Lyle stared at the road, seemingly unconvinced, and I continued, "First of all, there is Marty. He has some serious learning challenges and didn't have to go into Child Protective Services since he was already 18 when it all happened. Next is Hawk. He's smart enough but too full of impulsive energy. He already has a few black marks on his juvenile record, but nothing too serious. D.J., his next oldest brother, is super smart but had no patience with school and finally got his GED. Then we have Nate. He was the one who almost got beaten to death by his father. Then in court, the boy was asked to testify against him. He dropped out of school after ninth grade. Hawk, D.J., and Nate were all in protective custody for over a year while their father awaited trial, and that was really hard on them. I have my doubts about the quality of those programs, at least in this part of the country. They were essentially placed in a holding pen in Amarillo and expected to go to whatever school was nearby. All three ended up skipping out of school after attendance was taken and disappearing onto the city streets. They have had a terrible life. I feel so sorry for them."

Lyle was thoughtful for a while. "Well, looks to me like they broke the law, not going to school and all. I'm not too sure I feel as much sympathy as you do. Seems like they just need to pull themselves up by their own bootstraps and quit depending on your sister. Mack always said they were like half-grown puppies still sucking on her teats."

"Yes," I replied, "Mack would say that. But, you know, that is easier said than done. All those boys are damaged to some degree, especially Nate. But... I don't pretend I have the answers either."

"Well, I'll try to remember all that. Somehow for me, all four of them just run together in my head." He paused. "So, what about the others? I know Heather got put up there in Boys' Ranch. Never could figure out why they decided to take girls and still call it Boys' Ranch. But anyway, that leaves four others, doesn't it?"

"All the rest were with Susan during that time before Hilario got sent to prison. I honestly don't know how she managed it. Especially since Angie kept cashing in the food stamps for herself. It was an awful time, and, of course, Mack was right in the middle of it. He was damned if he did and damned if he didn't. That's when Susan became so desperate for money. But it was money we really didn't have..."

Lyle slowed down as we neared Carla's house. "I know all about that. It was really hard on Mack," he replied. "What about now? Where are they all now?"

"Well, the older boys are with Susan, and the younger three girls are now with Angie. Louie, the youngest boy, kind of goes back and forth between his mother and Susan. He's never had his own bed to sleep in. Angie gives preference to the girls." I paused as Lyle pulled into Carla's long drive. "I guess that's the run-down for now, except that Hilario, their dad, is in prison somewhere down around Waco."

"Okay, I thank you for that," Lyle said, slowing down to a crawl. "I tell you what – I'm just gonna drop you off. If I go in there and Carla gets to talking, I'll be here 'til sundown."

"No problem," I said, opening the door. "I'm already planning my own exit strategy. Thanks much for lunch and the ride."

Carla was well-known for several things – patience with her recently deceased philandering husband, nurturing care of her mama cows and baby calves who grazed over hundreds of acres of her pastureland, her generous heart, and her stream-of-consciousness conversations. My feet had just touched the ground when it started.

"Oh, my goodness sakes! I saw you the other day and then Susan said you were here, and then you called and I'm so glad to see you, and you know you can borrow this ol' car whenever you want, got it used from one of the Baptist preachers, and just can't seem to get rid of it and did you know that I've been down in Lubbock most of the week, seeing about my grandson who had surgery, you know he has trouble with his kidneys, or has Susan already told you about that? This is his fifth surgery, poor little thing, and you know his mother, Georgia, you remember Georgia, my daughter? Well, she is homeschooling all four of those kids, and I don't approve because if you ask me, they need to be out in the world, meeting people, she just keeps them penned up in that little bitty house they have, and she's a bright lady and my own daughter and so I don't know what happened there…"

I was looking forward to the chaos of farmhouse sorting by the time I was finally able to escape with Carla's Billy Graham-mobile.

Chapter Ten

Reunion Committee

I met the class of 1963 reunion committee at the county memorial building the next day to look at the downstairs Reynolds Community Room where our reunion dinner would be. The building was here largely because of the work of my mother and other like-minded community leaders. Not to be outdone by other farming communities that dotted the High Plains, the city fathers and mothers formed a committee to raise funds for a new library and museum in the early '80s. The library, on the ground floor, was a sterile substitute for the sweet, musty odor of the old library I remembered. This new building was completed when water still flowed abundantly from 12" irrigation pipes, and the local farmers could depend on bountiful harvests. Civic pride was at a height, and Picnic Week, a celebration of the town's founding, brought thousands to town for the parade and barbeque. The high-school band marched down Dip Street, followed by farmers proudly driving their air-conditioned cab tractors and combines.

This was traditionally the time for high-school reunions, and members of our committee had been planning for months. The locals, who planned every reunion before, decided it was time for some help from classmates who moved away. That included me. Cindy didn't make an appearance today, but Norm came this time. Even though our eyes had to adjust to new wrinkles and pouches, he came up to me right away. "Well, I'll be danged. Aren't you Dalinda Stanlan? I ain't seen you in a coon's age. Ya'll still living up in West-consin? In't that where you're a' liven'?"

I was tempted to tell him that no, I didn't live in West-consin, I lived in East-consin, but I refrained. Instead, I said, "Norm, is that you? Oh, my goodness, it has been a long time, hasn't it?"

"It's me, okay. Still here, poking along. I'm not sure I'll be any help gettin' this reunion put together, but I come to see what was a' goin' on."

"We'll find something to keep you busy," I replied.

Penny, our no-nonsense treasurer, got right down to business, ending any small talk. "Now Maria Cruz can cater on Saturday night. She'll do the Mexican casserole like she does on Wednesday noon Senior Citizens – 'course she'll have the iced tea and trimmin's too. It'll be $15.00 per person. Now I know that's high, but it is Picnic and it is our 50th reunion."

"So, if we add $5.00 for other expenses, that'll make it $20.00," Marcia added.

"Whew! You're breaking the bank there. That'd be at least $50.00 for Billy Don and me when you throw in Friday night's food." Johnetta, the most frugal, was clearly worried.

Penny, ignoring Johnetta, continued, "Of course, there's no alcohol in the Reynolds Room, but ya'll knew that, right? And we better make the Friday night shindig a BYOB. Remember Doug at our last get-together? We don't want that happening again."

Johnetta chimed in again, ever hopeful, "Let's keep it simple – sandwiches and that kind of thing for Friday. We're all bringin' somethin', right?"

Marcia wore bright-green eye shadow under her glasses and looked much the same as when she shouted through the megaphone and shook her pompons on the football field. She too ignored Johnetta and pulled the big photo album out of her bag. "Ya'll, let's go sit down and talk about this a minute, okay?" She led the way toward the downstairs door. The three men in the group hung back, not too sure of their role with these take-charge women.

"Ya'll need us anymore?" asked Van.

"'Course we need you, what do you think you're on the committee for?" Penny shot back. "We got lots to figure out, so come on down and sit a minute."

"Yeah," Marcia insisted, "I really need you for this part. I'm makin' up a book about everybody that's died. I need to know about the vets. They're the ones I'm most worried about missin'."

Johnetta was still struggling to maneuver the steps. As happened times in the past, she seemed forgotten and left behind. "Ya'll need to wait for an old lady; my knees ain't like what they used to be." She giggled at her own joke, stepped heavily down from the last step to the floor, found a chair, and settled herself. I smiled at her sympathetically, thinking how much she reminded me of a soft, pink marshmallow, with her smooth, baby skin and soft, fuzzy sweater. Her lap was ample and her smile placid. She had become the kind of woman who was perfect for rocking babies to sleep.

"Now," began Marcia. "I need you men to look over this list and see if I've missed anyone. Gene and Van, you two were in Vietnam, weren't you?"

"Yep, enlisted the same day, or we woulda been drafted. Went through that whole dad-gum war together." Van was the talkative one. Gene nodded and got out his pouch of Big Red tobacco.

"I didn't know you were in Vietnam!" I turned my head, surprised I never knew this. But like in other wars, once 'the boys' came home, war was the last thing they wanted to talk about or remember.

"Yep," continued Van, "we was there all right. You remember Dennis, don't ya? He was with us a while too, but he didn't make it."

"Oh, I am so sorry," my voice sounded hollow, and the men looked at me as they must have looked at so many others who had no clue as to what that experience was for them.

"Okay," continued Marcia, "I'll add him to the list. You know, I pretty near forgot about him. In't that sad? Now, if you see anyone I've left out, just write their names down right there and I'll add them to the book. We don't want to leave anyone out, especially our servicemen."

A few minutes passed while the men pored over Marcia's book. Several of us counted tables and chairs and checked out the kitchen; Penny briskly checking off her list. "Now, Johnetta, you all set with the decorations? Need anything from us?"

Johnetta still sat silently, watching the group. "Yeah, Penny, I'm all ready. My daughter took herself up to Hobby Lobby, and she's a'helpin' me. She's got a real good eye for decorating. She's already done up three, four houses, curtains and everything."

Van pulled himself up from the table. "I think we got this list a' straightened out now. Ya'll need anything else from me?" He checked his watch. "It's gettin' along about feedin' time for me."

Gene pulled down the bill of his DeKalb cap. "I gotta get goin' too."

"You'll get the tractor and the trailer for the parade, won't you?" asked Penny.

"Yep. Got 'er done. I'll have the whole rig up to the high school long about 9:00."

Penny turned to me. "And you ordered the banners, right?"

Gene spoke up again, "She done had them sent to me, Penny. Now you quit worrin', we got 'er under control."

Penny wasn't done yet. "They'll be on the side of the trailer, right? We want everyone to know who we are, and that's how they always do it."

"Yep, we're set." The men were already headed upstairs and to the exit door.

Besides ordering the banners, it was my job, along with a couple of other out-of-towners, to come up with a program. Greg, a friend and classmate who had been our local disk jockey in high school, saved tapes from that time which would be his part of the festivities. My job was to come up with some games and to reminisce about our school days. While in high school, I was on student council, editor of our school paper, and class historian. Not exactly high-school royalty, but dependable when the written word was needed. I was preparing memoirs of our school days for the big event. One of the stories I planned to tell was about Ellen, the class beauty, and Betsy, a red-headed pistol with a wicked sense of humor.

"So," I began, "has anyone heard the latest on Betsy?"

Penny jumped right in. "Well, you know we thought it was just back problems and all her smoking, but now her sister tells me they've diagnosed her with ALS, you know, Lou Gehrig disease? But now keep quiet about that. Marion told me that on the Q.T."

"ALS?" My hand flew to my mouth. "Oh no! Not ALS." I couldn't imagine my spunky friend so incapacitated.

"That's what I hear. Nobody's seen her, of course, seeing as how she's still up there in Colorado – been there since she married that boy from Tech." Penny loved to be the first one to share bad news.

"That is so hard for me to wrap my head around. That's an awful disease. So sad." I sighed. "Obviously, she won't be joining us. And neither will Emily. You know, she and Keith are on their way up to their condo in Wyoming. I talked to her last week."

"Well," snapped Penny, "she sure could have planned that trip at a time to stop by for our 50th. She doesn't have a good excuse like Betsy. As a matter of fact, that goes for Ellen too. I guess she thinks she's a bit too good for us now, seeing as how she's gotten rich on Kansas City real estate. She's on her third husband too, and I expect he's just as rich as the last two. Her email said she had a big closing scheduled, so that tells you how we rate."

I stayed around a bit longer to reminisce with the women and to ask about other missing classmates who seemed to have disappeared into the ether. Our class benefited from the lack of professional jobs for women in the '50s and '60s, because most of our teachers were women – extraordinary women who were denied opportunities in other professions. They knew how to spark our creativity and bring out the best in us. Our valedictorian, like three other class members, earned a doctorate degree. He invented an important new drug and taught at a university in one of the Carolinas. He was the one bringing the old disk-jockey tapes.

"Ya'll know about Rob, don't ya?" piped up Marcia. "Well, the last we heard of him, our class president as you remember, he earned a Ph.D. and was growing orchids in Idaho or Iowa, or one of those places. Just can't imagine that, what with him being the star of our football team and all. Don't know why he doesn't bother to come see us. You'd think after all these years, he'd come around."

"Maybe it's still too hard for him," I offered. "You know, after what happened with his dad."

"Now, help me remember," Marcia chimed in. "Was it after our senior class picnic that we found out about Jim?"

"Well, I'm surprised you don't remember that, Marcia." Penny was the authority. "We got off the school bus and the Methodist preacher was there. He told Rob and Ellen, who was his girlfriend, remember? She collapsed on the spot with all that moaning and crying. The rest of us couldn't get off that bus until they all got into the preacher's car. Then Mr. Cooley, our band director, got on the bus and told the rest of us."

We were all quiet for a minute, remembering that moment so many years before. Jim, Rob's father, a beloved farmer, was a stalwart of the community. When he didn't come in for lunch, Rob's mom went out to the fields and found him pinned under his tractor. No one was sure how long he'd been there when she found him. Three days later, the church was packed to overflowing with mourners.

"I don't think Rob was ever the same after that," Penny added. "But those things happen farming. You just gotta get up and get back on the horse."

"I suppose," said Marcia, "Sure didn't work that way for Rob. Not for Ellen either. They broke up after that, and now no one really sees either of them, and they were the king and queen of prom. Seems like they could at least pay us a visit now and then."

"I'd guess he's made another life for himself," I said, ignoring Penny who arched her eyebrows and gave me a withering look. I continued, "John and Greg are coming, though. I'm really looking forward to seeing them. John was also a professor and taught at a conservatory of music. We had all been good friends in high school, part of the marching band. Today, we would probably be called nerds or something worse. In 1963, we were known as squares."

"I sure hope they didn't forget their share of the program," Penny declared, back on task. "You never know when someone's so far away." She paused. "I guess Mary Beth's coming. Can you believe she and her husband have all these art galleries in New Mexico? She even told me they spend their winters in Mexico! Can you imagine that?"

Mary Beth had been an especially shy but talented classmate who was good at art. She married another artist, and between the two of them, they owned several successful galleries in Santa Fe and Taos.

"Another one not coming is Lonnie," continued Penny. "Of course, he calls himself Lon now. Anyway, at least he sent a nice letter, plus a big check. You know, he works down in Midland-Odessa and is some kind of big-shot executive with an oil company. He's on his second marriage to some foreign woman, and he has a five-year-old daughter. Can you imagine? Having a little one at our age?"

Right now, we were all remembering our age, even though when I was with these women, 1963 seemed like yesterday. That was when we teased our hair and went through cases of Aqua-Net hairspray. Hours were spent rolling our hair on gigantic rollers, or orange juice cans, then sitting under bulbous, plastic, hair-dryer bonnets until we were ready for the 'comb out.'

Toward the end of our senior year, the whole town turned out when our girls' basketball team went to state and then breathlessly followed the town gossip when the young woman who was our senior girls' forward eloped with the star forward of the boys' team, threatening to disqualify us for the state title. In the year of our graduation, many of us were ready to move on and spread our wings, yet many would limp back home to work on family farms or in the hardware store. Some would take off caps and gowns and never be seen again. Others would always live right down the road from one another, still gathering black-eyed peas from the same patch. Our idea of the future was living on Mars and driving flying cars. Flags flew high on the 4th of July and on Picnic Day, and many classmates went off to Vietnam. It never occurred to any of us that the water wells might someday run dry.

As I walked out of the memorial building, I was in a nostalgic mood. Each major contributor to the building had his or her name engraved on a bronze plaque on the entrance wall – the size of the contribution determining the size of the plaque. My mother and father were commemorated on one of the larger ones, next to other leaders of the community. These were people whose parents and grandparents lived in dugouts and endured the Dust Bowl, stubbornly refusing to leave the land even during the darkest days of the Depression. They deserved the plaques which would still be here years after the Ogallala aquifer ran dry.

I headed toward my sister's house. Earlier in the week, I received the appraisals for all the property in the trust. We had the data we needed to really get down to the business of how to manage the farm – what to sell, what to keep. Also, I needed to let her know what Irv, down at the Auto Sales Barn, offered for the crippled pickup.

It was lunchtime when I pulled into my sister's driveway. Inside, I found her frantically pulling cushions out of the couch. She didn't seem altogether too pleased to see me.

"You already back? That didn't take long," she said, examining a gum-covered nickel.

"No, I think we have it figured out," I replied. "Why don't we go out for lunch and go over all this paperwork together."

"I can't right now. I have to feed these kids. I'm looking for money in the couch. You'd be surprised how much goes down the cracks."

"Can't Angie feed her own kids?" I was tired of these answers.

She gave me a dirty look. "Are you saying I shouldn't feed my own grandchildren?"

"No. I'm saying that their mother should have to be responsible. And their father."

"Fat chance of that." She plopped a quarter into a nearby jar. "They're out of food stamps for the month."

"Well," I replied, trying to stay focused, "this morning, you said you wanted to discuss the appraisals."

"I do. You just have to understand that we can't talk exactly when you want to."

"So, when's good for you?" Now I was impatient as well as hungry.

"I don't know. I never know. I'll come out there when I get all the kids fed." She pulled another coin out from behind the couch cushion.

"Don't you have money from the check I just wrote you?"

"No." She glared at me. "I had to use that to pay the bills. You know? The bills? Or don't you have those?"

I sighed and bit my tongue. "Do you want me to pick up food for you and the kids?"

There was a moment's hesitation. "You mean you'd buy them lunch?"

"Yes, or I could go to the store and fix something here for us."

"Half of them won't eat it. They like Sonic burgers, or burritos. That's it."

I did my best to not lose my temper and call them all spoiled brats, but that wouldn't solve the problem. I opened my purse and pulled out two 20-dollar bills. "Here, take this. It should help to feed them. I'm going out to the farm. Come on out when you can."

Susan took the money and stared at me as I walked back to Carla's 23-year-old car. I would find something to eat at the farm.

Chapter Eleven

Dance Dress

I didn't see Susan again until later the next morning. Gradually a semblance of order was emerging at the farmhouse. I designated a corner of the living room for the items I wanted to keep – a cut-glass crystal vase belonging to my grandmother, sterling silver serving pieces, photos, paintings, and other mementos. Susan was most interested in the larger items, since she hoped to buy a larger house and use some of the furniture, so the items she wanted to keep went in one end of the living room on their way to the basement. I brought up the idea of her moving to the farmhouse, since it was larger and in better condition than the house, she was in. But she insisted she wasn't interested in living in the farmhouse because it was so difficult to get to town in bad weather. The pavement ended two miles from the farmhouse, and the dirt roads became impassable with sticky clay when it rained.

I was making headway with all the sorting, but time was running out, and nothing was settled between my sister and me. I was beginning to wonder if she was just making excuses to avoid difficult conversations. I spent the past couple of hours pulling clothes out of the closet in the room I used to share with her. Neither of us had lived there for over 40 years, but our high-school skirts and blouses still hung on the hangers, and old dolls peered down from high shelves. If there was one thing our mother insisted on when the farmhouse was remodeled, it was plenty of room for storage. For years, she told us to come clean out the closet and take what was ours, but we both had other priorities. She saw no reason to clear it out if it wasn't hers, so wire hangers holding small blouses with Peter Pan collars were intertwined, locked into permanent embrace.

Several more substantial hangers held dozens of fabric-covered belts, the dresses they belonged to long ago given away to church clothes closets. All of these would go in one of my large, black, plastic, garbage bags. As I reached for a box on a high shelf, I lost my grip, and it tumbled down on top of me, spilling a cascade of dusty fabric. The bright yellow tulle, with red polka dots, looked vaguely familiar. I was cramming it into the garbage when it all came back to me. The fabric was left over from my sister's tap-dance dress long ago. It triggered a flood of memories, especially about my mother and her struggles with being a good housewife and mother while still wanting to realize her full potential as an educated woman during the 1950s.

As a woman, she left her daughters a complicated legacy. My brother, being a boy, was granted enormous freedom. There was no vegetable peeling or dishwashing for him; no 10:30 curfew or lectures about the dangers of dating. I was quite young when I addressed this injustice with my mother, probably while playing with one of my shapely 'Storybook Dolls.'

"I wish I were a boy," I complained.

"Why do you want to be a boy?" my mother asked from her place by the sink.

"Boys have all the fun. They get to be outside and go to work and shoot guns and have adventures. Girls just get married, have babies, and become housewives."

She sighed. "You don't have to be a housewife. Girls can be doctors and lawyers and get jobs. You don't even have to get married and have babies if you don't want to."

This was news to me.

"I wanted to be a doctor," she continued, "but when I was in college and was first introduced to the operating room and saw the sight of so much blood, I fainted. That was when I decided to become a teacher."

She had been a teacher for two years following her graduation from Baylor University, continuing a long tradition of teachers in the family. Her mother, Noona, graduated from Normal School and taught school while my grandfather was in the service during World War I. Mother's grandmother, Lucy Canary Conroy, the esteemed 'mother of the county,' was a teacher before her marriage. Mother's great-grandmother, Mary Bousfield, also taught. If it was good enough for them, then it was good enough for her, reasoned my mother.

Her explanation about my career choices was not helpful. I was a child, post-World War II. Women gave up war jobs to the returning veterans and went back to the bedroom and kitchen. Advertisers were aggressively marketing to the housewife, selling them electric dishwashers, mangle irons, sewing machines, and prepared cake mixes. Bright, happy women in colorful aprons and high heels danced across kitchen floors, shined to a high gloss with the latest Johnson Wax product. Home economics became an important major for women who went to college to earn what was called their MRS degree. On the one hand, girls were encouraged to get an education, but on the other hand, society told them to stay home, raise children, and keep house for their husbands.

My mother was a shining example of these conflicting expectations. She was a born leader – organized, eloquent, passionate, and smart. In high school, her small-town debate team went to state competition. I've no doubt she could have become a physician if she persisted. However, she also yearned for children and a family. There were few role models then for doing both. Of course, by that time, there were a few teachers who were married with children, but since that was decidedly a nurturing profession, the 'professional' part of it was downplayed, and the 'nurturing' received top billing. Teaching was almost considered volunteer public service, since it certainly did not pay enough to support a family. It was the teacher's husband who was considered the real breadwinner.

Nursing was another option for educated women, but, again, few women worked professionally and raised a family. By the time I declared to my mother my wish to be a boy, my mother was deep into the homemaker role, trying her best to fit into the mold. Besides Reader's Digest and Life Magazine, she subscribed to Good Housekeeping, Ladies Home Journal, and Better Homes and Gardens. However, she did not have a green thumb or natural love of food and cooking like Mimi did. Her satisfaction came from organizing people, serving on committees, and leading civic, fundraising campaigns. But in the Eisenhower days of the '50s, when no one wanted to appear anything but contented and happy, she hadn't yet verbalized this.

All this came back to me as I recalled the significance of the red-polka-dotted yellow tulle. All the little girls in the county signed up for Miss Lillian's dance classes held on the outskirts of our little town in a cold, empty storefront. To her credit, Miss Lillian did her best to make it into a real dance studio, installing ballet bars and covering the sheet-rocked walls with mirrors. Noona and Granddaddy were paying for the lessons for my sister and me. Noona believed in cultivating an appreciation for the finer things in life, dance being one of them. I was to take ballet since I was pronounced 'clumsy' – and this was bound to help – while my more coordinated little sister got to take tap dance which was all the rage. She was six, and I was ten.

Miss Lillian announced a recital/performance for spring, sending all the moms in town into a flurry of fabric and thread buying. In those days, no one ever heard of a store that sold dance outfits and, even if they existed, would never have been caught dead in one. The fabric of choice for the tap dancers was tulle – yards and yards and yards of slippery, stiff, yellow tulle that had to be gathered tightly and sewn onto a bodice that would fit a tiny six-year-old. Neither sewing nor cooking were my mother's forte. In fact, she actually hated sewing. But it was what women did in those days, and Mother was certainly not one to be left behind in the dust, so sew she did. Night and day; day and night. The bodice was only slightly easier to manage than the tutu, because the fabric was a satiny early attempt at polyester – red with yellow polka dots.

As the recital drew near, her hours at the machine stretched into the early evening, then past bedtime. It began again as soon as we were safely packed off to school and my little brother occupied with his toys. The day before the recital, the dance outfit still lay in two pieces, and the most difficult part lay ahead, attaching the skirt with its miles of gathered tulle to the unraveling polka-dot bodice. The sewing machine whirled late into the night, interspersed with muffled words that sounded a lot like those we weren't supposed to say. Finally, with my sister's tutu as complete as it ever would be, she collapsed into bed.

The morning of the recital dawned bright and clear. Strangely enough, I don't remember anything at all about my own costume. Perhaps it was a hand-me-down from a prior Miss Lillian's Dance Studio recital. In any case, it was there, ready for me to be zipped into. But there was a problem. My sister didn't want to get up. Her head hurt and she felt sick. Opening the top of her pajamas, my mother gave a gasp of disbelief. Her little chest was speckled with what could only be chicken pox.

That's when she crumbled – my mother – not my sister. She sank to the floor and laughed until she cried, or maybe she cried until she laughed. The costume swayed on its hanger above her, finally complete, never to be worn.

I smiled to myself, thinking of my mother's determination, and her frustration. I was anxious to see if Susan remembered the fabric, and the story, like I did. Jack, the big, gentle German shepherd, suddenly rose from the floor where he was napping, alerting me to a visitor. Even though the big box fans blowing through the house muffled outdoor sounds for me, the dogs always heard the cars or trucks.

It was Susan. For once she was all alone, and I met her at the door, forgetting all the business we needed to discuss.

"Hi! You will never guess what just fell down on me from a shelf in our closet."

"What?"

"Well, come look for yourself." I led the way through the kitchen and hall to our childhood bedroom. "Do you recognize this?" I held up the scratchy, brightly colored fabric.

"It's a net. Maybe a mosquito net for circus animals? It looks like something a clown would wear." She gave a little laugh, and for a moment, the sister I remembered was in the room with me. "Or was that left over from the doll clothes Mimi used to make for us?"

"No, look again," I said. "This really brings back memories for me. I think I was probably 10 or 11 and you were 6 or so. Remember? It was when Noona decided we should take dance lessons from that lady who came to town and opened a studio down on the highway in that old strip mall."

"Really? I guess I remember it vaguely. What does that have to do with all this yellow-and-red nylon?" Susan still looked confused.

"You got to take tap-dance, but not me. I had to take ballet," I continued.

"You did? I think I remember that I wanted to take ballet." Susan looked thoughtful as she stared down at the bright tangle of fabric. "But you know what? I do remember that I got tap shoes. I loved those. And you were so jealous! But I really don't remember anything about a dance recital."

"You don't? Mother worked for weeks on your costume and you came down with chicken pox on the day of the recital, just hours after Mother finished it."

"Oh! I do remember having chicken pox. It was awful. Mother covered me with that awful, pink, calamine lotion that made my skin stiff." She hesitated, then continued, "You mean she made my costume? Out of this stuff and sewed it herself?"

"Yes. She worked on it for weeks. Isn't it funny how we each remember different things? I thought for sure you'd remember, but all you remember is being sick. Well, anyway, I remember Mother sitting down on the floor next to your bed and crying. I didn't even have to go to school that day because she was sure I would come down with it too."

"So, did you?" Susan asked.

"I think I got it later, because I remember having to stay at Noona's, since Mother was taking care of both you and Mack. Both of you had it. I guess I performed at the recital, but that's not what I remember. What I remember is that we had just gotten our first T.V., and Mother let us watch television while she went back to bed. It was a black-and-white T.V., and all we got was an Amarillo channel. After Captain Kangaroo was over, all that was broadcast were these honky-tonk women with long hair and fringed cowgirl shirts, standing in front of a curtain and behind a microphone. They played gospel and old country-western on guitars and accordions and had these whiney, nasal voices. I have no idea where Mack was. Maybe he was watching T.V. too. Or maybe Mimi kept him for the day. We stayed with our grandparents a lot."

Susan was quiet for a moment. "You know, I don't really remember Noona very well. Mostly, I just remember her being sick and Mother taking care of her. It really bothers me I don't remember..."

"I was gone by the time she got leukemia – away at college," I said. "I remember that when I was little, she insisted that I wear those ugly, heavy, saddle, oxford shoes and keep them polished. Also, she was always worrying about the hem of my dress not being straight. Oh, and lots of other things... I have so many memories of her."

Susan picked up the red-and-yellow tulle with a sigh. "I don't, but I remember lots about Mimi. She is my role model. She was the only one that gave me unconditional love. Mother was always so hard on me. I used to tell my friends I was raised on guilt and red Jell-O. Mother made Jell-O for almost every meal. Remember?"

This was a conversation the two of us had many times. Our memories were different.

Our mother was a strong-willed woman with a large heart but definite ideas about how her children should be raised. As a teenager, I tangled with her many times, yet, as an adult, I realized she was the product of her time and, in many ways, a positive role model. Susan, on the other hand, harbored strong resentments even though our mother was always there to help her out when Angie would dissolve into screaming tantrums or when Susan was short on either time or money. I was miles away, with little family support, while my sister remained close-by, depending on family in many ways.

Susan continued, "That's why I try to give my own grandchildren unconditional love – it's what Mimi did."

This is when I should have kept my mouth shut, but, instead, I said, "Yes, but Mimi certainly never paid for everything we wanted. I remember the doll clothes and quilts she made for us and how she enjoyed having us around, but she gave of herself rather than money or things."

"Are you saying that I give my grandchildren everything they want?"

"I'm saying you are supporting them and enabling their parents to sit back and do nothing to help." Before I realized it, the words came tumbling out of my mouth.

She threw the crinkly fabric on the floor and turned to walk out of the room. "You have no idea what I do!" she screamed. "You don't get it at all. You never had an adopted child or nine grandchildren. I didn't come out here to hear your almighty advice. I knew this would happen. That's why I stayed away."

I shook my head and counted to ten. "Okay. I'm sorry. I shouldn't have said that. Please, let's go sit down for a minute. I'm ready for a break – I'll make some iced tea."

She headed to the front porch, her hands shaking as she lit a cigarette. I gave her a few minutes to calm down as I pulled out the ancient ice-cube trays and found two glasses that weren't dirty or packed. It was taking all my self-control to refrain from screaming back at her that I was sick and tired of her avoiding the truth. Instead, I carried out the tea a few minutes later and sat down on the front steps. "Do you want to see the appraisals?" I asked, trying my best to keep my voice even and neutral rather than my go-to sarcastic. "I think you'll be surprised."

"I don't know," she replied in the injured tone I became accustomed to. "I'm really mad and I can tell my blood pressure is going up." Neither of us said anything for several long minutes. "Okay, I might as well look at them," she finally said. "And what about the pickup? What did you do about that?"

"It's at Cy's. He should be calling me before long." I did not want to have another knockdown drag-out about the pickup right now.

We spent the next hour with the appraisal papers and land plats spread out before us on the kitchen table where we had shared so many family meals. The animosity cooled a bit as we tried to decipher the complicated papers. Our mother died the day Lehmann Brothers collapsed. While everything else in the economy took a nose-dive, investors decided that farmland was a good bet. From 2008 to 2013, the price of land in our area went from $200.00 per acre to $800.00 per acre. We didn't have cash, but we certainly had land. We were, as our father used to say, "Land poor," which, now that I thought about it, didn't really make much sense.

Since my brother's death, both Susan and I were signatories on the farm-business checkbook, but I was the one designated to make the decisions. This would be the case until the family trust officially ended two months from now. Even though I was the trustee in charge, because I was so far away, Susan also had the ability to write checks. This shared responsibility involved lots of phone calls and coordination. Before either of us wrote checks, we had to inform the other. I wanted to make sure everything was above board and all the books wide open for her inspection. She vacillated between being suspicious and being totally disengaged, depending on what was happening with Angie and family and whether or not she needed money. However, during the school year, she did work four mornings a week, teaching adult ESL and GED classes. With the grandchildren demanding so much of her, she definitely had less time than I did.

"So how do you think we should work this out now that the trust is ending?" I asked.

"Well, I guess we'll do just like we planned, except now Mack is not a part of it. We will form a partnership and pretty much keep doing what we are doing now but dividing everything 50/50," she said this, forgetting that her share would now be less than 50% because of the money she already took out. The final accounting would come in September when the trust officially ended. I decided not to bring that up right now.

Instead, I took a deep breath. "I think that the way it works right now is really clumsy. Only one of us should have our name on the checking account. That person could be in charge of the money – paying the bills and taxes, and all that. Then the other person could handle day-to-day things, like renting out the farmhouse and working with Jerry Bob and Skeeter or whoever we decide should rent out the land."

"So, are you saying you should handle the money?"

"With everything being online now, that would certainly be easier to do from a distance," I said. "Besides, you said yourself, you don't want to do that part."

"So, you're not going to move back here and help me with this?"

My mouth fell open and I rolled my eyes. I was incredulous.

"Susan," I began, "that was never part of my plan. We talked about that."

"But that was before Mack died. I thought that now you would come down here and help me out. I can't do all this by myself."

I shook my head. This was much more complicated than I even imagined on my worst days. "Okay, well, why don't we sleep on it? We also have to talk to Stu and Andy and get their input."

"I don't see why you always think accountants and lawyers have all the answers. I really don't trust them any farther than I can throw them. Why don't we just work this out between us?"

"Well, I don't know about you, but frankly, I need their advice. If you don't want to meet with them, then I'll just go by myself. Our meeting is scheduled for next Wednesday."

Susan picked up her purse and sunglasses. "It's too hot in here. I'm leaving, okay?"

"Wait," I said. "We also need to go through the things in that locked file cabinet. I talked to Lyle and he said he'd help us figure out what all that gold and silver is worth. Is there a day we could do it next week?"

"You are always in such a yank to get everything done – do this, do that. Hurry, hurry, hurry! You make me tired. I never know what I'll be doing next week, and I don't want Lyle knowing our business either, so there." She slammed the iced-tea glass down on the table.

"Okay, fine. Lyle and I will just do it ourselves and let you know what we figure out," I replied.

"Oh yes, that is what you'd say, isn't it? No. I will come out so I can be here too. Nobody is cheating me out of anything." The dogs followed her out the door, hoping for a walk, as I sat with my head in my hands.

Chapter Twelve

Home Chat, Brownies, and Church

As I labeled boxes that afternoon, I racked my brain, trying to think of what I might have said to make my sister think I would be moving here. When our brother died, it was so unexpected. There was so much to think about that my memory of that time was probably not very reliable. Maybe when I told her I would be here to help, she assumed I meant I would be here indefinitely. Certainly, I spent enough time here since January. But Susan had a way of taking things out of context and making assumptions about what I was thinking without confirming it. It was time for me to make things very clear.

I also wanted a reality check. The norm here was so topsy-turvy that I sometimes wondered if I was using good judgment. There were several friends at home that were excellent listeners, but they weren't always available. My three sons were my best check on reality, especially since they knew, only too well, the situation with my sister and her family. But they all led busy lives with kids and jobs, plus the issue of inconvenient time zones for phone calls. That left me with Joyce. I owed her a call anyway, since she called and left messages a couple of times. I would run things by her and at least get another opinion.

She answered on the first ring. "I was wondering when you'd get back to me. How are things in Texas?"

"Rather tense," I said, pulling at a persistent hangnail.

"What's up?"

"It's my sister. She stays so angry all the time. I feel like I'm walking on eggshells."

"What's she mad about this time?" Joyce asked. As usual, she was always interested in other families' pathologies.

"I'm not sure," I replied. "That's the problem. Yesterday, she asked me when I was moving down here."

"What?" Joyce replied with alarm. "You're moving there?"

"No, no. She somehow got it into her head that was my plan." By now, my cuticle was bleeding.

Joyce paused. "Oh, for Pete's sake, that would never work."

"You got that right," I replied.

"So, what did you tell her?"

I sighed and realized I was pacing back and forth as I talked. "Well, I just said that was never part of the plan. Maybe, though, I've just avoided telling her directly, I don't know. I'm just trying to keep the peace until the big mess with the trust is over."

Joyce was matter of fact. "Doesn't sound like that's working. You need to level with her. Tell it like it is."

I sucked on the bleeding cuticle as I considered this. "I don't know, Joyce. She seems so fragile – or maybe brittle is the better word. It's like if I say the wrong thing, she might crack or shatter – fall apart. She is so nervous and insecure."

"Well, of course she is," Joyce replied with typical Joyce authority. "She's had to live with that daughter of hers and take care of all those kids. If it were me, I'd be in a mental ward by now."

"So," I asked, "what do I do?"

Joyce avoided my question for now. "Have you seen her? Your niece?"

"Lately, we avoid each other. She knows how I feel about what she has done to this family. If she comes around while I am at Susan's – and she always comes around for money – then I am polite. It's not worth a screaming confrontation. She's like dealing with a two-year-old."

Joyce continued, "And your sister is still supporting her and her family." This was a statement, not a question.

"Yes. And it's always the welfare of the kids she brings up," I explained.

"Of course. Don't you see it's emotional blackmail? She's using you."

"Who?"

"Well duh – both of you. Angie blackmails Susan, and then Susan blackmails you because she knows that if she brings up the grandchildren, you'll give in. Didn't she do that to Mack too?" Joyce was clearly impatient with me. "I mean, I can hardly blame her. Take my little granddaughter now.

She's my one and only, and probably always will be. If her parents told me to bathe her in chocolate milk, that's exactly what I'd do. Those kids are our weak spot. It's where your heart is tender, and especially where your sister's heart is tender."

"Yeah, but aren't the kids a legitimate concern?"

"Sure, but not when they're being used as pawns in an emotional game of Russian roulette."

I could always count on Joyce to express her opinion. No active listening 'I-messages' for her. I had other friends for that. "Okay. You've given me lots to think about. Everything fine at home?"

"Oh, you know, the usual. I watered your plants at the condo. It's been hot, then cool, then hot. Book club is coming up. Of course, I read the book three weeks ago, but I need to call everyone and remind them to get busy. You're going to be back by then, aren't you?"

"I sure hope so. That's my plan."

"Oh, and what about that big reunion? Have you seen any old boyfriends yet?"

"It's a week away, and no, I haven't."

"Well, I know you'll make an effort to be back for your Up-North group, even if book club doesn't rate." Joyce made no secret of the fact that she resented not being a part of a group of women who spent four days at a cottage in Northern Wisconsin.

"Joyce, I promise I will do my best to be home in time for book club," I replied. "But I may have to read the Wikipedia summary this time. Hey, I gotta go, but thanks so much for being my sounding board."

"Okay, I'll let you go, but you have to promise to give me the rundown on all those old, high-school flames. I'll be awaiting an engagement announcement."

"Very funny. I'll try not to disappoint you."

I hung up and sat on the porch, contemplating what Joyce pointed out to me. Finally, Shane, the oldest and sweetest of Mack's dogs, nudged my knee. It was time for a walk.

The dry grass crackled as I set off into the pasture. Thunderheads like mountains loomed above. The air was sultry, teeming with energy. There was tension in the moment – both within and without. The dogs completed their circuit of the pasture quicker than usual as the faint echo of thunder rumbled across the sky. We made it back home just as the first big drops plopped against the concrete earth and the wind arose, blowing dust ahead of the storm.

It was a fast-moving front, and by suppertime, the sun was out again. The earth smelled of birth – fresh and newly washed, awakening to life after weeks of parching thirst. It was times like this that reminded me of my father. Nothing thrilled him more than rain, even when it came at an inopportune time for the crops. That was when he would bounce through the house, whistling a tune, stopping in the kitchen to give my mother a slap on the rump. Later – after the roads dried out some – he would take us kids for a ride in the pickup, pointing out the playa lakes now filled with water. He would turn up the radio or sing songs to us like, "Sioux City Sue, Sioux City Sue, your lips are red, your eyes are blue, bet my heart and soul on you, Sioux City Sue..."

With his knees holding the steering wheel, he would reach for his pipe and pouch of Prince Albert tobacco. The sun reflected off the shallow water as we drove through the pasture, Daddy calling to 'his girls' who were the young heifers grazing in the grassy field. Sometimes he would let us ride in the pickup bed and toss them big pellets of food that reminded me of Tootsie Rolls. Then we drove toward home, anticipating the homemade ice cream our mother always made when we celebrated rain.

There was no ice cream for me tonight, though. I was restless and soon searching through the pantry and fridge for something sweet, preferably chocolate. Mack subsisted on chicken breasts and broccoli, so it was doubtful I would find anything hidden in a corner. Unfortunately, the last time I shopped, I failed to make provisions for just such a moment. Like a nicotine addict desperately searching through ashtrays for the leftover butts, I pulled everything out of the old freezer at the top of the refrigerator. At the bottom, buried under layers of frost, was a plastic bag that looked promising. I yanked it out, and Voila! Success!!! Sure enough, it was a huge brownie about four inches square. It was double wrapped in commercial cellophane like the kind of thing you might pick up in an airport coffee shop. 'Double-Fudge Organic Brownie' was clearly printed on the label.

I found a dull knife, tore off the wrapping, and began sawing off a piece. Even frozen hard, it was undoubtedly one of the best brownies ever. Soon, I returned for another small piece, then another. Before I knew it, I consumed the entire thing. While on my sugar high, the dogs and I walked out to look at the stars in the moonless sky. As I rounded the corner of the house, I stopped

121

in my tracks. In front of me, about 30 degrees above the horizon, were four, bright, rectangles of light, each the same size, glowing in the dark. The dogs didn't seem to notice. There was no sound; nothing to indicate danger, yet my heart pounded in my ears.

What was this? A nighttime mirage? Some strange prairie phenomenon? As I walked closer, the lights seemed to stay in place. Above them gleamed the stars and planets. What could this be, greeting me as an apparition, challenging my common sense? I crept closer and startled when the phone in my pocket chimed.

"Matt? I am so glad you called – so glad!" I'd seldom been so happy to hear my son's voice. I began to feel wobbly as I turned back toward the house, keeping the phone close to my ear as I warily watched the lights over my shoulder.

"Mom? What's wrong? You're breathing like you just ran a race."

"Oh my God, I don't know what's wrong," I replied.

"Where are you?" he asked, alarmed.

"I'm outside, at the farm. I went to look at the stars, and now, well… I just saw the strangest thing."

"What? What did you see?" he demanded.

"I don't know. It's like some creepy extra-terrestrial object – four rectangles of light hanging in the sky." There was silence on the other end of the line. "Matt? Are you still there?"

"Yes, yes, but I'm not so sure about you. Have you been drinking?"

"No. No! I've been working like a dog. You don't believe me, do you?" By now, I was yelling into the phone.

"Okay, calm down. Tell me exactly what is going on." Matt was the steadiest of my sons in crisis situations.

"I just told you," I said, my voice rising. "I just saw the craziest thing."

"Okay, I'm coming to take away your wine. Why don't you go back in the house and lock the door? Are the dogs with you?"

"Yes."

"Are they acting scared?"

"No!" I cried, semi-hysterical by now. "They're acting like they want to go back to the house and to their beds."

"That's a good idea. You go in and take a nice, hot shower and go to bed, okay?"

"Okay. Hey, isn't this funny? I mean, think about it. I saw lights in the sky – weird lights – in the sky." I giggled.

"Mom?" Matt was using the voice he reserved for his children when they were being unreasonable. "This has all been too much for you. I'm going to call you back in an hour and check on you. How about that?"

"Okay, sweetie. Now, you want me to do what, besides a cold shower?" I was trying to suppress my laughter.

"Get rid of the wine and go to bed. I'll call you soon."

"Bye-bye." I clicked off the phone and headed into the kitchen where all the lights seemed to be pulsating. I felt dizzy and was babbling to myself. In my foggy state, I reasoned that the brownie had much more sugar in it than I realized. After all, I'd eaten a huge portion. I grabbed the empty wrapper from the counter and reached for my reading glasses as they seemed to recede from my reach.

There it was, in small print, the list of ingredients prefaced by 'For Medicinal Use Only: Four doses cannabis. Take only as directed.'

Okay! That explained it! I stumbled into the shower and watched, fascinated, as the water ran over my body and down the drain. Wow. This was amazing. Why hadn't I noticed it before? When my son called again sometime later, I explained, between bouts of hysterical laughter, what was in the brownie. He didn't know whether to be relieved or to get on the next plane to come and get me. But I must have convinced him I was okay, although I felt awful. It occurred to me that I needed to call my sister and let her know I was dying. My reasoning went something like this: if I didn't call her and let her know, she would be so angry when she found me dead the next morning. Fortunately, I decided to go to bed instead. Finally, after tossing and turning for several hours as the bed pulsated toward the ceiling, I vomited copiously into a conveniently located empty box by my bed. I turned over and fell into a deep sleep.

The next day was Sunday. Despite my escapades of the night before, I awoke feeling fine, except for being ravenous. Not only was I hungry, but I also felt the need for some spiritual nourishment. I considered going to my childhood church, but the roads were still muddy after the rain. There was also the issue of what church to attend.

Susan got her feelings hurt if I didn't attend church with her, but I felt more comfortable in the one I attended as a child. A few years back, Susan moved her membership from the Presbyterian Church of our childhood to the Methodists, two blocks over. She told me she did it because she was convinced that Angie and her children would attend Sunday School if they would just hold class midweek. Since the Presbyterians would not accommodate her, she decided to try another. Now, if I decided to attend church, I had to decide between the church of my childhood or the one she currently attended. Actually, it wouldn't matter much. Both had ancient organists who made even the most joyful hymn sound like a dirge. The ministers were both 'stated supply,' or substitutes, since neither church could afford a permanent preacher. My spiritual community was elsewhere, but if attending church with my sister would smooth the way toward an amiable agreement, I was all for it.

Then it occurred to me. There was no way Carla's old car could make it through the heavy mud roads to town. The decision was made for me. This Sunday, I wouldn't attend church at all, thanks to the rain.

So instead of grabbing a quick bowl of cereal, I made a real breakfast of bacon, eggs, toast, and jam, then enjoyed my coffee before going back to packing and sorting. More boxes were now labeled, ready for the Community Clothes Closet or marked 'Give Away.' A few were marked 'Save-Susan' or 'Save-Vintage.' I had my own 'Saved' boxes containing a few items too good to toss that I hoped we could sell online or at a resale shop. There were a few garments, like my mother's wedding dress and my great-grandmother's black mourning clothes, that I was tempted to save. Of course, unless I wanted to leave them here at the mercy of my sister and niece, I would have to find a way to get them home. I sat down on the edge of a damask-covered parlor chair that had seen better days. At one time, someone left a smoldering cigarette on the upholstery just long enough to leave a yellowed indentation. What was I going to do with all of this? Why did my mother leave this for me? It wasn't fair. I took aim and threw a ragged silk blouse at the 'Throw-away' box which I noticed, with satisfaction, was now overflowing. I congratulated myself, heaved my body to a standing position, and marched to the kitchen for a coffee refill.

On Sunday mornings, the radio only broadcast sermons and services – not even country and western for these children of the Bible Belt. That was saved for much later in the afternoon. Right now, an enthusiastic evangelist was cautioning us heathens in radio-land to beware of any Bible if it wasn't the King James version, as all the others were the work of the Devil.

"Now, I tell ya'll honestly, as Christian folk. Do not let Satan tempt you from the righteous way – the only and real word of God is not found in newfangled, what is called, revised editions of the Good Word. I am here to tell you that you cannot revise God's holy word, brothers and sisters. We want our religion straight – just like Moses got it from the Almighty up there on Mount Sinai. I tell you truly, the man, or even the woman, who thinks their souls will be saved from damnation by reading some fancy college boy's idea of the Holy Word is not going to be with me and the disciples at the right hand of God in eternity."

I could almost hear him working up a sweat.

"No, brothers and sisters, I'll say it again – you only find the true word of the Lord in God's own handwriting given to Moses long ago in the, I'll say it again, The – King – James – Bible."

I couldn't believe what I'd just heard. But of course, it wasn't the facts, or the truth, that mattered here. It was the emotional appeal to the lowest common denominator. You could argue until the cows came home that Moses would have been totally baffled by Shakespearean English, but the facts would not matter. In fact, they definitely got in the way and were therefore disregarded entirely.

I clicked off the radio as I considered my own spiritual journey – a childhood wandering through the stumbling blocks erected by fervent believers.

It is difficult to believe now, but as a child in my little town, the church you attended defined who you were. That being said, almost every church in town practiced some form of Calvinistic Protestantism. There was the First Baptist Church which Noona attended. Granddaddy was a member too, but he spent Sunday morning reading the Amarillo Globe News. Noona, my grandmother, spent the morning praying for his soul. Her church was on Crosley Street and was made of creamy-colored brick with a bell tower that played 'The Old Rugged Cross' or a similar hymn every day at noon.

The Methodists were a block away on Bradford Street; they had tan and light-gold brick. The Presbyterians on Darnell Street had red brick. A few blocks down the same street was the Church of Christ which had cream-colored brick similar to the Baptists. Not to be confused with the decidedly more progressive United Church of Christ, they didn't allow pianos or organs and were fond of telling us Presbyterians that we were going to hell since we didn't go to the Church of Christ. Then there were the Holy Rollers on the edge of town in a little wooden clapboard.

On the east side of town was the Assembly of God. They had an L-shaped building cobbled together from two trailer houses moved to the same lot. The Roman Catholics were way on the south side, away from the main population, because they were ruled by the pope and might convert us if we got too close.

We might have had our denominations tattooed on our foreheads since communication between them was highly discouraged. When there was the occasional 'mixed-marriage,' like between a Methodist and a Baptist, the woman was always expected to defer to the denomination of her husband. There must have been some law, written in stone somewhere, that decreed this, since it was strictly upheld.

Our religious affiliation also determined what kind of car we drove and where children sat in the public-school cafeteria. Baptists drove Buicks and Pontiacs. Methodists drove Fords. Presbyterians drove Chevrolets and Oldsmobiles. Church of Christ drove Chryslers and Mercuries. Since we were supposed to avoid the Catholics, nobody paid attention to what they drove. All we knew was that they bought their cars in Bethel, the German-Catholic town in the next county. As long as we observed these unwritten rules, all faiths were tolerated and everyone was friendly and got along okay.

By the time we got to high school, we had friends from other churches; it was just that we spent so much time with 'our group' of kids: Sunday School and youth group on Sundays, Wednesday prayer meeting for some, Sunday night church for others, plus Bible school in the summer and church suppers most anytime. However, even as a young teen, I began to question the system and began to feel the stirrings of a rebellious nature. Part of that was because, much to the consternation of Noona, I had a Roman Catholic boyfriend who was a perfectly nice person and drove a Model T which he resurrected from the junk yard. This led to many years of spiritual searching – separating the religious chaff from the grain – until I was able to reach a deeper sense of spiritual truth. Now I was again confronted with the beliefs of my childhood.

This morning, after the brownie of the night before, I felt a bit like a time-traveler who awakened from sleep and found herself in the 1950s.

Chapter Thirteen

Bradford Street House

The word got out about my Saturday night adventures via my sons' text messages. First, I had a phone call from Pete, son #2, in Oregon.

"Mom? Are you okay today?"

"Yeah. I'm fine. You must have talked to Matt. Can you believe what I did?"

"Well, I am not surprised about what you found. When we were there for the funeral, we found a stash under the bed."

"You did? Why didn't you tell me!!!" I asked.

Pete paused. "I guess we didn't think you wanted to know. We knew Mack used for years. Remember that time we went skiing in New Mexico when we were in high school? Well, we were staying in the same place he was, and he didn't try to keep it a secret."

"He didn't? It's a good thing I didn't find out for sure until now." I exhaled slowly, rubbing my eyes. "He never told me. I guess I suspected that he used, but I didn't want to admit it."

"Hey, Mom, don't worry about it, okay?"

"He probably started years ago after his accident while he was still married. I have a feeling he used the hard stuff for a while, and that's what led to the divorce."

Pete continued, "Look, that's not what I want to talk about. I think you need to go home. Matt said you were talking about seeing strange lights? I mean, that tells me you gotta get out of there. Remember when we had the meeting with the lawyer and accountant after the funeral, and all three of us said you should just sell the farm? That's what you need to do. Get out of there."

"But you don't understand. I'm the executrix of Mack's estate, and the trustee of the trust. I have to finish this job. Besides, I'm not convinced selling the farm is the right decision."

"Mom, that place is awful." There was a moment of silence, as he probably realized how this would go down with me. "I mean, I know you grew up there, and that Tutu and Pawpaw worked really hard to farm it and keep it for you, but none of us want it... I know that's hard to hear, but can you imagine us trying to work with Angie after something happens to Susan? I mean, look what you are going through. With her, it would be much worse, and you know it."

I sighed, considering this. "I know how you feel, but I'm not sure you know how I feel. It's really hard to let it go. All my life, it was drummed into me how important it was to never, ever sell the land."

"I know, but that was then. Mom, the water is running out. And it doesn't look like anybody is looking at putting up wind turbines on that land anytime soon. Things change. It isn't like when you were a kid."

"Okay, okay. I hear what you're saying. I will think about it."

"Are you sure you're feeling okay today?"

"Yeah. Actually, I feel pretty good. But, you know, I just remembered about the lights! Did Matt tell you about that?"

"Yeah, he told me," Pete sounded skeptical. "You really need to take it easy; you know."

"Okay, don't believe me, but I know what I saw. I'll go outside right now and see if I can figure out what it was."

"All right. But no more brownies today, okay?"

"Ah, come on," I teased. "Okay. I'll be good, but there is another one still in the fridge. I think I'll take it home to show the girls when we go up north. Otherwise, they'll think I'm making it up."

"Oh my God," Pete replied. "Now I know you're losing it."

"No, it's just in retrospect; it's quite funny and a great story." I was enjoying this by now. It was really a turn-around for my behavior to shock my sons.

Before I forgot again, I went outside to check out the strange lights. The barn on the other side of the house looked the same, but I decided to get the key to open the padlock and look inside. The dogs loved the inside of the barn because it was filled with mice and other critters to chase. But I was always careful, since we once found a huge rattlesnake coiled in the corner. Fortunately, Jerry Bob's nephew, Skeeter, came along and swiftly decapitated it with the edge of a spade. He was the man who did the actual managing and farming, with Jerry Bob being the silent partner providing the cash.

Usually, the inside of the barn was dark, but today, it was brighter than usual. I looked up and realized the lights were on. We forgot to turn them off the day Susan's grandsons went inside. Then I noticed something. High up on the inside of the steel structure were four, small, vertical windows. Oh my god, what I saw were the lights from the barn windows! Because it was so dark, what I didn't see was the outline of the barn itself. So, it looked like the lights were hanging by themselves in the sky, when in reality, it was only the light shining through the windows on a very dark night. Mystery solved.

Since I was still in an upbeat mood, I decided to call Susan and tell her the story, sure that she would be as amused as I was.

I was wrong. Her voice went up a couple of octaves as I talked to her. "Oh my gosh! You got rid of it, didn't you? What if the boys get their hands on it? I cannot believe you would eat something like that. That's just awful."

"Okay, okay. Just settle down. I'm okay, and you don't have to worry about anything."

"Well, that's what I always thought about Mack. He wasn't always in his right mind. Now I know why. No wonder Mary Rose divorced him. Where do you think he got it?"

"Don't know. Maybe I'll talk to Lyle about it. Maybe he knows. Oh, and by the way, we have a meeting out here with him on Tuesday to look at everything in the file cabinet, and, tomorrow, we need to go look at the Bradford Street house so we can put it on the market."

"You always have so much planned. I don't see why you have to be in such a hurry," she replied.

"In a hurry?" I was incredulous. "I've been here almost three weeks! I want to get this done so I can go home."

There was silence on Susan's end. Then, "Isn't this your home? This is where we grew up."

I took a deep breath before responding, "Yes. This is where I grew up, but it is not where I've lived for the past 50 years. It is not home for me anymore. I am ready to go home."

"You really want to hurt me, don't you?" she replied in her injured voice.

"That has nothing to do with it, okay? I know this is where most of your family is, but it is not where most of my family or my friends are anymore." I was trying to keep my voice even and calm.

"It's always about your friends. Family here really doesn't matter to you, does it? You used to be a person who cared about other people. You're just not the same person you used to be at all."

"Okay. We're not going to continue this conversation. It's not getting us anywhere. I think the roads will be dry enough tomorrow so that I shouldn't have any trouble getting into town. What time do you want to meet at the Bradford Street house?"

There was a click on the other end of the line. I sat, looking at the silent phone, shaking my head. If frustration had stages like death and dying, I was now moving quickly into the apathetic arena, totally paralyzed by an impossible situation.

By the time Chris, son #1, got around to calling, I was almost finished boxing up the memorabilia in my childhood bedroom. Just like his younger brothers, he was convinced that I would be doing everyone a favor if I just washed my hands of the farm and all that went with it.

"So, Mom, I hear you had quite an interesting time last night," he began.

"Let me guess, you've heard from your brothers."

"Yep. We all think you need to take a break from there. It's getting to be too much," he said. "In fact, it would be better to just go ahead and sell everything so you can get on with your life."

"So, tell me, Chris," I said. "Do you think I'm being selfish for even considering that option?"

"What? Of course not. You would be doing Susan a favor to force her to stand on her own two feet. She needs to grow up. How can the others learn to be self-sufficient if she has never set that example? She's always depended on someone else."

"Oh, I don't know. That just doesn't feel right... I mean, selling the farm doesn't feel right. There is some guilt involved. Do I have the right to do it? Is that the, well...you know, the Christian thing to do?" I usually avoided these questions with my minister/pastor son, but not this time.

"Okay. So, pray about it. Take some time to discern what is the right thing to do in this case. You need to reflect and get away from it for a while. Your conscience will be clear as long as you deeply consider the best way forward. Oh, and of course, ask for guidance from above."

"Thanks, dear. I needed to hear you say that. Things are really a mess around here, and I need all the help I can get." Chris didn't usually use 'God-talk' with me or the rest of the family, but he knew I was asking for spiritual advice right now, not necessarily advice from my eldest son.

By the next morning, the sticky mud had dried into hard clumps, so Carla's old car was able to bump slowly into town. Susan left a message, saying she would meet me at 10:00 to look at the house on Bradford Street, and I was looking forward to getting this part over with. This was the house my mother bought for my niece and family as more babies arrived. It covered over 3,000 square feet but only had two real bedrooms and two baths. Instead, there was an enormous family room, plus a finished basement.

After baby number six arrived, Angie convinced my mother to convert the three-car garage into another bedroom which added almost a thousand more feet. The same year, the foundation cracked, and the roof sprang a leak. The following year, the doorframes all fell out as a result of the crumbling foundation. By the time the last child arrived, a year later, the damage due to poor construction and severe weather was nothing compared to the damage done by an alcoholic husband, a bipolar wife, assorted dogs, cats, birds, and other animals, not to mention nine undisciplined children.

I arrived before Susan and tried the key in the lock. It wouldn't turn.

"Hey, let me try mine," Susan said, coming up behind me on the drive. "You know it's full of bugs, don't you?"

I swallowed the bile rising in my throat as I contemplated what lay in front of me. I thought about bailing out but told myself I just had to deal with it. "Well, no matter what, we need to look at it and put it on the market," I said. "We're running out of money fast."

"Mother paid $156,000.00 for it," Susan said, trying her key in the lock.

"Yeah, and then added a $25,000.00 addition when she converted the garage to a bedroom. What does the realtor think it's worth now?"

Susan looked up from the door, exasperated. "This one doesn't fit either. Maybe I grabbed the wrong key. Mack changed the locks not long ago, and I keep getting them mixed up. I'll have to go home and try to find the right one."

Nothing was ever simple here. "Okay," I replied. "Just tell me quick what the realtor said about the house."

"Oh. Well, she said we could put it on the market for $52,000.00." Hilario ruined this house, you know. It's his fault we can't sell it for more.

"Did the realtor just do a drive-by? I'll bet we'll be lucky to get $30,000.00," I said under my breath. "Go ahead and get the key. I'll check out the backyard while I wait."

I walked around the outside to what used to be a gate, now overrun with weeds and failing off its hinges. What I could see of the back looked like a junkyard. Various parts of riding toys, with or without wheels, body parts of dolls, and various pieces of clothing were strewn around. Trash was everywhere. I hated to think what it must have been like when Angie and family lived here. Discouraged, I turned around and sat down on the front steps to wait for my sister to return. Too bad she couldn't see the humor in the brownie story. We needed something to lighten the mood.

After what seemed like many long minutes, she returned with the right key and we pushed against the door. It finally opened into a foyer where the tile was coming up from the floor. The house smelled of mold and chemicals. The front room still held a crude animal pen where Angie kept the dogs' latest litters of puppies. We turned left into one of the two large bedrooms with adjoining bath.

"Oh my gosh, it looks like someone threw a bottle of Pepto Bismol into this bedroom!" I shouldn't have been surprised that both rooms were painted a vivid, bright pink; it was Angie's favorite color. "And look, all the fronts are gone from the cabinets and drawers in the bathroom! What happened here?" I said, turning angrily to my sister.

Susan was immediately defensive, "It doesn't work anyway – I mean, the shower. It leaks."

"The one in the other bedroom too?" I replied, disgusted.

"Probably."

"And the furnace is kaput too, right?" I said.

"Yeah, and the air conditioner. Mack never would fix anything." Susan visited the house daily through the years Angie and family lived here, so this was old hat to her.

I looked up the wobbly, iron, spiral steps. "What's upstairs?" I asked.

"You mean that little loft? Mainly dog poop and a bed."

"You're kidding. Old dog poop? Wonderful. And how the hell did they get a bed up there through that tiny opening?"

"How do you expect me to know? I wasn't here." As usual, Susan felt no responsibility for any of the problems we faced.

Now I was really angry. "So, we have a house with a cracked foundation, a leaky roof, showers and toilets that don't work, Pepto Bismol walls, and old dog poop ground into ratty carpeting? Plus, we are paying taxes and insurance, and we have to keep the utility bills paid or they'll turn off the water and electricity." Susan didn't reply, and I realized she wandered into the backroom.

"What?" she asked.

"Never mind," I said, throwing up my hands and threading my way through the trash.

"Huh?" She obviously tuned me out.

"I said, never mind."

Angie and the kids moved out six months ago after the foundation began to sink, but mainly because of the cockroach infestation. As we walked into the kitchen, we saw the shiny backs scatter into cracks around the countertop, still covered with greasy dishes. Susan didn't seem to notice, or if she did, pretended not to. Instead, she headed straight through the kitchen and into the backyard. I followed her, picking my way through the trash.

"You know, Angie used the garage back here for a cat house, don't you?" she said.

"A cat house?" I asked, imagining this extra, detached, two-car garage filled with cats.

"Yeah, until they started running away."

"So, even the cats had enough, huh?" I replied.

Susan gave me a disgusted look. "It wasn't Angie's fault. Mack wouldn't fix the fence and they got out. Same thing with the house. He wouldn't fix what needed to be fixed."

I remembered my brother's version of the fence/house story. He fixed it all several times, but it always got torn up again by the kids and their friends. I decided not to bring this up.

Susan continued, "This house was a lemon from the word go. One of the worst mistakes Mother ever made. And she did it despite all our protests."

I agreed; she was right about this. "Then she spent money turning the attached garage into another bedroom," I added. "I wonder if she had the beginning of dementia even then."

"Remember when she insisted that Daddy buy a motor home, but by then, he had given up driving and Mother was afraid to drive it out of town?"

"Yeah," Susan agreed. "They spent one night in it and then never used it again."

"That was quite a while ago, wasn't it? When the lake still had water? I guess that was about the time she gave Angie $900.00 to buy a fancy baby crib and entered all the Reader's Digest Sweepstakes, thinking Ed McMann would show up at her door with a million dollars."

"No," Susan disagreed. "It was all psychological. She gave Angie everything she wanted herself – a house, a new car, a backyard swimming pool. She was compensating because Granddaddy was an alcoholic."

"Maybe," I replied. "But I think it was the early stages of some kind of dementia."

"You always think you're right, don't you? You weren't here to see what happened, so get down off your high horse."

"Okay," I sighed. "So, we're starting this again? I thought we were trying to decide what to do with this house. What do you think we should list it for?"

Susan turned toward the house. "I just want to get out of here. This house depresses me."

"Wait a minute!" I demanded. "Just wait!"

I watched as she continued walking, ignoring me. I hurried to catch up and grabbed her arm. "I say we take the best offer. See if that guy who buys up houses wants to look at it. Do you have his number?"

"I'm leaving," Susan said, breaking away from me as she walked through the house to the driveway. "I've got to eat."

"Go right ahead," I screamed at her. "But don't be surprised if I burn this whole place down."

I stomped to the driveway as she backed out and pulled away. Right now, I wanted to get rid of everything and fly off to Tahiti. But not before I chased down my sister's car and rammed it with the Billy Graham-mobile. This was a satisfying fantasy for a few minutes. But instead, I pounded on the steering wheel, swore, and headed back to the farm.

Why couldn't she see what we faced? This was just one of the falling-apart houses in the trust. There was also the farmhouse, though it was definitely in better condition, but filled to the brim with leftovers from four generations. Plus, there was an old duplex, built in the '50s that had been in the family forever. Both sides rented out to Vietnam Vets and friends of Mack's who were just glad to have a place to live. Mack knew them since childhood and felt it was one thing, he could do to help them. But the old duplex, like the other houses, showed serious signs of neglect. Neither Susan nor I wanted to keep it. That we did agree on. We also had this sorry excuse for a house, the farm, the old pickup, a newer pickup, plus other rusting farm equipment, four dogs, and a stack of unpaid bills. Had my sister ever done anything to stop Angie, Hilario, and the kids from trashing the house? Why didn't she warn me about the condition it was in?

Chapter Fourteen
Toogie, Guns, and Gold

So, this was where the rubber met the road. Nine children. Father in prison for child abuse. Mother refusing to work and thinking she was entitled to family money when she already spent much more than her share, mostly by stealing from her grandmother. My sister paying the rent, even the 'bundle' for T.V./internet/phone, plus utilities and money for food not covered by food stamps. The children were always at my sister's while their mother watched T.V. or played videogames.

We had a house bought by our mother, now empty and trashed, worth a fraction of what she paid. In addition, there was cotton and wheat acreage gasping for rain. The younger brother I adored was dead, and I was the one who had to figure it all out. Added to all that, according to my sister, I was a bad person because I wouldn't help support my sister's family. When I pointed out that she took more money out of the farm trust in five years than she earned working, she screamed at me and walked out, telling me how selfish I was. Her grandchildren needed the money.

She knew how to hit where it hurts. Compassion for others runs in our family. Noona adopted the Burgess family who lived in a trailer house on the edge of town. She hired the daughters for housework and later helped pay for two years of junior college. She visited every 'shut-in' in town, bringing soup and cookies. Mimi took produce from her garden to all the neighbors and made a special effort to invite children of those of a different race and color to the farm to be our playmates. Daddy taught us to treat every person we met with honor and respect. My mother paid for the daughter of a farmhand to go to nursing school and started a daycare center for the children of migrant workers after a child was left in a car on a hot summer day and suffocated while waiting for his parents to finish chopping a row of cotton.

However, somewhere along the way, my mother's desire to give others a hand-up morphed into something much more destructive than helpful. I thought it was undiagnosed early stages of Alzheimer's. My sister disagreed. She was convinced that it was a deep-seated reaction to having an alcoholic father.

My mother was an adored only child, surrounded by a loving extended family who enjoyed a high standing in the community. After all, her grandmother, Lucy Canary Conroy, was known as the 'Mother of Tumbleweed.' Unusual combinations of family names being the norm for her family, my mother was named Tula Malinda. Her friends chose to call her Toogie, (pronounced TooGee) for reasons unknown. To her grandchildren, she was Tutu.

As a child, she never lacked for anything she needed, since her father owned a successful car dealership, and her mother made sure that she was exposed to culture and education. As a young woman in the 1930s, she had a solid group of girlfriends known as the Sub-Debs. As I was going through old photos, I found many black-and-white pictures of these girls posing together, obviously enjoying themselves and each other. Even decades later, Mother regularly kept in touch with these friends of her childhood who never aspired to be the 'debutants' of the town, instead happily claimed their second-class status. If there were hardships endured during the Dust Bowl days of the Depression, she seldom talked about them. Instead it was her group of friends who filled her life with simple pleasures.

I also found letters written to her by her many boyfriends, one with a shocking nude sketch of my mother. Reading the letters, I learned much about her, including the fact that as a teenager, she regularly sneaked out of the house at night to go for joyrides. Dance was strictly forbidden by her mother's Southern Baptist Church, yet letters revealed that she and her friends had a secret hideout where they danced to the Big Band sound. One of her friends had hospitable grandparents who encouraged the young people of the town to gather there. This worked perfectly because both elderly people were almost stone deaf, so none the wiser about the dancing going on in their attic.

These activities never interfered with her studies though. Her high-school debate team went to state, and she was named Miss Tumbleweed High School, a great honor in our little town. Her college years, from 1938-1942, were also the years right before and at the beginning of World War II. Most of the letters from boyfriends were filled with anguish – should they enlist? Should they wait to be called up? Would the United States be drawn into war? Others were from boyfriends who already signed up, proclaiming their undying love:

Flying Cadets
Hancock College
Santa Maria, California
Jan. 14, 1941

Well, I guess that you have decided that I have fallen for another woman down here and have just neglected to write you and tell you about it, but I haven't! No-siree. I just couldn't love anyone else because you are so kind, sweet, and considerate. In fact, you are my idea of an ideal wife, and you are going to be my wife, aren't you? I guess I would die if you should say 'no.' I love you, though more and more the longer that I am away from you. Sometimes I get so lonesome for you that I feel like just doing something to get sent home so that I can be with you.

I have been listening to Guy Lombardo's orchestra. They played 'You are my Lucky Star,' 'Down by the Ole Mill Stream,' and 'Auld Lang Syne.' These made me feel like crying, but you don't want me to so will change the subject.

This stuff they call flying certainly is wonderful. It is impossible for me to think of words to describe it. I just came down from 41 minutes' instruction. I did some beautiful spins and S turns, but I was lousy doing power stalls and overshot the field the first time I tried to land.

The upperclassmen aren't too hard on us; they are giving a dance in honor of us 'do-dos' and inviting cute, rich girls from Santa Barbara. That should be really swell. Some of them talk about us fighting Hitler pretty soon, but I don't think Roosevelt will let that happen. I plan to get me a sweet little girl before that – Ha-ha.

Don't forget me now. I want to come home and take a ride in one of your daddy's fine, new Chevys when I get my wings. Having told you all that I can think of, I will sign off until a later date.

Your Loving Sweetheart,
O'Dell

The mysterious O'Dell was an accomplished cartoonist and decorated his letters with drawings. On the last page of this letter was a pin-up of a shapely, petite, brunette woman with one exposed breast. My mother was a small, dark-headed woman with obviously lots more secrets than I ever dreamed. By the time she graduated from college, Pearl Harbor was a few months in the rearview mirror, and all the women realized it was up to them to keep the home front humming. Mother was no exception. She took a job as a teacher in another small Texas Panhandle town.

During the war years, many letters also came to her from her mother, my grandmother. They contained the town news, concerns about her studies and health, and often referred to 'Daddy's sickness' and my grandmother's failure to get him to attend church with her. She was convinced by now that only Jesus could save him.

It was only as a teenager that I realized that mother's father, my beloved grandfather, had a drinking problem. It happened one afternoon when I went outside to retrieve the sandals, I kicked off earlier. There I found him, passed out in his own backyard, trying to make it from the garage to the backdoor. I remember this as a time when I realized that someone, I idolized did not deserve his pedestal. Since I was alone at the time, I kept what I discovered a secret for several months, embarrassed for my grandfather. After another incident, however, I tearfully confessed to my mother what I saw. By now, she must have thought I was old enough to hear the truth. When she was a child, her mother would always refer to her father as 'being sick' and send her to her grandmother's house next door until the binge was over. Most of the alcohol was consumed away from home with his poker pals. When he did drink at home, it was always in secret and accompanied by a vast amount of guilt because, besides dancing, the other vice absolutely forbidden by my grandmother's church was the consumption of alcohol. The irony of it all was that some of the town's heaviest drinkers were also the biggest donors to their Southern Baptist Church. It was just that everyone pretended they were as pure as the driven snow. Hypocrisy reined.

Since the majority of our town's citizens were solid members of that church, or another like-minded one, that meant the whole county was dry. No alcohol sold or supposedly consumed. This only meant that everyone drank in secret. The nearest liquor store was 12 miles away in the next county. The name of the small community was Bethel, and it was made-up almost entirely of German Roman Catholics who enjoyed great prosperity as a result of the strict alcohol prohibitions imposed by the citizens of our town. More than one car of teenagers ended up in the cemetery after imbibing their newly purchased whiskey in Bethel.

My grandfather's drinking was obviously something that left its mark on our mother's childhood, but it was hard for me to connect this to her behavior toward Angie and family. Whereas my sister was convinced that she was trying to give Angie everything she never had and, therefore, quite literally, gave away my father's family farm, or at least any profit from it. Therefore, in Susan's mind, our mother was to blame for our present problems – memories colored by resentment.

As a teenager, I definitely clashed with my mother, but those days were many years behind me. When I thought about her now, I remembered a proud, practical, stubborn woman with deep convictions who never backed away from a fight for what she believed. She may not have been able to persuade our father to build her a new house, but she got the farmhouse extensively remodeled after I left home and always had a new car and enough money for whatever her Depression-era frugality desired. She was not a deprived child. It did not seem to me that she was giving her granddaughter money to make up for what she never had.

After our father's death, her behavior became unpredictable. For one birthday, after explaining to me that she couldn't get to the store to buy cards anymore, I gave her a collection of greeting cards she could use to send to her friends. I mailed them from Wisconsin, and when I called to see if she got them, she seemed delighted with the gift. A few months later, I visited her and, while looking for some wrapping paper, opened a large drawer. There, stacked in neat rows were hundreds of greeting-card packets, all sent as 'gifts' from the Vietnam veterans after each of their weekly requests for money. Somehow, I did not think this had anything to do with being the child of an alcoholic, except that perhaps she did become a people-pleaser, never wanting to disappoint. Maybe my sister and I were both right, for once.

What was very clear was that her granddaughter, Angie, took advantage of the situation to swindle her out of money. And as my mother became more detached from reality, Angie only became more insistent and aggressive, at one time telling Mother that her husband, Hilario, might come to the house with a gun if Mother didn't come up with the money needed. All during this time, before Mack was there to stop the financial bleeding, Susan seemed clueless about what was happening, or at least helpless to know what to do about it. Both Mack and I were left with an impossible situation, through no fault of our own. No wonder he became angry and frustrated at times. Now I understood so well. But Mack was gone. It was up to me to untangle the complex finances and relationships that lay at my feet in ruins.

At least the farmhouse was taking on a semblance of order. I separated out all the things I wanted to keep. A pod would be delivered from Amarillo where I could place my grandfather's smoking stand and my grandmother's small rocking chair, plus several larger boxes of dishes, vintage clothing, and linens I couldn't bear to part with. I gave up on trying to sort things with Susan and just decided to place all the items which didn't need to be trashed into one end of the living room for her to look through. A couple of the steamer trunks would be filled with items for her son, Will, my nephew in South Dakota, and for my three sons. I also sorted and labeled many of the financial papers and placed them in the file for safekeeping.

Tuesday was the day Lyle was coming out to help us determine the value of the gold and silver. I was looking forward to getting this part done. We planned to immediately take the silver and gold up to Stan's Safe Storage and place it with whatever was already there. We also needed to divide it between us and each get our own safety-deposit box. Perhaps then I could put everything else aside for a few days and enjoy my high school reunion.

Lyle arrived early and we sat down for a cup of coffee as we waited for Susan. I took the opportunity to tell him my brownie story and to ask him where it came from. Lyle chuckled and looked embarrassed.

"Well, I guess that's a part I missed. Mack asked me a long time ago, when he was worried about seizures, if I'd come out and check on him if I couldn't get it touch with him. It wasn't that he was worried so much about himself, but he didn't want his supply to fall into the wrong hands. I was supposed to remove all the weed and the guns. Of course, the night it happened, all I could think of was calling an ambulance and then letting you know. I made sure the guns were locked up, but I plum forgot about the other stuff. Sorry about that. I guess I was just too rattled… I obviously missed a few things."

"That's understandable, Lyle." I gave him what I hoped was a forgiving smile. "Let's forget that and get to the important stuff. So, where did he get the brownie?"

"Lanney. Remember Lanney? She was Mack's friend when he lived near Austin. She moved up to Colorado years ago, but every time she came through here, she would bring him some presents. They were friends from way back. You know," Lyle continued thoughtfully, "after Mack's accident, he used it to combat the headaches, but I think later on, he got hooked for a time on something else. Anyway, they were friends from his hippie days of the '70s."

"That accident really messed him up, didn't it?"

"Oh yeah. He definitely had a serious brain injury. It's really a miracle he recovered as much as he did, though he was never really the same..." Lyle stared down at his coffee.

"I always wondered," I replied, "why Mother and Daddy never took that guy's insurance company to court. He was drunk, ran a stop sign, and a young woman lost her life. That was a lawsuit for sure."

"Well," replied Lyle, "by then, your daddy had his stroke, and your mother had more than she could handle, taking care of both him and then Mack. I also think she was afraid that if they conducted a more thorough investigation, they would discover that Mack also might have been under the influence."

I stared at him for a long minute. "What do you think?" I asked.

"I really don't know. Mack never remembered the accident, and Mary Rose was such a wreck after her friend died and she watched Mack in convulsions out on the highway, that her memory of that night was not reliable either. I guess it doesn't matter anymore," his voice trailed off and he reached across the table to touch my hand. "The important thing is we knew his heart – his good heart – that in the end failed him rather than that dang-nabbed head injury."

"Thanks for being there for him," I said to Lyle, beginning to tear up.

"No thanks needed. He was always there for me too."

"I really can't believe he left all this silver and gold. He was such a private man. I think he enjoyed having his secrets."

The dogs suddenly ran out the doggy door, hearing the sound of an approaching vehicle. Susan was here.

Lyle looked at me. "So, how are things going with Susan?"

"Just about the way you'd expect," I said.

"I know how she feels about me," he said. "If it's just the same with you, I'd like to do this job as fast as possible."

"Oh sure. That works for me too. I really appreciate you doing this. Neither of us has a clue about how much any of this is worth."

"Well, get your paper and pen and we'll see what we can figure out."

I went to get my notebook as Susan came in the door. I knew that as much as Susan resented Lyle, she would be polite. We were genetically programmed for that.

"Good morning, Lyle," she said, pushing open the door. "I haven't seen you lately. Is everything going okay?"

"Oh yeah. I do miss that brother of yours though. We had lunch together almost every day."

"Oh, hi," I said, returning with the keys and notebook and walking past them toward the huge metal cabinet. "I hope I can open the lock. This is one very old file cabinet."

That was an understatement – it was the mother of all file cabinets, extremely heavy with industrial-strength drawers, manufactured before lighter materials were available. At first, the key stuck, but with Lyle's help, it finally opened. The top drawer contained a few miscellaneous objects, such as our father's wallet, some old title registrations from vehicles long gone, and assorted keys. Farm files filled the next two drawers. I removed them to a box to sort through later. The next drawer was very deep, and it was here we found the heavy plastic boxes filled with coin canisters. I pulled one out and opened a round two-by-four container. Inside were 25 silver dollars.

Lyle adjusted his glasses. "Okay, those are Silver Eagles. Probably worth about $20.00 each. You count the canisters and I'll figure out the total."

I handed Susan the heavy box. She could do the counting. I didn't want any accusations about being cheated. We waited patiently for several minutes.

"I count ten canisters in each box," she announced in amazement.

"Really?" I asked, looking over her shoulder. "Wow, that looks like it's worth a lot more than I thought."

"Now hold on," said Lyle, "Let's just see how many boxes like that we have. I'll figure out the total on my calculator."

I pulled out three more large heavy boxes, all filled with canisters of what Lyle called Silver Eagles. I passed them to Susan and pulled out what looked like heavy, plastic, shrink-wrapped packets. Inside were gold coins.

Lyle glanced at these. "Okay, those are American Golden Eagles. They're worth about $1600.00 each."

I looked at him in disbelief. "You've got to be kidding. They are worth that much?"

"Well," he pulled off his seed cap and scratched his head, "the value changes every day, based on the market. You'd have to look it up for today. I'm just giving a ball-park figure. Up yonder, at Stan's, they can give you the spot price, but, like I say, that changes daily."

There were 12 Golden Eagles, plus what I found out was a Krugerrand, some silver half dollars, and eight more of what Lyle called American Gold Buffaloes. In the back of the drawer was a large mason jar filled with quarters. I pulled that out last.

"Quarters?" I asked.

"Yep. He also collected quarters made before 1964. Those ones are solid silver. Nowadays, they put copper in them. Each of those is probably worth about $6.00 each."

"Oh my gosh!" I exclaimed. "Where did he get the money for all this?"

"He told me," Lyle began, "this was the money he got from that insurance policy when your mom died. He never trusted banks, so both of us began buying gold and silver. He was convinced the stock market would crash. The problem was he bought the coins at a high value. As I recall, your mom died the same week that Lehmann Brothers crashed. It was several months after that the insurance money came through, and that is when he bought. Everyone was getting out of the market and putting their money into gold and silver. It's not worth nearly as much as when he bought in."

"So," Susan added with smug assurance, "he really had quite a bit of money, didn't he? He always told me he didn't have any when I'd ask him to chip in something for Angie and the kids."

Both Lyle and I looked at her. Angie and family already depleted the farm account, and now we found out that Susan asked him to use his own money to support her daughter and children? No wonder he put the money in a place where there was no easy access. Otherwise, he would have fallen into the same trap as our mother and given in to the tears and tantrums of both Susan and Angie.

"But that's all he owned, Susan. Nothing else." I couldn't believe she would expect her brother to support her grandchildren.

Lyle cleared his throat and turned to Susan. "Mack believed in living frugally. He wouldn't even turn on the air-conditioner out here. When the temperature hit over 100, I'd find him out here in his underwear, with his feet in ice water and that ole fan a runnin'. He just didn't believe in wasting energy, or anything else, for that matter. I guess he expected that your daughter might do the same."

I waited for the explosion from Susan. In her mind, Lyle attacked her family.

She was examining the gold coins but spun around at his words. "So how do you know what my daughter needs or spends her money on? You don't even have kids. You have no right to judge her or my grandchildren."

I saw Lyle tense his shoulders. "Sorry, Susan. No harm meant. I was just thinking of Mack and how hard it was for him."

"Hard for Mack? He didn't have children either! He had no idea what it was like for them. That was the problem. He had no empathy."

"Okay. Do you have what you need from me, or is there something else I can do for you?" he said politely, reaching for his cap.

"I guess the only thing we still have to figure out would be the guns," I said. "Susan, is it all right if I give them to Lyle?"

Before she had a chance to respond, Lyle said, "No. No, I want to pay you for them. That's only fair. The only one I wonder about is that shotgun back in the closet there. That was your grandpa's. Do you think your son, Will, would want it, Susan?"

"Probably," she replied coldly, her voice strained. "I'll ask him."

"I didn't know there was a shotgun in the closet," Susan said.

"Well, that's good, 'cause Mack didn't want anybody to find it. Let's just leave it be until you check on it with Will, Susan. Okay?"

"Fine. Do whatever," Susan replied, still seething with anger.

I could tell Lyle was itching to get away, so I pulled open the bottom drawer of the file cabinet. Inside was a pistol and a small handgun with several boxes of ammunition.

"Here," I said. "Take these, and you can give us a check later. Why don't you figure out what they're worth and give us a fair price. Is that okay with you, Susan?"

"Sure. I'm sure you'll do whatever Lyle says anyway."

I got out my key and headed to the only closet in the house that locked. I pulled back the clothes hanging there and handed Lyle the shotgun. "Here. I'd rather you keep it for us until Will can come get it. We need to either sell or rent this house, and I don't want to keep it here any longer."

"Okay, if that's what you want." Lyle nodded toward Susan. "I'll keep it safe for ya."

Standing on opposite sides of the room, with the gold and silver between us, my sister and I watched Lyle walk out the door with the guns and climb into his pickup.

Chapter Fifteen

Stan's Safe Storage

Now that Susan and I had the gold and silver in hand, the plan was to take it to Amarillo where Lyle told us Mack stashed the rest of the precious metals, Stan's Safe Storage. So, the next day's 50-mile trip to Amarillo was an exercise in self-control. I was determined to take things a day at a time and get through this week without a blow-up with Susan because we still had to meet with Stu and Andy, the attorney and accountant for the trust.

The old pickup was semi-repaired and I needed to pick it up and get the Billy Graham-mobile back to Carla. There was no way I would risk driving either vehicle to Amarillo.

Susan would need to drive us. Her old van, however, was not much better. In the past few years, she went through a series of used vans, convinced that she needed a large vehicle to accommodate all the grandchildren. The fact that the children's mother drove a Mustang convertible with no thought to her own children was the fact that stuck in my craw.

A few months before, I brought this up when Susan was again requesting money from the trust to help pay the bills. Her reply was the usual – she was victimized by her own daughter. The story was that she gave Angie money to buy a used van. Angie bought the van, only to trade it in a few months later for the red Mustang. Of course, along with the new car came a huge loan with an interest rate at about 23%. To her credit, Susan tried to point out that Angie could not afford the payment, but that fell on deaf years. Both Angie and the loan shark went away happy – she because she now had a car, thoroughly impractical but sporty, and the finance guy because he knew that after a few months of payments, then a few skipped months, he would repossess the car and resell it to another sucker. So far, Susan managed to come up with the money because Angie, without a car, meant that all the driving fell to my sister.

If Susan refused to come to me for the money or I didn't give it to her, she would be the victim of abuse and harassment from her daughter, which she seemed powerless to prevent.

I arrived at Susan's after lunch, lugging the large tote bag containing the coins. The door handle on the passenger side of Susan's van did not work, so I waited until she reached across the seat and let me in.

"Hope this doesn't take too long," she greeted me. "I never know what I'll find at home when I get back. The kids invite their friends over and eat up all the food, and then there's nothing left to fix for supper."

"Is there somewhere else they could go so you don't have to worry about it?"

"No, I guess not. They are always here."

"Couldn't you insist they stay out of the house while you're gone?"

She gave me a withering look. "Yeah, right. As though that would work."

I decided that I would try to keep the conversation focused on neutral topics for this drive. We had to finish this task still speaking to one another. The car was a wheeled version of Susan's house. Old pieces of hamburger shone through greasy paper wraps, and month-old French fries were scattered on the floor, along with old chewing gum and spilled soda. The radio no longer worked, but thankfully the air-conditioner did. I was hoping for a semi-peaceful trip.

Susan headed out toward the Interstate, but instead of entering the onramp, she pulled onto the access road that was a part of the old Amarillo highway. I'd forgotten. She refused to drive on an Interstate, despite the fact that this was probably one of the least traveled Interstates in the country, the road ruler-straight, and one where you could see all the way to the next town with no problem. I bit my lip, searching frantically for something to fill up the silence.

"Oh, I forgot to tell you." I suddenly remembered. "I have all the family-history information I downloaded off Ancestry.com about the Conroys."

"You do?" she asked. One thing that fascinated my sister was our family history. "What did you find?"

"Well, now I know that James Frederick, you know, Granddaddy's grandfather? He is buried near Bowie, close to Wichita Falls."

"He is? I thought he died in Missouri."

"So did I, but not according to what I discovered. I guess he came to Texas with his two sons after all the other family members died."

148

The conversation continued in this vein for several miles. As we crested the rise leading down into the draw that eventually led to Palo Dura Canyon, Susan remembered something herself. "You know Cousin Jessie's saddle and the saddlebags we gave to W.T.?"

"Yeah. What about them?" I asked as I remembered our visit a few months ago from the curator at West Texas State.

"Well, they had them on display at the museum, and they didn't even let me know. I think that's awful. They don't even tell me when I can go see them. I had to find out from the lady at our local museum. Why did we even let them have them? We probably could have sold them."

She was referring to a fascinating piece of our family history. Our grandfather's first cousin was the daughter of a physician. When her younger brother died in the 1880s, she decided to become a homeopathic physician just like her father. Both she and her mother moved to Chicago for a year in order for Jessie to attend school. When she returned, she brought with her hundreds of small vials of 'medicine,' which she placed in a specially designed saddlebag. For the next 30 years, she rode from ranch to ranch, treating the cowhands and anyone else who needed help. When she finally died in the 1970s, our mother and one of her cousins were the sole heirs since Cousin Jessie never married or had children. It fell to them to clean out her home and dispose of all her belongings. Cousin Jessie was an eccentric woman and something of a hoarder, so the two women made many trips downstate to settle her estate. Many items ended up in the county museum in Bowie where she lived all her life. But her sidesaddle and saddlebags were special. For many years after that, Mother stored these in our basement, intending to get them appraised. After her death, it fell to us.

"Susan," I began. "Remember? We had that expert at the Texas Tech Pharmacy Museum look at the vials in the saddlebag. She said that they were so unique, it would be hard to find a comparable. The trust got a tax deduction when we donated it to them. Then I think the saddle and saddlebags ended up where they belonged, at the Panhandle Plains Museum at W.T."

"Well," she replied. "That's because you don't need the money like I do."

Once again, I decided to remain silent. We only had a few miles to go. The traffic picked up as we entered the outskirts of the city, but since we were poking along on the access road, I just watched it whiz by. Soon, we would have to turn onto a city street. "So," I began. "Do you know how to find this place?"

"Of course," she said. "I'll just go until I find 7th Street."

"Don't we need to turn left though?"

"You know I don't make left turns," she replied, her voice rising. "Just leave me alone and let me drive, okay?"

Thirty minutes later, we stopped at a gas station so she could ask directions. While she got out of the car, lit a cigarette, and walked into the station, I grabbed my phone and pulled up Google Maps. By the time she returned, I knew where we were and where we had to go. Now the dilemma. Should I tell her or just let her find the way on her own? I opted to keep quiet.

"Okay," she said, pulling the door closed. "We have to go back a few blocks and then turn on Georgia. That's a right turn," she added. "We should be just fine."

By the time we pulled into Stan's Safe Storage, my patience was stretched thin and a few new lines were taking up permanent residence around my mouth. But we avoided a major blow-up for the hour-and-a-half it took us to drive 45 miles.

Stan's reminded me of something out of a movie. There was a bell outside the door which we rang. A voice over an intercom greeted us.

"Yes? May I help you?"

"Hello. We are here to open our brother's safety-deposit box," I said. "He passed away in January."

"Name?"

The voice on the other end was efficient and suspicious. After explaining our mission, we were asked to have ready the information to access our late brother's box and verify our identity. After what seemed a long interrogation period, we were buzzed in the first door. Another door greeted us, then with a click, it opened onto a long, carpeted hall. All was silent. At the end of the hall was another carpet-covered door with a buzzer that went off when we pushed the door open. Above us, a security camera whirred, and after several minutes, the door magically opened into a glassed foyer. Behind a small reception window sat a ramrod, straight, older lady with steely gray hair.

"May I please see your driver's licenses and letter of testamentary?" she asked solemnly. Without another word, she turned and walked out of her little cubicle and was gone for several minutes. When she returned, a younger well-dressed man was with her.

"So," he began, "what do we have here?" Looking over his glasses, he examined our documents and finally looked up at us. "These look to be in order. Please follow me." Then, noticing my tote bag, he stopped. "What's in there, ma'am?" he asked suspiciously, probably expecting parts to an AK-47.

"Oh," I said, surprised I hadn't thought to explain. "This is more gold and silver my brother had stored at his home. We need to secure it here, if that's okay?"

"Mind if I have a look?" he asked.

I opened the bag, and when he was satisfied that I was telling the truth, he pushed a button. Another buzzer sounded and we were in an adjoining room. Every surface was covered with carpet. It smelled musty, with a faint overlay of mothballs and dust. No sound could escape, nor anything else. It looked like a library, with book stacks, except that the horizontal compartments were all secure storage boxes filled with someone's valuables.

His name was Larry, Stan's son, he explained. The stern lady behind the glass enclosure was his mother. She, he offered, had been working here since his dad started the business 40 years before. We explained that we needed to inventory Mack's box, then close out his account and open two new accounts, one for me, and one for Susan. Once he found out we were potential new customers, he became more talkative, telling us that he could give us the 'spot price' of everything in the box. Then, if we wanted to sell it, he would buy it. If not, we could deposit each of our shares in our own box, totally secure, he assured us.

He pulled Mack's box and ushered us into a small room covered on all sides from floor to ceiling with the exact same maroon carpeting. Putting the box on a table between us, he told us he would leave us alone to examine our treasure. The door clicked shut, and we were alone in an air-conditioned, carpeted cell. Both of us were slightly claustrophobic, so after he was gone, we opened the door. As far as we could tell, we were the only clients here anyway.

"Okay," I said to Susan, pretending to be undaunted by the creepy place, "How do you want to do this?"

"I can't breathe. There's no fresh air. I don't care how we do it, let's get out of here as soon as we can, okay?" She coughed, adjusted her glasses and pulled a pocket calculator from her purse. "I'll count first, then I'll give it to you to recount."

My farm-account spiral notebook contained all the financial numbers, the trust in one section, and Mack's estate in another. I started a new page and used the calculator on my phone to confirm the numbers my sister carefully added.

This part went surprisingly well. Soon we counted all the Silver and Gold Eagles, plus the Golden Buffaloes, and put aside a few foreign coins mixed in with the lot.

"I have to get out of here for a while," Susan said, putting her glasses away. "I need a cigarette and I have to find a bathroom. Let's get that guy to tell us what all this is worth so we can leave, okay?"

I went in search of Larry, explaining that we needed to finish this up as soon as possible. The carpeted walls were closing in and the unnatural quiet was unsettling. However, Larry was now in his element. As soon as my sister returned, we were treated to a lesson in coinage values, interspersed with story snippets from Larry's life. I was getting even more antsy, and I could tell that Susan's patience was long gone.

"This is all very interesting," I explained, "but we just need to divide this 50/50. Oh, and we need to add all the coins in this bag." I held up the heavy bag of coins from the farmhouse.

"Then when I get mine, I need to sell some," Susan added with a groan. "Will that take long?"

Larry was clearly disappointed that his life stories failed to hold our interest but excused himself to go 'look up the numbers.'

After long minutes of deliberation, Susan separated out a few canisters of silver and plastic-encased new coins gold. "I'm going into the next room to count this again. Then I'll put what I don't want to sell in my box. Do whatever you want to with yours." I packed my pile into the long metal box and stared at the numbers in my spiral as I waited for my sister.

Two hours after arriving, nerves frayed, we were again back at the window, presided over by Larry's mother who now introduced herself as Mildred. Now that we were officially part of 'the Stan's family,' she treated us royally, presenting each of us with our own Stan's key fob. Finally, after a more formal presentation of our very own Stan's Safe Storage key by Larry, we walked out into the blinding sunshine. Food was in order, plus a stiff drink, if you asked me, but, first, we had to find a place to eat that would suit both of us. A tall order.

"Would you like me to drive?" I asked. "I don't mind left turns, and we might get around faster." This comment was clearly a mistake.

Susan wheeled around. "You are not driving my car. First of all, you go too fast, and you don't know this town like I do. No. You are not driving."

I knew better than to argue. I needed to choose my battles. Her idea of a place to eat was cafeteria-style. Getting there, however, posed challenges. After a series of right-hand trips around several blocks, we finally arrived at the back of Furr's Cafeteria. By now, it was 5:00, and the senior citizens were lined up for the special. We took our place in line behind the canes and walkers and waited. All I could think of was the long drive back to the access road and then the slow ride homeward. A sign caught my eye on the other side of the street: 'All-Car Rental – We Beat Out All Competitors.' I would definitely be going home next week. How much would it really cost to rent a car and then drop it off at the airport?

I broached this subject as we ate. "You know, if I rented a car, it would save you a trip to Amarillo to take me to the airport. I think it might be a good idea. I'm not sure I trust the old pickup anymore, even if they do say they fixed it."

She was quiet for a minute. "Well, you can pay for whatever you want. That's what I mean when I say that you don't need the farm money like I do. And I know you don't like my driving... Well, I'll tell you this. I don't like yours either. Go ahead – do whatever you want. I don't care. I thought we could talk about the family history some more. That's something I really like, but I guess that's really not important to you."

"So, you're saying you don't want me to rent a car?" I asked.

"Do whatever. I don't care," she said, pulling her cigarettes out of her purse. "I'm going out to smoke."

As she walked away, I let out a loud sigh and dropped my head into my hands. Some things weren't worth fighting about. A rental car was one of them. A few minutes later, we pulled out of the cafeteria and headed in the direction of the access road, making right-hand turns. 'All-Car Rentals' receded in the background, and I braced myself for the bumpy ride home. The shocks in the van were long gone. We finally got on the road back home and I watched as trucks and cars blazed past us on the nearby Interstate. It had been a long day; my head danced with images of gold and silver coins.

"So," I began. "Did you ever in your wildest dreams think that Mack had all that money squirreled away, or that he would decide to leave it to us?"

"No," she replied. "I still can't believe it. I guess that's the money he got from Mom's life insurance after she died. My money from that is all gone. What about yours?"

"I invested mine, so I still have some," I said, deciding to be purposely vague. "But now you'll have half of Mark's portion, so that extra 25000 should be a relief to you."

"That will be my old-age money. I don't have anything else like you do."

"Well, I'm glad you have it now," I said, gazing out the windows as the prairie rolled by.

We drove along in silence for a while, until I remembered we had a meeting with the lawyer and accountant the next day. "Oh my," I began. "Do you realize we have a 9:00 a.m. meeting with Stu and Andy tomorrow to go over all the finances for the trust and Mack's estate?"

"So why did you have to plan it for this week?" she asked. "Of all weeks, this is the busiest! We have Picnic this week and you have your reunion."

"It had to do with their schedule. That's the only time they would both be in town."

Susan let out a sigh of exasperation. "Well, this is just great. I'm already worn out from today, and we have to go through another ordeal tomorrow. I just wish the whole thing was over."

"Well, so do I," I replied. "Let's just hope it goes smoothly."

"I hate these meetings. I never understand what they're talking about."

I knew both men would be happy to explain the financial terms to her again, even though they explained them to us both at the time of Mack's death, but I decided not to mention it. I knew that my comment would be misconstrued, and we were almost back to Susan's house. Then I remembered. I needed to take back Carla's car and get the pickup from the mechanic's garage. The trick was leaving the Oldsmobile with Carla without having to stay for the Carla monologue.

"Susan, I have a favor to ask," I ventured cautiously.

"What?" she said as she turned into town.

"I need to take Carla's car back and pick up Trusty Rusty from Cy's. Could you follow me to Carla's so I could drop off the Billy Graham-mobile and then take me over to Cy's?

"I need to feed the kids and, besides that, Carla's not home. This is the night she helps out at the weekly dinner at church, even though she doesn't go to church anymore."

There was a long pause as I tried to decide how to reply. Then, from my sister, "Oh, I guess so. This way, I won't have to get into a long discussion with Carla."

"Well, I guess that's one thing we can agree on." I looked at her with a wry smile. "Let's get this done quick." I knew that more than anything else, my sister needed a cigarette, and I could use a glass of wine...or possibly another brownie.

Chapter Sixteen

Accountants, Lawyers, and Farmers

As far as stress goes, Tuesday was just a warm-up for Wednesday. Susan was right. There was too much planned for this week. The days seemed to have collapsed in upon each other. This morning was our meeting about the end of the trust. Stu, the attorney, had an office a block off the square, just down the street from the Ozark Trail monument, emblazoned this year with – T.H.S. Class of 2013 Rules! 50 years ago, it was painted with the same thing, except then, it was the class of 1963.

The office was in a part of what had been, during my childhood, the ornate and sedate First National Bank. In those days, all the people who worked there were locals. No one needed identification or account numbers, because the tellers knew your parents and grandparents. Now the bank had the shiny sheen of plastic, with new counters and its own ATM, but no one knew the strangers who chewed gum and talked to each other while lazily examining your driver's license. The bank had gone through many permutations since my childhood, and now the big plastic sign on the front announced it as Wells Fargo.

I arrived at the office, armed for battle, my stuffed file folders and trusty farm spiral notebook tucked away in my Feed and Seed tote bag. Andy, our C.P.A., arrived next, then Susan. Stu greeted us, ushered us into his book-lined office, and seated us at his wide mahogany table. We could have been in a Dallas attorney's office once we moved past the reception area. Everything here gave off an aura of professionalism, smelling of leather and Old Spice. Indeed, both Stu and Andy could have practiced in any city of their choice, but both were homegrown kids who chose to come back and serve in the community that raised them. As a result, they were held in highest esteem and never lacked for clients or money.

Stu's secretary came in with a tray of coffee and water as we exchanged pleasantries. "Well, I guess I'll start," Stu said, stacking the papers in front of him. "Looks like today we're here to figure out the divisions of the assets of the trust that your mom and dad set up for you girls and Mack in 1990. Does that sound about right?" We nodded as he continued, "Now, Andy here has all the numbers, so I'll turn it over to him in a minute. I just want to review a few details and rules we need to follow." Stu pulled out his reading glasses and looked meaningfully at Susan and me. "As of September, about two months from now, it will be five years since your mom's death. That means we need to divide the remaining assets as per the trust agreement."

Stu paused to take a sip of coffee. "Of course, Mack's death has changed things a bit. Rather than ya'll each getting a third, Mack's part will now be divided 50/50 between the two of you as per his will. Next, we got to look at the assets and deduct what's already been withdrawn from the trust in these five years since your mom's death. After we do all that – and I'll let Andy explain that further – we end up with Dalinda at 56% and Susan at 44%. Do you follow me?"

I nodded. Weeks before, I ran the numbers myself many times. Susan looked surprised. "You mean the money, right, not the land?"

Stu shuffled the papers again and looked up at her over his reading glasses. "No, now, we talked about that, Susan. This does include the land and houses too. Even the vehicles are included."

I could feel Susan tense up. "Nobody ever told me we had to divide the land like that."

Andy chimed in next, "Now, Susan, that's right in the trust. It's been there since the beginning."

"How do you expect me to remember all that? Somebody should have told me." There was a note of rising panic in her voice.

Andy and Stu exchanged glances. They were seasoned warriors who had seen the same scene played out many times before, with just family names changed. They knew their lines. "Now, Susan," Andy continued pointedly, "Remember we had a meeting every year, and I explained each time that you could take money out but that there would then be less at the end to divide? Actually, since Mack died, you're getting more than you would have, had he lived."

"But nobody said the land…" Susan stammered.

"Well, the land, you see, is a big part of the assets," Andy explained.

"But we don't have to divide it, do we? We can just keep it like it is?"

"That's right. You don't have to divide it," Stu added, "But selling it is definitely one option. Another is dividing it up 56% and 44% and each of you still running your own part – probably still renting out to Skeeter and Jerry Bob. Then you would each get your part of the profits. Or you could just leave it intact, and one of you would run the show, like Mack did, and then just divide the profits at the end of the year."

"Well," said Susan decisively, "that's what we're going to do. We are not dividing it up or selling the land."

Stu turned to me. "Now is that your thinking, Dalinda?"

I paused. "I think we need to look carefully at all the options before we decide." Actually, this was all I'd been thinking about for some time, but I wasn't ready to commit to anything right now.

Susan turned to me. "Wait a minute. You and Mack and I talked about this before he died and we decided."

"Yes, but his death changed things. He isn't here anymore to oversee things." I turned back to Stu. "Could we look at the ways we could divide the land and still retain the integrity of the irrigation system and water wells?"

I could see Susan's knuckles going white as she gripped her pen. "I can't believe you are saying this. You would consider dividing up Daddy's land?"

I took a deep breath. "Yes, I think we have to consider all options."

"I cannot believe you are saying this," she said again, her voice rising in dismay.

Both men sat, watching patiently. They were used to watching the drama of family-farm conflicts. Finally, Stu spoke up, "Well, I tell you what. Why don't I give Skeeter a call and see what he would say about how to best divide up the land, just in case that's what you decide. That is, if you're both still planning to have him do your farming for you?"

"Yes," I said. "I know I would want him to continue. He lives right down the road and has done a good job. He'd probably be the best to know about all the irrigation wells and how they are tied together."

"I think that's a good idea," Andy added. "That boy knows his stuff. In the meantime, here's all the financials for the trust, as of June 30, 2013. Ya'll both need to look them over carefully and write down any questions you have. Then when we meet next, I'll address those." He turned to Stu. "You think we can get Skeeter in here and meet back next week? Dalinda, when are you leaving town?"

"I have an open return ticket," I replied. "But I'd like to leave by the end of next week."

Susan still seethed silently beside me. Andy looked at Stu. "You think we can get together on Monday, Stu?"

"I'll sure see what I can do, and I'll see if Skeeter's willin' to help. Is that okay with you gals?"

Susan finally spoke up, "I don't see what business it is of Skeeter's," she replied stiffly.

"He's just providing information, Susan," Stu explained. "Nothing more. I figure we need him for maybe half 'n hour at most and then we can finish up with you two, and Dalinda can be on her way."

I closed my spiral. "Sounds good to me. Thank you both very much."

Susan still sat, clenching her teeth. I gathered up my papers, including the new financial report from Andy. "Okay, Stu, give us a call when you get something set up with Skeeter."

"Will do," said Stu, rising from the table. "You two gals both look over all that and think about things, then we can figure it all out on Monday, or whenever it's good for Skeeter."

Susan stumbled to her feet, turned, and stalked out of the office. I followed close behind. This did not look like a good day for a friendly discussion over lunch. I needed to do some deep thinking plus some last-minute preparations for the reunion. Outside, the July sun practically blinded me. Susan pulled out her cigarettes and was leaning against her van as I yanked open the door to the pickup.

She gave me one of those if-looks-could-kill glances. "I cannot believe you could even think of dividing up Daddy's farm. You are not the person I thought you were." She threw down her still-lit cigarette, her eyes hard and her words bitter. I watched as she backed out and hit the accelerator, her way of expressing anger when on the familiar streets of Tumbleweed.

I sat behind the steering wheel for many minutes before I pulled out on the wide streets to head back to the farm. My sister was right. I was not the person she thought I was. A few months ago, the idea of dividing the farm would have been unthinkable, but that was before Mack died. Now, I saw the handwriting on the wall if we kept the farm intact. The business would now be on my shoulders. Susan couldn't even keep track of her own bills much less all the paperwork required for 21st century agriculture. If that was my role, everything I did would be second-guessed. It would be just like what Mack faced – from the many requests for extra money to the anger at not being consulted about every decision. I wasn't sure I had the needed patience to take on this challenge for the rest of my life. And, yes, I was selfish enough to want a life of my own away from the family farm. That was the part that my sister would never, ever understand.

All these thoughts ran through my mind as I drove the rutted country roads. However, I needed to put these aside for a while and concentrate on the stories I promised to tell for our reunion. I wrote two remembrances of our school days – one rather fun and light, and another darker and more serious. I couldn't decide which to use. I would like to use both but didn't want to take up all the time. Besides that, Penny reminded me more than once that our classmates wanted to visit with each other so to keep the memories short. I had three days to figure it out, plus all the rest on my mind.

Back at the farm, where I always left on the radio for security and comfort, Kenny Rogers was belting out his classic: "You need to know when to hold 'em, know when to fold 'em, know when to walk away, know when to run…" Before I had time to process this obvious message from beyond, the dogs suddenly barked and raced out the doggy door. A large, new-model, blue pickup was pulling up behind Mack's old one. Skeeter stepped down from the driver's seat. He was Jerry Bob's nephew, part of the third generation of Finches. It was he who actually operated our farmland, using his equipment and employees to do the actual work. Jerry Bob was more the silent partner, providing money and probably some unappreciated advice from time to time. The older Finches, Wyatt and Carrie Jo, his wife, were now gone, so it was their children and grandchildren who owned the manufacturing company and their farmland. All the Finches except Trenna Ray, Skeeter's mother, lived next to one another in what we always called Finchville, a mile away. Trenna and husband, both engineers, owned their own, small, manufacturing company on the other side of town. Skeeter's brothers and sisters lived near them and helped run their business, but Skeeter loved the farming part so chose to live in Finchville and manage the larger family-farm operation.

When I was a child, the large pole-barn home of Wyatt and Carrie Jo was the talk of the neighborhood because of its size and design. But there had always been other houses in Finchville. These were smaller houses Wyatt moved in to accommodate his hired hands and families. This was a common practice in that part of the country where small-frame houses had no basements so could be hoisted up and moved to a new cement-block foundation. Usually the new owner would update a few things, bring in water and electricity, then pass the house from one farm worker to the next as a part of the benefits of employment.

As children, we would occasionally play with the Finch kids when they weren't busy working on the farm or in the house with their mom, but we always visited one of these hired men's houses each week to take our laundry for ironing. One of the jobs my mother despised most was ironing men's work shirts which were usually made from a heavy khaki cotton – certainly nothing like the wash 'n' wear fabrics of today. Sometimes, if she wasn't too busy, Mother would sigh deeply and do the ironing herself. Then later, when Susan and I were older, the ironing became our job. But when we were young, the weekly ironing went to Mrs. Fronterhouse who lived with her family in one of Wyatt's houses. I guess there was a Mr. Fronterhouse, but I never saw him. I always pictured him as a Jack Spratt of a man, skinny and tall, as compared to his much more ample wife. Their house smelled of garlic, laundry starch, and slightly scorched cotton, but my dad's shirts always came back crisp and shiny, each on their own individual hanger.

Mrs. Fronterhouse would greet us with a wide smile at the door, her double chin almost meeting her extremely bountiful bosom. The rest of her was short and squat, and the Fronterhouse children clinging to her apron were squared-off versions of their mother. For my sister, brother, and I, the best part of Mrs. Fronterhouse was her name. It fit her so well. While our mother went in to gratefully pay her for her services and bring out the newly ironed shirts, we sat in the back of our station wagon and giggled helplessly as we watched the shirts, our mother, and Mrs. Fronterhouse try to make it out the narrow door.

In the years since then, the number of houses at Finchville had grown. Wyatt and Carrie Jo's house was joined by five other pole-barn homes. Skeeter and family were in one. His aunts and uncles and their families in the others. All were wide, sprawling affairs, neatly landscaped, with spreading yews and hardy cedars creating a wind break on three sides. Each had its own streetlight, so, at night, the Finch village was like a beacon for all those souls lost on the lone prairie. Except for Skeeter's mother, all the other Finches decided to do

161

away with the long-dress, long-hair requirements of their parents' faith. Now you could hardly tell them apart from plain ol' Baptists or Methodists. The women even wore nail polish, lipstick, and jewelry, yet, according to Carla, the local authority, they still practiced other aspects of their faith as before.

Skeeter greeted me as I came to the door. "Thought I'd come over and see if you'd like to take a little drive around the farm and see what's planted and all," he said, nervously fingering his feed cap. "I got a call from Stu, and he wanted me to come in and meet with ya'll about the land, so I figured it might be good to go over the whole place with you. I tried to get a hold of Susan but only got one of the kids answerin' the phone. He didn't seem to know where she was at."

Skeeter was about the same age as my own sons, and it was good to see him. "I'm so glad you came over, Skeeter. I feel remiss I haven't called you. It's just been so busy, trying to get everything done around here."

"Yes, ma'am, I know what you mean. Mama and Daddy passed away not long ago, and we're still trying to figure it all out."

"It's a big job, that's for sure. And I think a tour around the farm's a great idea. Do you have time right now?"

"Sure do, ma'am. If you don't mind sittin' in my pickup out yonder."

I looked at the shiny, blue Ford F-350 Super Duty parked beside Mack's ol' Chevy. "I think I can manage that," I said, smiling and grabbing my visor. "I'm ready anytime."

As we bounced along the narrow dirt roads, Skeeter was in his element. It was obvious he loved the land and took pride in showing me how he and his men were managing it. The first section of 640 acres was what we called 'R.J.'s section.' This is where my family's hired hand and his family lived when I was a child. Their house was long-gone now, but memories of it were very much alive. They were African American and hardworking. R.J. couldn't read well but was devoted to my dad and knew more about the land than anyone else. His wife, Verne June, worked in town while raising five children, all of whom graduated from high school and went onto good jobs. Their youngest daughter was the one my mother helped through nursing school. When we were children, they were my brother's playmates, all the children being much younger than my sister and me. R.J. died shortly before my dad, but all the rest of the family came to my mother's funeral which must have been hard for them. They were the only black family in the church that day.

But my mind was wandering, and I needed to pay attention to my tour guide. Skeeter was now the authority and I was the student, learning about my own land. "Now you got half this section in pasture. Th'other half's got a well, but it's not pumping out much water these days. Pretty soon, if we don't drill her down farther, it'll be nothing but dryland here."

"And that's pretty pricey, isn't it?" I asked.

"Yes, ma'am. Sure cost ya more than a couple of nickels, for sure."

"So, what about the Sutter Section?" I asked, referring to the next mile of land which was named for someone no one could remember. "What's the water look like here?"

"There's only about 30-foot of water in that well on the Sutter section – could drill down to hit the Santa Rosa but might hit saltwater. It's a gamble. 'Course I'm not gonna do anything unless I own the land – 's not worth it. Could spend hundreds of thousands of dollars and still not have more than a drop of usable irrigation water."

I sat up straight, surprised by his comment. "So, you're wanting to buy it?"

"Yes, ma'am, I am. If you're sellin,' I'd sure like to be first on the list for buying this. First of all, it abuts our property, and I know it like the back of my hand. Some of this just needs new wells and maybe a new sprinkler system. Other parts, like Sutter section, and R.J., well, we'd have to see... But I know for sure that that land on 12's got a mighty fine well. We've been producing a good yield there for several years. So...yes, ma'am, I'd sure like to make you an offer on it if you're a willin'."

I was stunned into silence. If any family could afford to buy the land, the Finch family could. It's just that selling never seemed a viable option until now. In my family, land was something you did not sell because it was irreplaceable. Also, the price per acre was not something most people in Herschel County could afford. I wasn't sure I was ready to let it go either.

Skeeter continued, "You know, you and Susan are really gonna need to put some money into this place pretty soon. It's been quite a while since your daddy did anything to improve the land, and we're a'gettin' behind, if you know what I mean."

He was right. Like any business, improvements and repairs were a necessary part of the bottom line. Susan and I had nothing to invest. Skeeter and his family did. I listened carefully to his assessment as we bounced through the pasture, surveying the land. Daddy would have approved of him. He was a good farmer – practical, wise, down-to-earth, farsighted. And it was obvious he loved this rough piece of Texas prairie.

Memories rushed out to greet me – times I rumbled over the same pastureland with my father and his contagious enthusiasm for the young heifers he called his 'girls' whom he nurtured so lovingly. I thought of all the people who created these memories for me, those who had lovingly nurtured me. They were all dead and gone. Susan and I were the ones left – grandmothers now – not young, bright-eyed women looking at a rosy future from the perspective of the 1960s. Yet it was these family ghosts we fought over. Our grandfather who broke the soil in 1916; our father who arose at 3:00 a.m. to set the irrigation pipes so that the precious water ran down each row of sorghum; my mother's fierce love of the little town her grandparents founded from their sod dugout in the 1880s. Then there was her vehement declaration as an 85-year-old as we tried to convince her to move to assisted living in Amarillo: "I will not desert this town. I will not desert this land."

There were ancient echoes in my head that told me to never sell the land – never, ever. Whoever owned the land ruled the world. Great and violent wars were fought over land rights, and we had our own little plot of land we were taught to fiercely protect. Never had I considered that the fate of this family farm would rest with me. That was not what was supposed to happen.

Skeeter cleared his throat, interrupting my thoughts. "So, now I don't want to be pushy or anything, but I do want you to know about my offer. And I'm glad to go in and talk to ya'll, Stu, and Andy. I sure can tell you what I think would be best if ya'll decide to split it between you and Susan. Now that's not the best way to do it, but family is family, and you got to make everybody happy."

I thanked him as I stepped down from the leather seats inside his comfortable truck. I wasn't sure of most things, but I was fairly certain none of this was going to make my sister very happy.

Chapter Seventeen

Sections and Lessons

My plan was to work on the reunion memory that afternoon, but the conversation with Skeeter and the meeting that morning distracted me, so I pulled out the farm appraisals from the file cabinet to look at again. Now I was looking at them from a new perspective – possibly dividing the land between my sister and me. There were four sections with 640 acres each, and a half-section with 320 acres. Like my dad's heifers, the sections were also given names or numbers. When my mother died in 2008, the land value was approximately $200.00 per acre – a bit less for pastureland, a bit more for irrigated. However, since the economic downturn, investors looked at land as a safe haven for their money. Consequently, after many years of stagnation, land prices in this flat corner of Texas were at an all-time high. The possibility of leasing to wind-turbine companies also added to the value.

As I examined the appraisal details more closely, it was apparent that each section was valued differently, depending on the availability of water. My father had been very conservation-minded early on and designed a water system that connected the farmhouse section and McMurry section to Section 12 which had the most productive well. The water ran into a reservoir and was then pumped out when extra water was needed. The other two sections were separate, each having both pastureland and cropland but diminished water wells, making pumping up the water a costly measure.

Skeeter knew all this and obviously wanted to make an offer to buy the entire farm operation. But I knew that selling was something Susan would never agree to, although she needed the money. For my sister, it was important to leave the land intact, with the two of us managing it together, each taking our share of the profit at the end of the year. This plan would mean we would be co-managers which I could not see working. We couldn't even sort through a box without an argument.

We could divide the land, but to divide it so that each percentage was correct was a challenge due to the different value for each section. That part would be complicated to figure out. I would need to come up with my own plan and then compare that to Skeeter's. Even if we were able to divide it 44% and 56%, it would be almost impossible to convince Susan that this was a good idea. The way the trust was written, I was the designated trustee and didn't need anyone else to make the decision, yet in the spirit of fairness and maintaining a relationship with my sister, I preferred to have her buy-in.

All this was too much right now. I needed more time here, yet I desperately wanted to get back home too. I finally decided to turn it over to my subconscious, or to God, or at least sleep on the problem. I would direct my fast-fading energy instead toward working on the reunion memory. It was a relief that I would not be the only one on the program. Greg would be replaying some of the tapes from his time as our local disk-jockey in the early '60s, John would play the piano, and Penny would sing her Patsy Cline favorites, just like she did at every reunion. Even that sounded appealing right now. I would just go back to a much simpler time and live in the world of my youth.

However, the ride around the farm was a reminder of the most life-changing events of my young teen years, bringing up the question of which of the story I should tell my classmates. I wrestled with this and decided I would tell one with a lighter tone and just suggest to my classmates that they download the other story if they were interested. As I finished labeling a few leftover boxes, I thought about the story I wouldn't tell my class – all that happened my freshman year of high school:

Segregation was a fact of life in the Texas of the 1950s. There was a separate school, separate bathrooms, and separate drinking fountains. In the Royal Theater, where kids got to spend their allowances on John Wayne movies, there was a separate balcony for the Sunset Addition kids. Our hired hands, R.J.'s family, were the Hendriks. They, and a handful of other families, were the lucky ones. They lived out in the country instead of across the railroad tracks in Sunset Addition where most of 'their kind' were supposed to live.

Because of the Hendriks, and the Micks, who lived across the road from Mimi, my sister, brother, and I spent time interacting with both families. The Mihlbauer family made no secret of the fact that this Jim Crow system was not the way things ought to be and went out of their way to teach us lessons of tolerance. The other side of the family, the Conroys, who lived in town, were kind and generous people but felt the social system worked fine as it was and was better left alone.

However, there were others in that dusty little Bible-belt town who realized this vast inequality needed to change. One of those was our pastor, a transplant from Minnesota, who preached about accepting others as brothers and sisters. Another was the editor of our hometown newspaper – a man who had the courage to speak out about segregation, the John Birch Society and later Barry Goldwater at a time when that was not popular in our corner of Texas.

In 1955, when integration hit the Texas Panhandle, it brought out the best and worst of us all. Terrible rumors swirled around town about the world being taken over by Communists and their allies on the U.S. Supreme Court. But for those of us who were fifth graders at the elementary school, it meant something else – Pearly May was now in charge of the playground, especially the big slide. She was one of the children from Sunset Addition who actually came to school. A large girl with huge, expressive, brown eyes, she was a force to be reckoned with. Apparently, she had not gotten the message that her race had traditionally been forced to be subservient to ours. Right away, she established the pecking order, not caring a hoot who saw her underwear as she slid down the big slide or commandeered the merry-go-round.

For most of us, it was a relief not to be bossed around by the 'popular girls' with their swishy, starched petticoats, poodle skirts, and smooth curls. But for too many people, Pearly May and her kind were a threat to the social order. Their fears were short lived because by the time we entered high school, Pearly May was needed to help support the family. Eighth grade would be her last. For all of us who knew her, she set the racial bar high, demanding respect for herself and many who would follow her.

Others were more fortunate than Pearly May and her family, like the Hendricks who lived on our farm. R.J., their father, was our top hired hand. As he aged, his hearing grew worse at the same time that my dad's ability to speak also left him because of his stroke. Yet, because the two men knew each other so well, excellent communication between them continued. It was just that nobody else could figure out what they meant. The Micks were another African American family who lived in the country. Beulah, the mom, looked for all the world like an Ethiopian princess – tall and regal. Their oldest son, Jimmy, excelled as an athlete and, as a senior, became the quarterback of our high-school football team. His four little sisters loved to sing and dance and would entertain us when we went to visit or when they came over to sample Mimi's cookies.

I was a sophomore in the marching band by then, which meant that every Friday, we all piled into school buses with our clarinets, trombones, and snare drums to accompany the team to 'away games.' Since the teams in our conference were sometimes a hundred miles away, we left right after school. Then we usually stopped somewhere for dinner at a restaurant where our food was preordered and ready for over 100, hungry, high-school kids, teachers, and parent chaperones. One particular Friday, our 'away game' was over a two-hour drive, and by the time we poured out of the buses, we were all famished. We filled the chicken restaurant and found seats. Soon, however, we realized there was problem at the door. The band director, football coach, restaurant manager, and my friend, Emily's mother, Nellie, were engaged in a very serious discussion. It seemed that our quarterback, Jimmy Mick, would have to take his supper and eat it on the bus. Even with Jimmy standing uncomfortably beside him, staring at the floor, the owner refused to let any 'of them kind disgrace his reputation.'

All of us waited and watched as the restaurant manager turned red in the face, gesturing dramatically as he pointed to the front door. Soon the word spread around that Jimmy couldn't eat with us. Quiet discussions began around the tables as we played with the salt-and-pepper shakers and watched from the corners of our eyes as the adults angrily negotiated with the red-faced manager. There were definitely two camps of opinion. One was determined that Jimmy eat with us, and the other equally determined that the 'Jimmy problem' shouldn't keep the rest of us from our dinners.

By now, a few of the football boys were pounding on the table with their silverware, demanding food. It was a tense few moments before Coach Randall, Mr. Blake, and Nellie signaled for silence. Our band director, Mr. Blake, stuffed his shirt into his pants, got out his handkerchief to wipe off his face, and made the announcement. If Jimmy couldn't join us, we were leaving without eating. Our chicken dinners would just have to grow cold in the kitchen. There was stunned silence and grumbling, but soon we were all back on the buses, despite our growling stomachs. Coach Randall assured us that hotdogs would be available for purchase at the football field and that we would all be better off if we sat down and shut up.

I remember angry classmates and parents, hostile glances and gestures. But more than that, I remembered that despite the protests, the adults with us did the right thing and stood up to the racist manager. Nellie had been particularly insistent, and she was a woman. That alone, in the early days of the 1960s, was truly amazing. We lost the game that night but won the high ground in a way that was even more spectacular.

In the 50 years since I last lived here, the children and grandchildren of those who at one time lived in Sunset Addition moved closer to downtown into houses that were vacated by aging parents of my generation. With a few exceptions, most of the Baby Boomer generation who went away to college never returned to take over the family home. Crawfords, Nickersons, Smiths, Barnes, Murphys, McMillans, and Hermans were replaced by the Hernandezes, Gonzales, Alvarezes, Garcias, Riveras, and Torres. All descendants of migrant workers who decided to stay put one winter and never returned to Mexico. In short, over the past half century, the demographics of the region changed dramatically. Gone were the small businesses of my youth and the farm jobs of a few decades ago. Today, the county was divided between the farmer-rancher landowners and those who worked at the local gas station, convenience store, or at the Super Walmart 25 miles away. The public school was a mix of brown, black, and white children – one of the only places in town where everyone was, at least theoretically, equal.

There were 100 kids in my graduation class of 1963. Of those, only four were minorities. All of them Mexican American. Today the class size was much smaller, as was the community itself, and the minority had become the majority. We always hoped that Theresa, Louisa, and Maria would come to one of our reunions, but like many locals, they stayed away. Years after the fact, we found out that Jose, a quiet, studious, young man, was the only person in our class to be killed in Vietnam. There were other Vietnam vets in our class who returned with both physical and mental injuries, but his was the only death. Many of the men avoided Vietnam by enrolling in college which granted them a deferment, or they joined the National Guard. It was generally men like Jose who were sent into battle. I doubted that Theresa, Louisa, or Maria would join us for our 50th either, even though they lived nearby. The old high-school tapes still played through all our minds.

All those who were at the restaurant that long-ago day probably remembered the story differently. I'm sure there were differing interpretations, depending on values and upbringing. Maybe using this as my reunion story wasn't such a good idea. Humor would be more appreciated. While I was lost in these thoughts, the phone rang. It was probably my imagination, but it seemed to ring with a certain urgency. Sure enough, it was my sister. It was obvious by her voice tone that Skeeter finally reached her and, because he believed in treating each of us the same, offered to buy the farm. She sounded surprisingly calm, yet there was steel in her voice.

"I'm not selling the farm to Skeeter," she began. "I told him that, so I don't want to discuss it any further. Got it?"

"Okay. I heard you. You don't want to sell the farm. Are you sure you've thought that through all the way? You're always strapped for money. This might be the time to think seriously about that."

There was a click on the other end of the line, and she was gone.

I was getting very tired of this. I understood the emotional pull of farm – I felt that too. But the bottom line was that the farm was now rented out. We received 25% of both expenses and profit. There were taxes to pay. The water was running out. And, right now, the price was right. My sons, and her son, Will, were not interested in the farm anymore. Their lives were elsewhere. The last thing any of them wanted to have to do was deal with Angie, yet if Susan died, that's exactly what they would be left with. In another generation, when all our parents' great-grandchildren inherited it, the farm would be split 15 ways. Maybe it was time for us to bite the bullet. It infuriated me that my sister refused to even discuss all the decisions that lay before us. I picked up the phone.

"It's me," I began. "Could we please go out to lunch next week and discuss all this like adults?"

All was silent on the other end of the line.

"Are you there?"

"Yes. I know what you want to do. You want to use all your big words and long sentences to convince me to change my mind."

"Look, all I'm trying to do is discuss our options, okay?" My voice was rising, just like my blood pressure.

"Yeah? That's what you always say." More silence. "Some of my friends will still be here next week. You know how everyone comes home for Picnic. That's the only time I get to see them and I'm not messing that up."

"Look, I'm sick of your excuses! It's always like this. You find an excuse to push away the problems rather than get down to the nitty-gritty and solve them. Your friends will only be here for a couple of days. I know that. But this is important, okay?"

"Fine, fine, fine. Whatever you say, big sister." Again, the line went quiet.

It was all I could do to keep from throwing the phone across the room. I grabbed my hat, called for the dogs, and went out for a walk. By the time I reached the run-off pond, I was beginning to think rationally again. I would let her cool off, enjoy her friends, and put this on the shelf for a few days. I had food to make for Friday's informal reunion gathering, plus more boxes to pack and label. I wanted everything, including the family conflicts, tied up neatly and packed away as soon as possible. But that was not to be.

Friday evening was designated as our informal reunion gathering. This involved preparing something for the picnic which would be held at the country home of Gail and Charlie Swanson. Along with the Finches, the Swansons either owned or rented out much of the county farmland. Gail had been a part of the infamous 1963 girls' basketball game which won the state title for A.A. schools. She was one of those people that everyone liked, even though she was also the envy of all the classmates who remained in the area. She and her husband had a beautiful country home with Southwestern decor, and an outdoor living area made up of a series of adobe-bricked patios with tables and chairs tastefully placed. It was the perfect place for summer entertaining and had been the site of all of our other reunion gatherings. However, for the special 50th celebration, it was determined that a 'more formal' setting with a dinner was more appropriate. Some classmates would only attend one of the two events, and since the picnic only involved bringing something to contribute to the meal, it attracted those too frugal to fork over money for an event at the Memorial building.

I decided to make baked beans, so I made a trip to Rob's Supermarket in town. Since it was the only place in town to buy food, I was sure to run into either an old friend or neighbor. When this happened, one did not cut off the conversation abruptly. In fact, the last time it happened, I ended up having a 30-minute conversation with a woman who took care of my dad at the hospital during his last illness. I owed her my attention and time yet found it very draining to have to dredge up painful memories. Consequently, I tried to get in and out of the store as soon as possible, avoiding painful, time-consuming conversations with people who remembered me but whom I did not remember. Rob's was the kind of place you found all over this area of dwindling population and changing demographics. Sugary cereal and snacks took up two aisles, while wilting 'fresh produce' was pushed into a damp corner. Today there were three aisles devoted to Mexican food, whereas, in my childhood, you couldn't even find a tortilla in the local grocery. But I chose the right thing to make – I had no problem finding the kind of beans I needed. I was making a beeline for the checkout when I felt a soft hand grab my elbow.

I took off my sunglasses and looked down into the wrinkled, smiling face of Mary Meyer.

"Well now, you aren't goin' to walk right past me without saying a hello, are you, Missy Dalinda Adelia?"

"Mary," I exclaimed, trying to sound happy to see her. "So sorry, I didn't see you. My mind must be a hundred miles away. How are you?"

This was the wrong question to ask. Mary was terribly proud of all her aches, pains, and surgeries, and also the fact that she just celebrated her 93rd birthday.

"Well, you know, I'm being honored on Saturday for a bein' the oldest citizen still livin' in my own house in Herschel County. I mean, there are others, but you know how older people get? Most of 'em don't have any mind left. But now, people say I'm sharp as a tack. So that's how I'm a doin'. And you must be here for Picnic. I tell you what, I just miss that little mother of yours to death. She was a sweetie, that one. Knew more about this county than anyone around too. I would be on the phone to her two, three times a day, since she and I remembered pretty much more than the rest of the county put together. You know, we started first grade together. Did you know that?"

"Yes. Indeed, I did, Mary. Mother talked about you like you were the one knew the most. I'm sure it is really hard to lose those your own age – those with the same memories."

"Well, bless your heart. I believe you do understand what I'm a talkin' about. So now tell me about your little family. Toogie, that sweet mother of yours, was always a' goin' on and on about them, but I haven't had an update in some time now."

I could tell this conversation could go on for much more than the 30-minute record. I thought fast: "Mary, I really would love to catch up with all your family too. I do kind of hate to have to have you standing here in the grocery-store aisle though. Do you think we could meet somewhere for tea or coffee sometime?"

"Oh, my goodness, honey. I know how busy you girls are. And don't you fret about me. I'm as strong as an old ox. I can pretty much stand here as long as you can. But I s'pose your class is a gettin' together for a big anniversary and you got work to get ready, isn't that right?"

I nodded and was ready to thank her for her perception when she moved closer and pulled me toward her grocery cart. "Now, before you run off, I just have to ask you about some gossip I heard. You know what a small town this is. So, anyway, I just have to hear it from you."

Mary looked expectantly at me as I racked my mind, trying to figure out what she was talking about. "I guess I don't know what you're talking about, Mary," I began.

"Well, like I say, it's just gossip, but someone told me you were thinking of selling off your daddy and mama's farm. I told them I just didn't believe a word of it. I know how much you girls love that land, especially because it goes clear back to your kids' great granddaddy. But anyway, I thought I'd hear it directly from you so I can set straight those town know-it-alls."

I should have expected this, but I was caught flat-footed. "Mary, who are you talking to these days?"

"Well, I'm not s'pose to say, but you know Carla and how she talks..."

Oh yes, I did know Carla. I was sure she was the first one Susan called after our last difficult conversation right after Skeeter called her. "Mary, my sister really depends on Carla as her sounding board. I'm sure that she is exaggerating all Susan's deepest fears when she passes on what has been told her in confidence. If I were you, I would just keep all this to myself and not worry about it."

Mary looked at me skeptically. "Now I'm gettin' confused. Are you sayin' it's true or not true?"

"I'm saying that you can't believe everything Carla tells you."

"Well, honey, don't you think I know that? But now, I tell you, I do know what your mama told me was the truth. That poor lady tried her best to take care of that good-for-nothing granddaughter and her kids, and what does Angie do but practically steal the clothes off her back in return. I told her – your mama, I'm a talkin' about – I told her that she should have the sheriff get after her and lock her up in the county jail for a while. That's what she needed. But you know your mama, always a' turnin' the other cheek. That's just how your family always was…"

Mary was off on a tangent and this was a good thing. Now I had a chance to get away. "Mary, you have been a devoted friend. Thank you for that. I bet you'll be riding a float in the parade as the oldest citizen, right?"

"Oh now, you just reminded me! Isn't that somethin'? You think I should throw down candy like I was some kind of beauty queen or what?"

There was a twinkle in Mary's eye as I quickly made my escape, promising to see her at the barbecue in the park after the parade.

Chapter Eighteen

Friday Night Gathering

With baked beans battened down beside me, I headed out to the Friday evening gathering. A spattering of pickups and SUVs were already haphazardly parked along the rough road that led up to the Swanson driveway. I spotted a man wearing shorts and a golf shirt – definitely not a local – carrying a grocery sack.

He gave me a sidelong look and then stopped short. "Hey, hey! Is that you, Dally?"

"It is!" I put down my pot of beans to give Greg a big hug. "You look just the same."

Greg pulled off his baseball hat to point to his thinning hair. "Oh, look a bit closer, and you'll see I've earned my battle scars. How in the world are you?"

"I'm fine, and you?"

"Good! You remember Julie, my wife? We flew in last night and drove down from Amarillo today, so you're the first one I've seen."

I greeted Julie who stood to one side, smiling, as all the spouses/significant others would do until their lips grew tired. None of them shared our memories, and I could well imagine how much of an outsider each felt. Greg and I were great friends in high school, part of the 'headed to college' group who participated in the school plays rather than the sports teams. He was now a retired professor, having invented an important pharmaceutical that was purchased by one of the large drug companies. Recently, we emailed each other, plus friend, John, since we were the designated '50th Reunion Program Committee."

"Do you think anyone will have some kind of glasses I can pour this into?" he asked, pulling a bottle of wine from his bag. "They said it was BYOB, so I hope that meant wine too."

"Surely we can find something that will work. Do you need a corkscrew?"

"Nope. Got a screw top bottle."

For some unknown reason, two card tables covered with red-and-white-checkered plastic were set-up near the end of the long driveway, at least a hundred feet's distance from the food. I rummaged under the one set up with liters of Coke and Sprite until I found some classy plastic ware that would have to make do. I turned back to Greg and Julie as a foursome approached from the road. All of us stared at each other, trying to make a connection between the real-life person and a memory of 50 years before. In a few minutes, we would all get our nametags – the stick-ons and markers were on the other card table – but right now, it was a guessing game. This time, it was David Bivens and Carl Johnston and their wives, two men who moved downstate and married out-of-town girls. There was hugging and backslapping and then the procession up the driveway to the open garage, the nametag table, and long tables set up with a growing buffet of chips, dips, and salads. Gail, the hostess, took the food from my hands and directed me toward the patio area where the group was quickly organizing themselves into small clumps of familiarity.

First, there were the locals who saw each other practically every day. They were busy chatting about the demise of yet another business in town. Then there were the 'girls' who were a part of our winning 1963 basketball team. Since they got together every couple of years, they were up on gossip the rest of us weren't privy to. As they compared manicures and pulled out pictures of grandchildren, their husbands or boyfriends excused themselves to find the beer cooler. A few single men grouped in a corner, wearing cowboy boots and Stetsons, thumbs in their belt loops, and cigarettes between their lips. The local married men, mostly farmers or small business owners, all wore their seed caps and Levi's. In another corner sat several women with dark pants and over-generous floral tops, who seemed to be in deep discussion about quilt patterns.

By this time, my friend John was also here. He sneaked up behind me and covered my eyes. "Guess who?"

"Oh, I would know that voice anywhere!" He was a professor at an Eastern university and recently came out as gay to some of us. Yet he knew better than to bring his partner to this gathering. If he had, that would have been the focus of the entire reunion rather than what it was supposed to be about. He knew when it was wise to reveal oneself and when that was counterproductive. For some of our classmates, his was the kind of lifestyle that sentenced you to everlasting hell, and that just wasn't the kind of conversation John wanted to be the focus of our reunion.

As more people arrived, there was a general milling around and peering at pictured nametags. We were searching for something that would connect the name and picture with the reality of the person who now wore it. There was Milton, notorious for flunking fourth grade, who was now a retired superintendent of schools. Leon, the small, dark-haired boy who always sat in the back row and now owned his own furniture company near Dallas. Mary Beth, the quiet, shy girl who we always asked to make our posters, owned a successful string of art galleries in New Mexico.

Then there was Deana, the curvy cheerleader, who got pregnant as a sophomore, disappeared for a time, and came back telling everyone that Johnny Paul Box, the star senior forward on the basketball team, was the father of the baby she gave up for adoption. She now sat, overflowing on a folding chair toward the back of the milling group, nursing a drink. Her eyes were heavy with regrets of a lifetime as she avoided contact. According to Carla, she was 'in treatment' and had been given a 'pass' to attend the reunion. Deana's mother and mine were long-time friends, and I made my way toward her to ask about her mother.

"Deana, do you remember me?" I asked.

Deana glanced up as she snuffed out her latest cigarette on the Spanish tiles. "Oh, yeah, sure. How are you?"

"I'm good. And you?"

"Perfect. I'm perfect," she replied with a sneer. "I don't know what I'm doing here. Who are all these people?"

"Well, you have to look at the nametags," I began. "We've all changed a lot in 50 years. Everybody here has had their own share of life's ups and downs, and it's taken a toll on us all…" Even though Deana lived in a nearby town, she carried the weight of her high-school reputation and never showed up for reunions.

Deana looked off into the distance and I changed the subject, "So, how is your mom? I'm so sorry, but since Mother died, I don't even know if she is still alive?"

"Oh yeah, she's alive all right. She's never going to die. She got remarried in her 80s, you know. Moved off to Arizona, then Utah. Finally divorced the ol' fucker and moved back here 'to take care of me.' Can you believe that? She wants to take care of me. Finally, she wants to take care of me. What a laugh, huh?"

I thought of Dodie, her mother, a tall, quiet-spoken woman with porcelain skin. She never quite knew what do to with Deana, seemingly surprised that Deana belonged to her at all. Yet when she and my mother were young, they were best of friends, both part of the Sub-Debs who dressed alike in straight, wool skirts and close-fitting sweaters. They remained close until my mother's death. "So, is she living with you now?" I asked.

Deana snorted, giving a dismissive laugh. "Are you kidding? I put her up in a nursing home in Amarillo. I can't have her living with me."

"Well, next time you see her, give her my best. Up until the end of her life, Mother talked about her friend, Dodie. I think they spent hours on the phone after they both got to the point when they couldn't travel."

"Why don't you go see her yourself?" Deana replied. "She's up at Plains Caring Place with all the rest of those drooling old people."

I looked again at Deana. Somewhere under that tough exterior, I could see a scared, pregnant, 16-year-old whose parents, with the best of intentions, shipped her off to Fort Worth to an unwed mothers' home. Their reputation was at stake in our little town because her father owned one of our three jewelry stores, and they attended the Baptist church. I was surprised she even came to the reunion since she skipped all previous ones. Since I really was at a loss as to how to change the direction of this conversation, I began the usual babbling I resorted to when in uncomfortable social situations. "I remember when your mom was our seventh-grade social-studies teacher, and she would walk around the room, making sure we were working on our maps of the Texas soil regions. Did you ever wonder why we had to learn that?"

This was obviously a topic that did not interest Deana. She was looking over my shoulder at someone approaching from behind.

"So, what is this I hear about our seventh-grade social-studies teacher?" I turned to see Marcia bearing down with the memory book under her arm.

Grateful for the interruption, I turned to her, "Marcia, guess who I found here?"

For a split second, there was a blank look on Marcia's face as she took in this new Deana. Recognition dawned slowly. "Oh my, is that you, Deana? We haven't seen you for so long. How are you, girl?"

"And who would you be?" asked Deana.

"Well, you know me... I'm Marcia. We were majorettes together, remember? And, huh, we twirled batons. Of course, you were a cheerleader, too...there for a while..."

"Looks like you've had some work done on your face, Marcia," replied Deana snidely. "I wouldn't have known you except for that nametag."

I jumped into the conversation at this point, "Marcia, you were just asking about our seventh-grade social-studies teacher, and remember, that was Mrs. Foreman, Deana's mom. Remember how she was so particular about our map work? Oh, how I loved working with all those colored pencils." My babbling returned.

"Well, I guess that didn't go into the long-term memory bank," replied Marcia. "All I remember is Mrs. Turner, our eighth-grade English teacher. And I'll never forget what we did to her. Nobody liked her, so one day we got her back," Marcia giggled.

I already knew the story Marcia was going to tell. This was one of those stories that was repeated at each reunion, growing larger each time it was told. Marcia was off and running, and it looked like Deana was engaged, at least temporarily. "So, we had English right after lunch, and we knew Miz Turner always had a little square of a Hershey bar as her dessert right after we all filed into class. Well, anyway, Ellen distracted her in the back of the room while Betsy and me went up to her desk and substituted Ex-Lax for the Hershey bar. Then we did this every day for a week. Finally, it worked, and for a few days we had some kind of clueless substitute who sat at his desk and read the Amarillo Globe News and let us talk all class period." Marcia shook her head and she giggled again. "Isn't that just the funniest thing you ever heard, Deana? And can you believe we got away with it?"

Deana was staring at Marcia with a blank expression, but I felt my feathers ruffle, having retired as an eighth-grade English teacher after teaching for most of my adult life. Somehow, this story did not seem funny to me anymore. Finally, Deana responded.

"Everybody knew about that, Marcia. You didn't fool anybody, especially ol' lady Turner. She knew all along. Told my mom all about it."

I watched as Marcia seemed to deflate right before my eyes. She cleared her throat and pulled back her shoulders. "Well, anyway, what I came over to ask is if you can remember anybody who died that we forgot to put in our book. I just don't want to leave anyone out, especially our vets. You want to look through it and see if we missed anyone, Deana?"

Deana gave her a hard look. "So, you came over here to ask me to look for dead people?"

"Oh, no, Deana. I really just came over to say hello and tell you how glad we all are to see you." Marcia was clearly rattled. I was trying to maneuver us closer to another knot of classmates who formed a few feet away. Laughter was coming from this group and that's what was needed right now.

Linda, another classmate, was talking about her elementary students and their foibles, and I wanted to listen to what she was saying. "I really need to go say hello to a few more people," I said to Deana and Marcia. "Have you talked to Gene and Linda yet, ladies?"

Marcia was quick to pick up on this, "Oh right, I'll talk to you later, Deana. I haven't even walked around to see who all is here." She reached down and gave Deana a sisterly pat on her arm.

Deana flinched and shrugged, not seeming to care one way or another.

So soon, I was listening in on Linda's retired-teacher stories. Right now, she was talking about five siblings who were in her class consecutive years. "Well, there was Dusty, Wendy, Sunny, Stormy, and Rainy Wilderdinger, and I had them all. Sometimes I wonder about why people name their children as they do, don't you?"

David, who now joined the group, piped up, "Sounds to me like a regular weather bureau, don't it? People 'round here have the darnedest names I ever heard of. Now I'm not sayin' that people down in my part of the state do any better, but somehow it seems a big part of 'em are up here. Like the wife has cousins by the names of Josie Rose, Polly Marie, Sonny Jon, Paulie Bob and Frankie Carl. Ever'body call them by both of those names all the time."

"I wonder why that is? I mean, that's in my family too but wonder why?" Linda looked around the group for help.

"Just custom, I reckon," Gene chimed in. "I'll bet you if you took a survey, practically everyone here has someone in their family they call by one of them double names."

"Well, I remember when everybody called me Dalinda Adelia." I added. "I mean everyone, not just my parents when they were angry. Now almost everyone at home just calls me Dalinda." My classmates lost interest, and I turned toward the drink table. That was when I ran, quite literally, into Odetta Ferguson and found myself staring into the freckles on her flattened chest as she loomed above me. As long as I'd known her, Odetta chose to stand about four inches closer to people than polite behavior dictated. She had always been tall, and now her Dowager's hump caused her neck to crane downward.

"So, Dalinda," she said, skipping formalities, "why did you get a divorce?"

This direct approach shouldn't have taken me by surprise, but I hadn't laid eyes on Odetta for 50 years and I'd forgotten what she was like. Besides that, my divorce was almost 40 years ago – hardly breaking news. "Yeah, well…" I hesitated. "That was a long time ago and…well, sometimes it just happens."

Odetta stared at me, obviously unsatisfied with my explanation. "So, who cheated?"

I opened my mouth, but nothing came out as Odetta continued to stare down at me. Finally, clearing my throat, I turned the tables. "So, what have you been doing since the last time I saw you?"

This didn't work. If at all possible, she inched even closer as I began to back up. "Why didn't you get remarried?"

I mentioned something unintelligible about not connecting with the right person as I struggled to come up with a way to extricate myself from Odetta's tight web. "Hey, can I get you a refill on your drink?" I asked rather too enthusiastically.

"No. I don't drink the stuff here. I brought my own."

And then, without another word, Odetta turned around to confront another classmate. As she turned her head, I noticed a drool of onion dip making a path down her chin. I sighed, remembering that my mother always told me that Odetta was a bit 'unusual' but that I was to treat her kindly and invite her to my birthday parties. However, after a couple of years of Odetta coming to my parties and spending her time following my mother around the house rather than playing with us girls, the encouragement to extend her an invitation stopped. Now as I turned toward the drink table to find John and the twist-off top bottle, I felt a stab of sadness for Odetta.

About that time, Penny stood up and clanged the triangle the Swansons hung above the patio. "Ya'll listen up. It's time to eat. We have more food than we know what to do with, so help yourself. But before we all form a line, I would like to ask James Caraway to lift us up in prayer. Now he's not a pastor, but he's the closest thing to it we got."

What she meant was that James Caraway was a devout Baptist. The only pastor in the group had been Tommy Dawes who did become a Southern Baptist preacher. As James hefted himself up from the sagging lawn chair, I turned to Linda who was still beside me and whispered quietly, "Whatever happened to Tommy Dawes? Didn't he become a Baptist pastor?"

Linda put her finger to her lips as James revved up to offer grace. After a meandering prayer, asking for everything but a blessing for the food, Linda put her hand to the side of her mouth and whispered to me, "The last anyone ever knew Tommy was a missionary in Israel."

"Israel? He is trying to convert the people in Israel?"

"Yep. That's what I heard. Of course, you know how it is here. You can't believe everything you hear…"

This was a piece of gossip great to share with John. Few people would appreciate the irony as much as he.

The food was spread out on card tables in the four-car garage. It was a banquet of barbecue, beans, tuna-fish sandwiches, fruit cocktail with Cool-Whip salad, various Jell-Os, brownies, chips, salsas of every kind and flavor, deviled eggs, and bologna rollups. I picked up my plastic cutlery and paper plate and joined my classmates in a polite line, winding around the tables. At the end of the food line were huge containers of lemonade and iced tea for all those who chose to refrain from alcohol. We all made our way to the closest seats with our sagging plates and found ourselves face to face with classmates we managed to avoid for years. For me, that person was Larry Jon Jacobson and a woman I presumed was his wife.

Larry Jon greeted me with a full mouth of bologna sandwich. "Well, now, aren't you Dalinda Adelia? I thought I seen you over a'jawin' your mouth."

"Hi, Larry Jon," I began. "How are you? Been a long time, hasn't it?"

"Well, we been here all along. It's you been gone up yonder in Yankee land."

I made eye contact with the woman beside him. "I'm Dalinda, and you?" I asked.

The woman eyed me suspiciously. "I'm Larry Jon's sister, Clara Jo. Don't you remember me?"

"Sorry, no. Were you in high school at the same time as Larry Jon?"

"Nope. Didn't go to no high school. Somebody had to stay home and take care of all Mama's youngsters." Clara Jo didn't seem eager to continue any conversation with me, but I could tell Larry Jon had more to say.

"Me 'n Clara still livin' out to near Viago in the old family place, trying to scratch out a livin' on that little ol' piece of shit my daddy left us. You 'member where we lived, don't ya? I'm a thinkin' we rode the same school bus, ain't that right?"

"We did," I replied. "And I think I remember where you lived."

"Well, you sure can't miss it." By now, the bologna sandwich was gone, revealing a few stained teeth next to large gaps where the others used to be.

"And why is that?" I asked.

"Well, ya'll remember J.T. Stovall? Well, when you're a'goin' north on the interstate, 'long about Happy – you know where that ol' barbecue place wuz when we wuz kids? Well, ol' J.T. got the Lord a while back and put hisself up the biggest dad-burned white cross you ever see'd – right up there next to I-27. Ya can't miss it 'cause it's all white and glowin' in the sun. Don't know what manner of sins he done atoning for, but I'm a here to tell you, there must be a' plenty for him to fork out those kind of dollars for 'at big ol' cross."

"So then," I asked, "what does this have to do with where you live?"

"Oh yeah, plum forgot. So, I live 'bout a mile directly east. You just come to that big ol' cross and make a left-hand turn, and pretty soon, there you are."

"Okay. Well, I think I'll have to check that out before I leave for home."

"Ya mean you ain't stayin' here now that your brother's dead and gone?"

"No, I need to get back home."

Clara Jo was growing impatient with our conversation. "Larry Jon, I need me some mustard. You think you could run up there and fetch it for me?"

I saw my escape route. "I tell you what, I need to go visit with a bunch of other people, so I'll just go get it for you and then somebody else can have my seat and visit with you a bit."

"Well, that's pretty neighborly of you." Clara Jo was warming up to me. "Just give me about five of them little packages. That should be a plenty."

After delivering the mustard, I snaked through the crowd toward a group of women in a corner of the yard and found an empty seat nearby. We greeted each other and I settled down to eat my food when I noticed that Donna, another classmate, was staring pointedly at the beer I picked up when I couldn't locate Greg and the wine. Instantly, I realized my mistake. These were the Baptist ladies. I was offending their sensibilities. Something in me decided to let them think whatever they wanted to think, which was probably that I was an unrepentant alcoholic. I took a big swig of the beer. Donna cleared her throat and asked, "You really like that nasty stuff? Because we have plenty of Diet Coke if you'd rather have that?"

I swallowed a mouthful of tuna salad and turned to her. "Actually, this is not my favorite brand, but I really don't like diet drinks, so no, thank you."

Donna was taken aback by this and floundered around for another topic of conversation, "So, now where is it you live?"

Once again, I was saved. This time by Penny who announced that Van dusted off his old jukebox and would be spinning some golden oldies, so would we please give him a round of applause. I looked around for my old friends and finally spotted John and Greg sharing the bottle of wine. I excused myself from Donna, and not looking to my right or left, I headed toward more comfortable territory as the voice of Neil Sedaka told me that, "Breaking up is hard to do," and Shelley Fabares moaned about 'Johnny Angel.'

Chapter Nineteen
Picnic, 2013

The next morning, I arrived in town early for all the festivities. Like celebrations in small towns everywhere, this was an opportunity to stop work for a day, eat with the neighbors, and parade the kids with their decorated bikes. There were floats for all the town's organizations and businesses, horses and riders, and shiny, new, farming equipment. It was a time for homecomings, reunions, and family gatherings. The traveling carnival set up the old tilt-a-whirl and Ferris wheel on the square, hawkers tempted kids with snow cones and cotton candy, and grandparents shelled out money for rides on the bumper cars. Except for the addition of a bouncy castle, the celebration looked just like it did when I was a kid.

Each high-school class celebrating significant decade anniversaries rode in the parade with aging classmates atop hay wagons with banners on the side, announcing that they were the Class of 1953, or '63, '73, etc. Our class joined the other decades and lined up next to the high school, with the oldest having priority at the front. Van provided the hay wagon for the class of '63, the hay bales for sitting, and the very important ladder for the ladies. If the truth be known, everybody there needed the ladder, but we didn't bring this up. Some of us were at the celebration the night before, but for many, this was the first time we had seen each other for many years. Besides that, unlike last night, we didn't have the benefit of nametags since Penny insisted that our 'official nametags,' with our 1963 yearbook picture, be saved for tonight's celebration. This meant we all had to look carefully into the faces of these strangers before we recognized the 2013 version of their high-school selves.

I was able to hoist myself up the ladder with the help of the strong arms of Gene, now a Dallas physician. I found a place to sit and watched as he helped a parade of old classmates. As each one made his/her way to a hay-bale seat, a voice behind me tried to identify each one.

"Who is that?"

"Golly, I'm not sure. No, wait… I think that's Beth Pearson, isn't it? Oh, bless her heart, she's really put on the weight."

"Well, so has Virginia. Look at her. Oh my, I hardly recognized her, poor thing."

Somehow, the men who were several sizes larger than their old yearbook picture were less scrutinized. I turned around to see who was providing this running commentary, and there were Sherry and Wanda. I thought about reminding them that they probably wouldn't fit into their cheerleader outfits anymore either but thought the better of it. There was just the remotest chance that they might be able to wear their old, high-school clothes. Right away, I decided to talk to Beth and Virginia instead of Sherry and Wanda. Some of the women sat with spouses, if they brought them, and the same was true of the men who talked their wives into coming. But most of us seemed to head for either the men's side of the hay wagon, or the women's.

The person I was eager to see was my high-school friend, Martha. She now lived in Florida after spending several years abroad as a teaching missionary. We bonded in fifth grade when we both got puppies from the same litter and named them each Trixie. We rode the same school bus for the two hours it took to make its rounds to pick up and deliver all the kids who lived on the far-apart farms and ranches. Early on we learned to do our homework while the bus bounced roughly over the rutted dirt roads. She lived four miles east of me and was an only child with older parents. The house she lived in reminded me of a mushroom, built of a rough, gray stucco. Her parents seemed more like grandparents in their habits and attitudes, yet it was obvious that for them, the sun rose and set in Martha.

I looked around in vain for someone who looked like my old friend, but no one seemed a likely candidate until I saw a pair of deep blue eyes appear above the bed of the trailer. Making her way up the ladder was my friend. I rose to greet her and almost tripped on Al's size-15 cowboy boots.

"Martha? Is that you?" All the heads turned toward us as we greeted each other after all these years.

"Dally?" she asked. "I guess that's you, isn't it? I'll be darned. You look the same."

I scooted over to make a place for her on my hay bale and we began to catch up on many years of family news. As we chatted, I interrupted to identify old classmates as she noticed them.

"Who is that?" she asked, turning her head toward John.

"Don't you recognize him? That's John!"

"Oh my gosh, he has perfectly white hair. He looks like he just came from the beauty parlor. Is that his wife next to him?"

"Uh, no. That's Sheryl, Van's wife."

"Which one is Van?"

"He's the one standing there with the blue feed cap, talking to the women on horses."

Martha seemed to be digesting all this, trying to add 50 years to the memories she carried in her head. "So, which one is John's wife?"

"Oh. Well, John's not married."

"He's not? I wonder how he avoided all the women who must have set their sights on him. Isn't he a professor or something?"

"Uh huh," I replied. Something warned me not to go any further with this conversation. Martha may have traveled extensively, but she still adhered to the strict religious beliefs of her childhood. I decided to change the subject. "Martha, I know you were in the Middle East for a while, but I never knew exactly where you were. What was that like?"

"Well," she replied, "I really can't say where I was, but I can tell you that bibles were outlawed. So, you can imagine the rest."

I thought about this a few seconds, remembering that when my son was in Saudi Arabia, he discovered that Bibles were indeed outlawed, except in the Western oil-company enclaves. Somehow, I couldn't imagine my old friend in such a repressed society, but that seemed the most likely place. I turned to look at her. "Wow, I bet you met some fascinating people."

Martha looked at me as though I just suggested she strip naked and march down the street. "Heavens, no. I stayed in the compound most of the time, teaching the missionaries' children. I had no desire to really get to know the people outside."

It was apparent that Martha and I were separated by more things than 50 years of time. Still, there were wonderful memories we shared, many spent on the dusty, old, school bus bouncing down the country roads. Our conversation turned to those days as we greeted classmates as they painfully clambered onboard the creaky hay wagon. We both remembered Peggy Rice who was the bus bully. She sat in the backseat with a huge bag of M&M's which she was too stingy to share. When not popping another candy into her big red mouth, she heckled the younger kids and made fun of Martha and me concentrating on homework. Even though the bus stops were miles apart, Peggy's was right before Martha's, and by the time we reached her house, the M&M's bag would be empty. When she finally lumbered off, we breathed a sigh of relief that we had a few minutes without her overbearing presence.

Just as we were on a roll of remembering, the county sheriff rode up to us on his chestnut quarter horse. "Ya'll doin' okay? It's about time to start movin' down the street. The old-timers already passed by the courthouse on the other end."

He was talking about Mary and her contemporaries, and I wondered if she threw out candy to the kids like she said she would. I would have to be sure to look her up at the park after the parade ended. The marching band in front of us a few units struck up our school-fight song which just happened to be to the tune of On Wisconsin, and I felt right at home. Van's tractor sputtered into life, pulling along its load. Behind us, the ladies' riding club clicked to their horses, and we were on our way. Martha and I turned to visit other classmates as we crawled past our old high school and down Dip Street. It wasn't long before I spotted Mary. Her parade-riding duties were over, and she was standing next to Carla, watching the rest of us pass by. You couldn't miss Carla. She wore a bright red hat, with loud yellow jeans and a dazzling-white western shirt. A few years back, she was a part of the Red Hat Club in town, but there was some kind of falling out, and as a protest, Carla always stood next to her former club members, wearing her red hat without the required purple dress. She stood out like a sore thumb which was exactly what she wanted to do. Mary, with her cloud of white hair, stood beside her, clapping and waving as we passed by.

The whole parade route was 15 blocks long, and since we were toward the front, we finished in time to watch all new farm implements, proud owners sitting high in the air-conditioned cabs of combines and tractors. The 4-H float came next, followed by several more riding clubs, then the kids on their decorated bikes, and finally a large group of vintage cars, trucks, and farm machinery. Then it was over, and everyone made their way to Conroy Park for the barbeque. Each honored class was assigned a different corner of the park where we were supposed to congregate. Even if you weren't part of a class celebrating being from a decade ending in a three, this was where we got to see classmates who were in other classes, many of whom we knew as well, or better, as those from our own class. Someone tapped me on the shoulder, and I turned around to face Bill Daley, a man who was in my sister's class. Like so many others, Bill's mother and mine had been good friends, and our families were close when we were children. I always thought of him as just an irritating little kid, but in his case, the years had been kind.

"Just wanted to say hello," he said. "Do you remember me from long ago?"

"Oh sure," I replied, thinking of his relationship with my sister after high school. He broke her heart, and life for her was never the same. The man who stood beside me looked like an AARP ad for Viagra, with his thick silver hair, neatly pressed slacks, and golf shirt bearing the logo of an expensive club near Dallas. Susan told me that his law firm worked for some of the richest people in the state, and that he regularly golfed with celebrities. "How is your mom?" I said. "I hear she is in custodial care here."

"Yes, she doesn't even know who I am anymore, but I try to get up to see her a couple of times a year. You're still up-north somewhere, aren't you? I suppose taking care of the farm down here is hard to do now that Mack isn't around anymore."

I ignored his question about the farm, instead gave my standard answer about living in Wisconsin. Then I inquired about his family, but his mind was elsewhere.

"You wouldn't know where you can get a decent cup of coffee around here, would you? I can't believe this place and how it's changed," he said with faint disgust.

Strangely, I found myself bristling, suddenly defensive about my old hometown. "There really isn't a Starbucks or anything like it any closer than Plainfield," I said. "But you know, most of us that went away to college never returned, and then farming became so mechanized that there are lots fewer jobs than there used to be. That's been hard on the entire economy."

He gave me a strange look. "Well, that's no excuse for letting this town go to pot. They could at least pick up the trash and get rid of all the junkyards."

"So," I replied, "how long are you staying here?"

"Oh, I'm not staying here at all. I have to catch a plane later this afternoon. Just stopped by to say hello to a few people." He looked down at his phone and continued, "In fact, it's about time I got around to talk to a few more people

189

before I have to leave." He paused and put the phone back in his pocket. "Oh, I almost forgot to ask, how are you and your sister doing with your farm since your brother died? And, by the way, I was sorry to hear about that."

He didn't sound sorry; he sounded like he was in a hurry. "We're doing just fine," I lied. "Right now, I'm just cleaning out the farmhouse."

"Okay, well, let me know if I can help out," he said, making exaggerated motion putting on his Ray-Ban sunglasses. "Hey, I hear that Charlie Swanson's done well for himself. I thought I'd see if he needs any legal advice." He winked at me and I watched as he headed across the park to visit the class of 1973. Then I remembered. Susan told me that he and his friends, like Dr. Phil, were heavily involved in real-estate investment around here, thinking there might be a boom in wind energy. He heard the rumors about our farm and was trolling for a business deal. That was the reason he sought me out, not at all to renew an old friendship. I had to remember to tell my sister about this.

People were moving toward the barbecue line, and I joined a few classmates and headed in that direction. County residents who lived here at least 50 years received free barbecue as 'old timers.' They got to go through the line first. My sister qualified for this special treatment and I spotted her, trailed by the four youngest grandchildren as they picked up cups of iced tea, balanced food on paper plates, and found seats at designated 'Old Timers' tables. I was sure the Chamber of Commerce members who were serving the food felt the kids deserved a meal too since they were part of her household. I had to admit, there was kindness here, if not good coffee.

Since the barbeque line was long, I decided to head over to the Memorial building before eating to make sure tables were set up for the evening's events. I especially wanted to be sure there was a working microphone. Johnetta was already there with her bags of Hobby Lobby decorations, two daughters, and various other female relatives. Bright placemats were set on each table, and a volcano of crepe paper sprouted from the center of each table in colors of red, yellow, orange, blue, green, and silver. Johnetta beamed at me across the room.

"Don't this just look great?" she asked. "We've been working since before the parade. Prob'ly even missed the barbecue so we could make sure everything is set for tonight. It just turned out so nice, don't you think?"

"Oh, Jonny," I purred, using her childhood nickname. "You have really outdone yourself. It just looks great. Wherever did you get the decorating gene?"

"Well, you remember my mama, right? She always was doing things up, making it special, even when we didn't have two pennies to rub together. She just had the knack. So, I guess I got it from her." I could have sworn that Johnetta was blushing as she acknowledged my compliment. With Johnetta, a little went a long way.

"I'm just here to check out the microphone and be sure it works for Greg and me."

"It's right up yonder on the stage. I reckon it works, but I wouldn't know about that stuff. Good thing you're a checkin' it out before tonight. I am so excited! I think we all did just a great job organizing everything, don't you?"

"I do," I assured her, walking toward the raised platform she called the stage. I plugged in the mic and tried a test, only to be greeted by an earsplitting feedback squeal. I hoped it would just work fine, but now that it was screaming at me, I needed help. Before I went to round up Greg, I tried a few things to settle it down and finally got it to working by adjusting switches on the sound boxes. With a sigh of relief, I told Johnetta I'd see her later and headed back to the park to grab some barbeque and find Greg to see if he wanted to double-check the microphone before tonight.

The various class groups dwindled by this time, but there were a few people still eating lunch in the 1963 corner of the park, and I headed that way to join them. On the way, I noticed that Susan was with a few of her friends who always returned for Picnic, and she seemed to be having a good time. I was relieved, because maybe she'd be in a better mood for Monday's meeting with Andy, Stu, and Skeeter. She made brief eye contact, then quickly turned away. As I watched, I saw the four children with her break away and run toward me. They came to a halt, panting with excitement.

"Aunt D'linda, Aunt D'linda, can we have some money for the carnival? Grandmommy told us she doesn't have any and to ask you."

Four pairs of brown eyes were shining up into mine as I had a flashback. I remembered doing the same thing when I was a child – asking my grandparents for carnival money. It wasn't that my parents didn't have the money to give us, it was because our mother did not want us on the carnival rides. Her cautionary words still echoed in my head:

"Those rides are not clean, and besides, they are dangerous. I just heard about a little girl who was killed on a Ferris wheel. Besides that, those men that work there…they are nasty dirty. There is no reason you need to be on carnival rides. We'll go to the rodeo tonight, and you can see your friends there."

Of course, her words had no effect. I knew that if I hit up my grandfather, he would give me enough money for at least a couple of rides. And Mother would never know the difference, because she always had plans with her own old friends at picnic time. I wasn't the grandparent of these children, but I did identify with what they were feeling – their friends were getting to do something that happened once a year and they wanted to be a part of it. I reached into my purse and pulled out several five-dollar bills. I was irritated with my sister because she told them to come ask me, but at the same time, I understood her lack of money. Carnival rides were not in the budget. As I handed out the money to all the eager hands, it occurred to me how very hard it was for my sister to say no to these children. All we had to do as children was to ask our grandfather, and the money was ours. The only people in these children's life was their grandmother, and she couldn't afford such extravagance for four or more kids.

"So, where are your brothers and sisters?" I asked.

Josie, the spokeswoman for the group, gave me the kind of look I remembered when I asked my own children what, to them, should be obvious. "They're teenagers, Aunt D'linda. They pretend they don't care about the rides anymore. All they do is hang out by the snow cones since that's where the cheerleaders work. Their friends usually share their carnival tickets with them anyway."

"Oh, right," I agreed, suddenly realizing that, to them, I was as ancient as the dinosaurs.

"No," piped up Treenie, the youngest. "J.T. and Marty aren't at the snow-cone place. They're smoking cigarettes and drinking beer behind the church."

"Hush, Treenie," Josie said, turning to give her younger sister a reproachful look. "Just hush!" She turned back to me. "Okay, well, thanks, Aunt D'linda. Thanks."

I stood and watched as they ran with excitement toward the old carnival rides. If Susan would agree to sell the farm, or even part of it, she could afford a few small luxuries for her grandchildren. Yet her refusal to even consider selling was adamant. Monday's meeting would not be pleasant.

With the meeting on my mind, I picked up a 'takeout' barbeque, deciding to go back to the farm to rest up for tonight rather than do any more socializing.

I was almost back to the pickup, when, from the corner of my eye, I saw a cloud of white hair and a large red hat coming in my direction. I pulled the visor down over my eyes and made a beeline toward the pickup. Today was not the day to explain the farm dilemma to Mary and Carla.

Chapter Twenty

Reunion Night and the Little Store

By the time I arrived at the Memorial building that night, the surprise of seeing classmates in their older form had worn off. Instead of noticing all the differences between us, I noticed the many similarities – the thinning, gray hair; the wrinkles won through a lifetime of triumphs and defeats. The local men wore their new creased Levi's and pearl-buttoned western shirts, while those from more urban areas wore new creased slacks and freshly pressed dress shirts, yet they all shared the same memories. The women wore pants and roomy tops, probably made in some Asian country, which covered ample tummies and hips. One of the differences between well-off and not-so-much being the quality of the jewelry – real silver with diamonds, or discount-store specials. We were ready to put aside our differences and remember when we were teenagers in the '60s and elementary kids during the Eisenhower years.

Greg had his old reel-to-reel tape recorder set up in the front of the room, and he assured me that the mic worked fine. Since no alcohol was served here, we got right down to the business of looking around the room at all the items contributed by classmates for display and our silent auction. Someone brought a photo of our second-grade class, all the girls in saddle shoes and little plaid dresses, and the boys with slicked-down hair, either grinning broadly or sulking in the back row. Another classmate found a discarded section of the bricks on Dip Street, which immediately ran up the second highest bid for the auction. Close behind was a plaque that read, 'I laughed so hard, the tears ran down my legs.'

Some brought mementoes to display, like yearbooks, football letter-jackets, and cheerleading uniforms. Someone even found an old, girls', junior-high P.E. uniform to bring. It brought back humiliating memories of the showers and changing rooms in the ancient junior high where I struggled to pull on the horrid one-piece pea-green garment with the ballooning legs and tight waist-elastic. It was school issued so had been worn by countless embarrassed girls since the 1940s. At least for all us females present, it provided for shared groaning, as absolutely no one had fond memories of those days in the stone-cold gym.

Jancy and Tim, our girls' basketball forward, and her star football-player husband, who shocked the town by running off to get married our senior year, brought pictures of their 50th anniversary. Despite the dire predictions about their marriage, they looked better than any of the rest of us. They were both vibrant and happy great-grandparents who looked 20 years younger than the rest of us. Pictures of their children, grandchildren, and great-grandchildren smiled up at us from their table display.

Penny clicked a spoon against a glass to get our attention: "Okay, ya'll, it is so good to see you here today to celebrate our 50th reunion. We have a wonderful program prepared for you after dinner, but first, a few announcements. Everybody should get in line and go through the kitchen to get your food, then find a place at a table. Now, don't start eating until we are all served. Then we will have a word of grace before eating. Okay, now ya'll go get in line."

We all filed through the kitchen to pick up our enchilada dinner plate and then found our places at a table preset with huge glasses of ice and pitchers of tea. Tables were marked as either 'sweet,' or 'unsweetened,' meaning the tea. After making this decision, some of us gravitated toward those folks we saw most often, but others made it a point to join classmates we rarely saw. Greg and his wife were still fiddling with the old reel-to-reel tape recorder and called me over just as I sat down next to Marcia and her husband, Butch.

"Go get your iced-tea glass." Greg grinned. "We have something we think you'll like."

I headed back to my seat, picked up my glass, excused myself from those at my table, and went back up to where Greg and his wife, Julie, sat with the massive tape recorder.

"Here, give me your glass," he instructed. If it hadn't been Greg, I would have been suspicious, but I thought I knew what he was up to. He brought up a bag from below the table holding the huge recorder and poured a light amber liquid into my glass. I took a sip. He winked at me as I noticed John negotiating his way toward us around the tables. "Just thought you might need a bit of courage for this crowd."

It was strange, the fear we felt when we stood in front of our peer group. All of us on the program were used to speaking in front of classrooms of kids and adults. Yet here we were shaking in our boots as we confronted these old classmates who, despite the years, were still our most critical audience.

After dinner, Greg took a slug of his iced tea and called the group to attention. "So, it is so good to be here!" he said. "I thought you all might like a trip down memory lane, so I brought some old tapes I found. These are from the days when I was spinning the '45s on K.T.U.U. when we were in high school." There was loud applause, and he clicked the creaky tape recorder to life. Suddenly, we were back in the '60s and Greg's higher and younger voice was telling us about the newest hits, 'Puff the Magic Dragon,' and 'Blowin' in the Wind.' Somehow, we couldn't help but sing along to the familiar words from those carefree, teen years so long ago.

Then it was my turn. I took a sip of my spiked iced tea, cleared my throat, looked out on a sea of expectant faces, and began, "Not long ago, I read an article that insisted that the last good year in the United States was 1963. Well, that was our year. I'm sure we all remember our graduation night. That's when we had to wade into the high-school auditorium because a sudden severe thunderstorm flooded the town."

There were murmurs of agreement.

"If you remember, after our ceremony was over, we learned that Silver City was blown away by a tornado, killing 30 people. Those were our neighbors, so things were really never the same after that. At the end of the summer, many of us went away to college, work, or the service, and watched in horror when our young president was assassinated in November of that year. After that, it was other assassinations, then Vietnam, Richard Nixon, and all that has come after. Computers and technology changed our world in remarkable ways, and most of the small farms of our childhood disappeared, and the towns they surrounded were changed forever.

"But tonight, I thought I'd remind you of a simpler time when we were in fifth grade in the old junior-high building. This is a story I originally wrote for a group of people who did not share our memories so had to be told about what we all know so well. The story is about me and two of our missing classmates."

I continued, a bit tongue in cheek. "Now, according to Penny, Ellen is in Kansas City, closing a big real-estate deal, and she is going to be so sorry she missed this story."

Based upon Ellen's appearance at our 40th reunion, she was still the class prima donna, but she was our prima donna. Surely time mellowed her a bit, and even if she were here, we could poke gentle fun at her for being a bit too big for her britches, so there was knowing laughter from my audience. I cleared my throat and changed my tone of voice for the next part.

"Sadly, our dear friend, Betsy, passed away last year of Lou Gehrig's disease. So, I hope this brings back happy memories of her, as well as Ellen."

Marcia and Penny both took off their glasses and wiped their eyes. I took a big sip of tea, cleared my throat, looked out on a sea of expectant faces, and began:

"And I know all of you remember our principal, Dooley Dinwoodie."

The whole group groaned in unison. Then from somewhere in the middle, a comment I was expecting.

"You mean ol' Dim Dinwitty? I can still hear that big ol' boomin' voice over the junior-high P.A. system tellin' poor ol' Buddy Sims to report to the office immediately if not sooner."

Now Penny added her two cents, "I was so scared of him. Remember, there was a boys' staircase and a girls' staircase? If he caught us on the wrong staircase…well, we were sure we wouldn't live to tell about it." There were chuckles of agreement. "We were sure he had an electric paddle in his office."

"Yep," one of the men agreed, "I can still see poor ol' Buddy walkin' to his doom with them scuffed up ol' shoes of his."

"Does anyone know what happened to Buddy? Anybody ever heard from him?"

I looked out over a sea of shaking heads. Then Van spoke up, "He's probably in prison somewhere. Poor kid, never really had a chance, did he? I mean, with that family of his. Well, I even remember a time when his mama put him on the school bus after she slicked down his hair with bacon grease. Like to fumigated us all outta that ol' bus."

It was time to retake control of the audience, "Okay, well this story isn't about Buddy or Mr. Dinwoodie. It's about the Little Store. Remember? It was across the street from the junior high. I know some of you men got to go there instead of having to eat the lunchroom food, but us girls were forbidden to go."

Marcia jumped in, "That's because the boys got paid real money for helping their daddies plow and plant, so they had their own money. Us girls were just supposed to help our mamas with the washing, ironing, dishwashing, pickin', and cannin' for free!"

"That's exactly the way I remember it, Marcia," I agreed. "Also, I remember that the Little Store smelled like fried onions, hamburgers, and dill pickles. And that scraggly, weedy lawn that served as its parking lot was filled with all these rough-looking men – I suppose they were actually older teenagers – with leather jackets, cigarettes, tattoos, and old black cars from the 1940s. And do you remember the woman who worked inside and flipped burgers? I remember her wearing a sack-feed housedress and dangling a Camel cigarette from her lip."

I paused. "She was not one of the ladies who attended Missionary Society meetings with my grandmother at the First Baptist Church."

"Now, wait a minute here," Martha spoke up. "That lady was related to one of my cousins, I think. Wasn't her name Pearl? Something like that."

"Naw, her name was Gert somethin' or another."

My story was rapidly going off-track. "Well, I guess we could argue about this all day, but anyway, what I do remember for sure was you could get a greasy burger for $.20, add cheese and it came to $.25. Cokes were a nickel, and you got them in a glass bottle out of a red-and-white vending machine."

"Those were the good ol' days!" piped up a female voice from the middle of the room.

"Okay, now, I know all of you know about Betsy and Ellen. This story is about what happened to them and me when we were in fifth grade. Ellen was already getting curves and Betsy was perky and cute with her twinkly brown eyes, curly red hair, and that smattering of freckles across her face. I, on the other hand, looked like a chubbette ad for Oshkosh B'Gosh, and you guys called me '16 Tons.'"

All the women giggled in recognition, while the men looked embarrassed.

I paused for a sip of my spiked tea, and from the back of the room I heard someone ask, "Ya'll got that song on the recorder? Be real fun to hear it again."

I turned to look at Greg who shook his head. "Nope, Jerry. Sorry about that."

"So, anyway," I continued, "I wasn't exactly one of the cool kids, and when Ellen and Betsy asked me to go with them to the Little Store, I jumped at the chance. I was willing to do the unthinkable – use my lunch money at the Little Store instead of the school cafeteria. Most of my story doesn't have to be explained to you, but since not everyone has the same memories we do, for others I had to explain what to us is obvious. So, anyway, this is where my story begins, and with your permission, I will read it to you."

I looked up, relieved to see nods of approval and I began:

"The Little Store

Like most of the girls raised in the '50s, I had clear irrevocable rules for right and wrong. Minding your mama was right. Not minding was clearly wrong. It was that simple. But Mama clearly didn't understand about the complexity of fifth grade social structures and the perils of not fitting in.

The big day came. It was a Friday and I wore approved fifth-grade attire – rolled-up blue jeans, penny loafers with a dime in the fold, not a penny, and a red plaid shirt, untucked, with a blue bandana tied around my neck. The week before I convinced my mother to let me get a *'lawnmower'* haircut which was all the rage that year. Photos of the time show me at about four feet 11 inches, 125 pounds, round face with cat-eyes glasses, short bob with squared-off bangs accentuating my ears which stuck out at right angles from my head. I thought I was very cool. Definitely ready to take on anything the Little Store could deal out.

Later known as The Hornet's Nest, the Little Store hunkered down in gray decay across from the junior high. A black 1940-ish coupe idled in front, the door ajar. A lanky, leather-clad, young man lounged in the front seat, a Lucky Strike smoldering between his fingers, and his lips pulled back in a leering smirk. His stare had to do with Ellen who joined us even though she was a Baptist and even more strictly forbidden to cross the street than Betsy and I who were Presbyterians, therefore had freedom of conscience. No one would have guessed that she was only 11 years old. Already her body curved seductively, and her black hair gleamed in the autumn sunshine as we bravely made our way across Austin Street to the other side.

His name was Leo – we knew that when he uncurled himself from the tattered upholstery and stood up. His name blazed across the front pocket of the faded leather jacket.

'Do you think they have a bathroom?' I asked, trying to look at anything but the leering Leo.

'Shhh!' Ellen and Betsy were acting like we did this every day. The problem was that all of a sudden, I did need a bathroom, but the idea of returning to the school restroom was of the question. We came this far and there was no going back. Betsy got to the door first. She banged the screen behind us as the whining sounds of the Carter family greeted us from the jukebox. The smell of greasy hamburgers and onions was an improvement over the school-cafeteria smell of overcooked broccoli and cauliflower. Betsy led us to a side booth while the line of older boys eyed us, whispering under their breaths. Pearl, the cook and waitress, stood behind the counter, the ash from her cigarette bending dangerously downward toward the hot sauce and napkin rack. Her bosom was covered with a white apron smeared with grease and catsup, but she gave us her best attempt at a welcome.

'What can I get for you young ladies today?'

Betsy unwrapped her lunch money from her knotted handkerchief. "I'd like a cheeseburger, French frieds [sic], and a coke."

'Me too,' echoed Ellen.

Now it was my turn. My mother never let me eat onions since she was convinced that gave you gas. I was willing to break the rules by going in the Little Store, but eating the forbidden onion was going too far. 'I want a cheeseburger with no onions, French fries, and a Dr. Pepper.'

'Coming right up, ladies.'

An unknown cowboy moaned out his misery on the jukebox and we sat there, pretending to be cool. My heart bumped around in my chest. We only had 15 minutes before we had to be out in the schoolyard with the rest of our class, so it was a relief when Pearl delivered our burgers – shiny with grease, covering an entire plate, fat pickles sticking out from the inside. This was the life.

It was about then that a shadow passed over our table in the form of Leo. He leaned down with both hands pressed against the booth, his keys dangling from his belt loop. 'So, what's your name, pretty little girl?' He was staring right at Ellen. Usually confident, she was a deer in the headlights.

'Ellen?' she replied tentatively. Her answer came out like a soft question.

'Well, Ellen, how'd you like to go for a ride in my little coupe out there?' Ellen swallowed the last bite of her burger in one big lump.

'I gotta get back to school,' she squeaked.

'Naw. School's for sissies, baby. All you need is strong man like me to take care of you, honey.'

My fear was reflected in Betsy's face.

'You could ask my sister,' Ellen continued bravely. 'She likes cars.'

'So, is your sister as pretty as you are?'

'Oh yeah. She was prom queen last year.' The ethics of sacrificing her sister to save herself was not a part of her fast thinking.

'Prom queen? Well, how d'ya like that. The sister of a prom queen sittin' right here in front of me.'

'She's older than me,' Ellen persisted.

'Oh yeah? How old would that be?'

'17.'

'And how old would you be?' For the flash of a second, I could see Ellen's struggle. Should she be honest or sophisticated? For Ellen, this was a hard choice. 'Are you babysittin' these little girls or what?'

Ellen's words came out in a whisper, 'I'm almost 12.'

Incredulity passed over Leo's face. He stood up slowly. 'Ya'll gotta be kiddin' me. I thought you wuz the babysitter for these little girls here.' Betsy and I shrunk down behind our cheeseburgers. "Well, I tell you what, sweetheart. Ya'll come back and see me in a few years. Hear now? I don't feel like a messin' with somebody's kid sister right now."

We watched him saunter back to his car, kicking open the fly-infested screen door with his boot. Ellen left her fries and coke untouched. 'I think I need to use the restroom too.'

Without another word, we all headed for the door – trying to ignore the catcalls coming from the line of boys leaning up against the coupe. Then we were running across the street with our bandanas flying. Our school-cafeteria friends looked on with amazement as we threw ourselves down next to the monkey bars.

'Where ya'll been?' Norman Peters was the first to ask.

'We just went over for candy,' Betsy lied.

'I'm a gonna tell your mamas ya'll went to the Little Store.' This was what Norman did best.

'You are not!'

'Am too.'

'Git outta here, you ol' tattletale.' Betsy was on a roll. 'You think we couldn't tell plenty a stuff about what you do on the school bus if we figured to?' We may have had Norman over a barrel, but everyone else in 5B knew too. Our lives passed in front of us. In a little town like ours, the news would reach home before we did, and there would be the devil to pay.

Just then, the rev of an engine silenced everyone. It was Leo leaning out the window. 'Hey, I forgot to ask you, darlin', what's you sister's name?'

For the rest of our time in junior high, we only saw the outside of the Little Store from the school side of the street. Several brave seventh and eighth graders later ventured across to get their wax-candy ruby lips or harmonicas, or to buy their Lik-M-Aid, but we never joined them. Much later, Ellen would herself be chosen prom queen and Betsy the F.F.A. Sweetheart. Even I got rid of my glasses and lawnmower haircut in time to be elected Marching Band Sweetheart – evidence that we had all arrived at a place safe from peer ridicule.

Never again, though, would I enter the Little Store. Several classes of junior-high kids continued to be attracted to that ramshackle ol' store until it was torn down to make way for low-income tract housing – bland and harmless – teaching no lessons."

There was applause and laughter as everyone began sharing their own memories. Soon, everyone was listening to Al as he related another shared memory. His was impromptu so carried more credibility as far as storytelling goes.

"Ya'll remember the belt line?" he began. Loud groans erupted from all the men as he continued, "As I recall, it was the upper classmen boys who stood on either side of 'at ol' sidewalk down Audry Street, each about a yard apart. Then they would all unbuckle their belts with the big, ol', silver buckles and start snapping the leather. All the ninth-grade boys would be in a line, ready to run down the sidewalk and take their hits. And I remember watching the freshmen when I was in eighth grade – I guess the whole damn school got to watch – ain't that how ya'll remember?"

There was unanimous consent as he continued, "Well, anyways, I was a watching and feeling sick to my stomach, thinking of next year when it would be our turn to run through, and then somebody – I won't say who – right next to me grabbed his crotch and let out a string of really bad swears and took off for the door to the building. But he didn't make it in time. We all saw he crapped his pants, right there, just looking at all those pale-faced boys shakin' like leaves, preparing themselves for their initiation into high school."

All the men were nodding. Somebody in the back piped up, "Wasn't that ol' Pat Sweet that done that? You know he moved away that year. Never did have to do the run."

"None of us did, remember?" John spoke up then. "It was Nellie and my mom, plus some others who went to the school board after that because somebody got welts so big, they had to go to the doctor. After that, I guess they decided it was dangerous. Can you believe, though, that no one stopped it before that?"

Al answered, "Nope. The deal was there was a group thought that would be provin' your manhood, or something like that. Nobody was willin' to speak up, 'cause they'd be called a sissy or something worse. We were the first class didn't have to run the belt line... Can't say that made me sad, but there were people thought we were being coddled by our mommies, and they told us that all freshman year, as I remember now."

For a moment, all the men present shared a common memory – their fear of the belt line, and their relief when that trial by fire was no longer a requirement for a young man to enter high school in 1958.

Then it was Marcia's turn. She came to the front to show everyone her memory book.

"Now, I want ya'll to stand up as I read these names. This is all the classmates who are no longer with us. After that, I'll hand it around and you can look at it. Notice that there's a little American flag right by the names of our veterans, so say a little prayer for them as we remember their sacrifices."

There was a shuffle of moving chairs and creaking knees as the class stumbled to their feet. Marcia read all 22 names, almost a fourth of our class. "Okay, now I wonder if someone could please help me out here. John? How about you? I think we need to all sing together our Alma Mater."

A reluctant John struck a piano key, hummed a starting note, and we bumbled our way through a distinctively off-tune version of Our Dear T.H.S.

Penny made her way to the front, flashing smiles. "Okay, now I have had a bunch of you askin' me to sing, and I'm so inspired by all the love I see here that I am goin' to do it."

There was loud applause as she belted out a good Patsy Cline imitation of 'Crazy' and then, encouraged by more applause, her version of 'I Fall to

Pieces'. Penny's eyes shone with tears as she looked out at all these older friends. Then she said, "I just think we need to do one more thing here before we start to visitin'. We need to read our class roll, and then if anyone knows about anybody we just couldn't find, please raise your hand and tell us what you know."

There were 100 people on the roll, and most of the unlocatables seemed to have dropped off the face of the earth, with one exception. When Penny read the name of Buddy Sims, a woman rose from the back of the room as we all turned to look. She and the man with her must have slipped in unseen sometime in the last few minutes because we hadn't noticed them before. "Well, ya'll, I'm Jessie, Buddy's sister, and this is Bud right here beside me." Standing next to Jessie was a tall man with a shock of white hair and piercing blue eyes. He raised his hand.

"I'm here all right," he began. "My sister throwed me in the car and made me come 'cause I was too shy to show up by myself. Ya'll remember I was always that bad boy ol' Doolie Dinwoodie would always call to the office over that intercom. Well, after growin' up some, I done all right for myself, and I just wanted to come back and say hello, but I was plum scared to do it. Hope I get to visit with you, if you're a willin' to visit with me after all these years."

For a split second, Penny was stunned into silence, then recovered. "Oh my, bless you heart, of course, we want to visit with you, Buddy. We're so glad you're here! I'll just finish up readin' this list of classmates and then I'm goin' to let everybody visit a bit, just like you all want to do, before we announce the winner of our silent auction."

The program was officially over and we were on our own. I was glad to see that several classmates gravitated toward Buddy and Jessie. As I started to get up from the table, Marcia grabbed my hand. "Now, don't leave until I ask you one question. I've not had a chance, and I can't let you get away without asking. What is goin' on with your sister and all those kids? I hear that those older kids of Angie's aren't even goin' to school, and there's even a rumor going around you are thinkin' about bailin' out and selling the farm. Is that true?"

Before I could even reply, she continued, "Now I know this is none of my business, but you know I'm raisin' my own granddaughters since their mama died, and I'm pretty worried about those kids. I mean, they have to go to school. What can Susan be thinking?"

For a split second, I felt like pouring out the whole story and confiding in Marcia, but fortunately something stopped me. The grapevine here was alive and well, and it would take less than 24 hours before my transgression made it back to Susan. Instead, I squeezed her arm and replied, "I would love to visit with you about it, but I just don't think I'm up to going into it all right now. Sorry."

Marcia smiled and nodded, clutching the memory book close to her chest. "That's okay. Maybe another time?"

Suddenly, I was plummeted back into the world of 2013, and I had no answers.

Chapter Twenty-one
Meeting and Explosion

It was a relief to have the reunion behind me. We all left with the promise to meet again in five years, despite knowing this would probably not happen for most of us. I hoped that Susan would be in a better frame of mind after being surrounded by supportive old friends who came to town for Picnic. Most of them only had a vague idea of what her life was like now and still viewed her from the perspective of many years before, which was good for her.

The meeting with Stu, Andy, and Skeeter on Monday was a crucial one, and I wanted it to go well. So, I decided to be strategic. I would invite Susan to go to lunch with me afterward so we could relax. If I offered to pay, she would probably accept. She was under the impression there was still a chance we could share the farm, but more and more, I was leaning toward some kind of division, with each of us managing our own acreage. The dicey part was dividing it up equitably so that I received 55% and she received 45% of all the assets. Skeeter knew the land best. His assessment was crucial. By the time the meeting was over, we should have a fairly good idea about who would get which land, based on what he recommended. Once the land was divided, I would no longer be responsible for her decisions, nor she mine.

We could both keep Skeeter as our renter-operator-farmer, or we could choose someone else. This way, each of us would have autonomy. If she wanted to give everything away to Angie and her children, that would be entirely up to her. It would also make it easier for my sons when I was no longer here. I hoped they would never have to deal with their unpredictable cousin and her family.

In my mind, it was all very logical and well-planned. I would be very calm, non-threatening, and kind, presenting this as a benefit to both of us and our families. I even rehearsed my talking points so I would be prepared for her arguments. Since I hadn't talked with her all weekend or since our last big blow-up, I decided to call her and make arrangements for Monday. I picked up the phone to call just as I heard the now-familiar rattle of her van coming into the farmyard. This was typical. Usually when she flew off the handle, she would resurface a few days later and act as if nothing ever happened. I was ready for her this time as she came through the backdoor with empty milk cartons hanging from her fingers again.

"Hi. I came out to get some country water. We're all out at home and I hate the city water. How was your reunion?"

"Oh, it was good. Everything went pretty smoothly, and I think everyone had a good time. How was your weekend?"

"It's always good when I get to be with Barb and Debbie. They are so supportive and loving."

I was fairly sure I knew what was going through her mind: *They are just the opposite of my judgmental sister.*

However, I let it go and got right down to business. "Hey, what do you think of going out for lunch on Monday after our meeting with Skeeter, Andy, and Stu? My treat. We need a chance to just relax and talk."

Her back was turned to me as she filled up the empty milk cartoons, so I couldn't see her face. "Okay. I guess so. I sure get tired of Mexican food, though. Wish we had just one regular restaurant here like we used to."

I thought about this a minute. "We could drive to Plainfield and eat there."

"No. That's okay. I get tired of driving too. We can just go to El Sombrero, I guess."

So far, so good. Maybe we could work this out in a civil way after all. I helped her fill up the rest of the bottles and carry them out to her van. But, of course, there was still the meeting to get through.

On Monday, I walked into Stu's office, feeling optimistic as I took my seat at the broad mahogany table. Skeeter was already there, and he and the other two men rose to shake my hand. We chatted about the weather as we waited for Susan who arrived breathless and shaking a few minutes later.

"Sorry," she began. "I ended up having to help find Josie. Nobody knew where she was."

"Josie?" asked Stu.

"Yes, my 13-year-old granddaughter."

"Did you find her?" I asked.

She looked at me for the first time and settled herself into a chair. "Oh yeah. She was at a friend's house, but she hadn't told anyone she was spending the night. I looked several places before I found her. It's so frustrating when she does that."

I wanted to ask where Angie was and why she didn't go looking for her daughter, but I knew how that would be received, and Stu was ready to get down to work. He put on his glasses and looked across the table. "Okay, I want to thank Skeeter for being here and giving us his opinion about how to divide the land, if that's what you girls decide to do. I think our job here today is to come to some agreement about the trust and how to proceed from this point. Am I right?"

Susan and I both nodded and turned to Skeeter who smiled kindly at us across the table. "Well, thanks for having me here," he began. "First, I want to say that I would really like to buy the land if you're a'willin' to sell. I know it like the back of my hand, and I promise to take care of it just like your daddy would have done."

Susan was sitting beside me, so I couldn't see her face, but she cleared her throat and shifted in her chair in a way that told me that for her, this was not welcome news.

Andy interrupted at this point, "That's sure something to consider, but right now, I think we want to hear about how to divide the land so each of these fine ladies can figure out what they want to do with their part."

"Right," said Skeeter, pulling out a plat map and laying it flat on the desk. "Well, you see, what makes sense is to keep together Section 12, the McMurry piece, and R.J.'s section. That whole kit and caboodle is connected together with an irrigation system. The way I figure it, with the value of the farmhouse included on the home section, plus most of the Sutter section, that would divide it up just about how you want it, 55 and 45."

"So, is the farmhouse in the 45%?" asked Susan.

"Yes, ma'am. At least that's the way I figured it. Ya'll could figure it any way you want."

Susan considered this for a long minute. "So why don't we include Section 12 in the 45%? And you might as well say it, that's what would be mine."

The men all exchanged glances, then Skeeter spoke up, "Well, ya see, that section's irrigation is all tied in with the McMurry and R.J. sections.

Otherwise, ya ruining that system ya'll's daddy set up, and it's still performin' really good. I just wouldn't mess with it."

"But that's not fair," Susan started. "Why can't I get Section 12 and the good water instead of my sister?" So far, she avoided looking at me, but now, she shot me a glance. "I need it more than she does."

Now Andy spoke up, "But we discussed this, Susan. According to the trust, it has to be divided fairly, and since you already took out a quite a bit of your share, there's less left now. We could divide it so you would get Section 12 but then you wouldn't get the home section with the farmhouse, so it looks like to me, you'll have to make a decision – I mean, you and your sister." He looked back and forth between us.

I could see the anger building up behind Susan's eyes as she tapped her pen on the table. "I do not want to divide up the land at all. I told you that. I want to leave it like it is and have us manage it together like we talked about when Mack was alive. I don't see why we can't still do it like that."

"That's still an option, Susan," I began. "But we have to look at this from a practical level and we're just trying to figure out what will be best." This was such a big decision and, to be honest, I wasn't too sure about what I wanted either.

Everyone was quiet for a few seconds, then Skeeter spoke up, "Now, I have to tell you all. I really don't want to buy any of the land unless it includes Section 12. That's where the good water is. Now, I don't want to cause any hard feelin's or anything like that, but I think you all need to know where I'm a'comin' from. 'Course, if you don't want to sell…well, that's up to the two of you. Now, if you're done with me here, I think I'll be takin' off, if you don't mind?" He looked at Stu and Andy and they nodded, stood up, and held out their hands. Skeeter knew exactly when to exit.

"Thank you for comin' in, Skeeter. Sure do appreciate your help." Stu was ushering him out the door while Andy turned back to Susan and me. "So, ladies, it doesn't look like you're ready to make a decision, but I want to advise you that it takes a while to get all the papers in order whatever you decide to do, and this trust of your parents is coming to an end mighty quick, so the sooner, the better."

It was my turn to speak up, "I tell you what, we'll mull it over and get back to you by Wednesday. Would that be okay?"

"Yep. That works for me," Andy replied. "Is that okay with you, Susan?"

"Oh, sure. Just rush everything through, like usual. But like I already told you, I'm not selling the land." She retreated into her default setting, slightly sarcastic, with a hurt feeling's overtone.

I turned to Andy who I could tell was as eager to end the meeting as Skeeter. "Could we plan on meeting again about 9:00 a.m. on Wednesday? I promise we'll have a decision by then. I can't stay here any longer, and we could remain indecisive for several more weeks unless we have a deadline."

"I'll work it out with Stu," Andy replied as he gave a long sigh and stood aside so that we could go through the door. "See you on Wednesday morning, unless you hear from me otherwise." Susan was still pouting, but as I followed her out to her car, I made a point of ignoring that.

"Well, I'm ready for some lunch. How about you?"

"Whatever you say," she replied. "I really don't care."

"It's a nice day, shall we just walk down there? It's only a couple of blocks."

"Do whatever you want. I need my car because I'll have to pick up food for the kids after we eat, and I don't want to have to walk for blocks, carrying food containers. I'll just meet you there."

She pulled out her keys and cigarettes and climbed into the van.

I talked to myself on the two-block walk to El Sombrero. I rationalized – I have to be the one in control to balance out the emotional. We are having lunch here because I decided that she will be less likely to explode if we are in a public place. I pushed open the door and saw my sister sitting at a back table. Surrounding her were cowboys with manure hanging from their boots, and families with kids playing with saltshakers and drinking straws. The soft-spoken waitress brought us huge tumblers of ice water. "Special today includes two enchiladas and an iced tea for $4.95." Like most of the town's population, her Mexican heritage gave melody to her English.

"I'll take that." Susan didn't bother to look at the menu. Most days, she ordered takeout from here.

"How about the Mexican salad?" I decided.

"Chicken or beef?"

"Chicken with lots of greens."

"Greens?"

"Lettuce."

"Drink?"

210

"I'll have a Diet Coke."

"*Gracias*," our waitress said, smiling shyly and taking our menus.

Susan was already hostile, but I plunged ahead with my plan, ignoring her foreshadowing mood. "You know," I began. "I feel like we are on a bicycle built for two. I look around at the scenery yet want to go fast enough to get there before dark. You want to take all the time we need, no matter when we get there." She sipped her tea and looked at me. "What I am trying to say is that you are deliberative and take your time. I'm more decisive. There's nothing wrong with either of us; it's just that we're different."

Susan looked down and seemed to think about this for a minute, pulling at the paper on her straw. Then she said pensively, "But I want us to be a team, like what we talked about before…with Mack."

"I've been on lots of teams," I blithely continued, "Collaborative groups, committees, all kinds, and I know that teammates can disagree. It can become a real problem after a while, especially within families…"

She frowned at me, not liking my answer. Clearly, her idea of a team was different from mine. "Yeah, but haven't you ever heard of teamwork – you know, working together?"

"Sure, but let me tell you what I think gets in the way. Not long ago, I was talking to Ava, my granddaughter…"

"I know who your granddaughter is," she fired back.

"Well, I'm never sure, since you've only seen her once," I replied. "Well, anyway, when I was playing with her, she refused to let the Prince Charming doll be in the castle with all the princesses from her Disney collection.

"So, Ava," I asked, "why can't Prince Charming come into the castle? 'Grams,' she said with exasperation, 'he's not on our team.'"

"You see?" I said, looking at my sister. "Already the concept of team, the battle of the sexes, preschool style. The fact is that you and I aren't on the same team. We do not both have the same goal in mind. The family farm symbolizes something different for each of us."

I should have stopped right there and paid attention to the salad the waitress placed before me. Instead, I tried a different angle. "Look, on a team, there are people with different strengths. I've been on countless teams for most of my life."

"There you go again. You said that before. You're just like Mother."

"What?"

"Always being the know-it-all, putting me down."

"It's just that you are more deliberative and I'm more decisive," I repeated. "We're just different and that's why it is hard to work together."

"I am not hard to work with," she said, looking at me coldly.

"No," I stumbled on. "No, what I'm just trying to point out is that some people in any group are working from their emotions, while others are looking at things intellectually. The rational has to balance the emotional – you have to look at both sides."

"So, I'm emotional?" her voice rose now, and she stabbed at her enchilada.

I blathered on, "It looks to me like you see everything through the lens of your grandchildren's needs, which is perfectly understandable—"

"Putting me down all the time. That's what you're doing. I'm. Not. Emotional!"

"There's nothing wrong with being emotional—"

"I said I am not emotional!" her voice was now shrill and out of control. She clenched her fork, then smacked it down on the table. By now, people at nearby tables were listening to the unfolding drama. Suddenly, she threw her napkin at me and pushed her chair back, crashing the one behind it to the floor. The other diners stopped eating, their forks in the air.

"I said I'm not emotional!" she screamed and stumbled toward the door, leaving her food uneaten and me to stare into my Mexican salad, my heart beating double time.

That was when I decided – I couldn't do this anymore.

The customers looked from the slamming door back to me. I shook my head and tried to eat my salad, but my appetite was gone. After a few minutes, I signaled for the waitress, picked up the check, and headed outside as the eyes of the other diners followed me out the door.

This time, Susan wasn't going to get away with just running away from the problem. She had to confront the issues we faced. I got in the pickup and drove to her house. Without knocking, I marched through the house where several of the grandchildren peeked out at me from under blankets spread on the pullout couch. The T.V. was on full blast, and leftover food littered the room. The kids gave me bewildered looks as I headed out to the backyard without as much as a hello. I knew I would find my sister there, smoking.

"So, there you are," I began. "Thanks a lot for embarrassing us in front of the entire town." When she remained silent, I pulled up an empty milk crate, which served as a lawn chair, and sat down. "I'm really sick and tired of your attitude, and I came to tell you that I intend to tell Stu to divide up the land just like Skeeter advised. I'll take 12, R.J., McMurry, and a fourth of the Sutter section. You can have the rest."

For the first time, she looked at me and then blew smoke directly in my face. "You can't do that. I have a say too, you know."

"You are wrong about that. If you had been willing to talk to me and negotiate, then maybe you would have a choice, but not now. I have controlling interest, so according to Stu, I can call the shots and that's what I intend to do."

With shaking hands, she snubbed out her cigarette. "You are mean, mean, mean, mean! You are not the sister I used to have. You only care about yourself!" her voice carried into the neighborhood. "You can't do this. You can't! That farm was Daddy's, and before that, Grandpa and Mimi's. You have no right to it! You are not even related. I will no longer call you sister!" She got up from her chair and stumbled into the house, slamming the screen door behind her.

I sat there, stunned. I tried to get up. I realized I was shaking and unable to rise. My knees were like water. I put my head in my hands and let go of tears I repressed for too long. The blare of irritating cartoon T.V. music was the only noise I heard from the house. Susan remained inside. No way was I going through the house to get back to the pickup.

After what seemed like a long time, I was able to get up and walk around to the gate which was wired shut. Tears were blinding my vision as I struggled with the wire. I wiped them clumsily on the sleeve of my shirt and tried again. After twisting and pulling, I was finally able to pry it open.

I had to get out of here. I needed to talk to Stu, but first, I needed to do something about the heavy stone that settled in my heart.

My mind was a jumble of grief, anger, and frustration. I pushed the old pickup beyond its limits as I drove back to the farm, and it wobbled dangerously from ditch to ditch on the rough dirt roads. The only thing I wanted to do was head out into the pasture with the dogs – my go-to place when I was a kid, and again now. It was far from what most people would think of as a place of peaceful reflection, with its cactus, yucca, and occasional rattlesnakes, but for me, it provided solitude and a place to think.

It was nearing August and the fields were dry and brittle, the grass crunching beneath my feet as I walked, and dust billowing up around my ankles. But the dull yellow-and-gray landscape was brightened by splashes of bright yellow sunflowers, purple thistles, and pungent sage. I was confident the dogs would warn me of rattlesnakes. Some people found the flat plains stretching into the horizon a frightening reminder of an uncertain eternity, fearing what lay just over the curve of the earth beyond reach. For me, the sky itself became the landscape – bright and strikingly blue – with only the white tendrils of a distant jet to remind me of the reality of time and place.

This morning, I thought I had everything smoothly sorted out, with a clear path to resolution. But I was only kidding myself, righteous self-confidence obscuring my awareness of my sister's pain. She hit me with the one thing she knew would hurt me the most. That could only come from her own pain and frustration. What was it which brought us to this point? I thought of my grandparents who settled this very land. They were so sure they were doing the right thing when, at the end of their lives, they divided the original farm between their two sons, giving the better half to my uncle. They forgot, or chose to overlook, the fact that it was my father who stayed on the land, making it his life, while my uncle went off in a different direction. There were echoes of the prodigal son in more than one generation.

If that did not add enough overlay, there was much, much more. My story was further complicated by something I tried all my adult life to forget, or to at least push below the surface. Now my sister opened the forbidden Pandora's Box, and I had no choice but to confront it.

Chapter Twenty-two
Angel Daddy

It was the day after Mack's funeral. Susan's son, Will, and my two youngest sons, Pete and Matt, came for the funeral. Chris, my oldest, who worked in Ireland, was not able to come. Since Susan and I both had sons here for the funeral, it was a perfect time to clear out as much of the farmhouse as we could before they headed back to their jobs. I'm not sure which one found the actual box, but all three suddenly appeared beside me, serious expressions on their faces. Pete, my second oldest, spoke for the three of them.

"Mom, look what we just found. We opened it and realized it's something you'd probably want to go through first. It's got all these letters and stuff... I think they are from your real dad."

I was busy scrubbing out the refrigerator and was caught off-guard. "What are you talking about?"

"This, Mom." Pete held out a square cardboard box labeled '1944.' I never saw it before, but even before I opened it, I knew it contained everything I avoided for so long.

I nodded. "Yeah, I want to look through it, but I think I'll wait until later... I want to finish this job."

"Are you all right, Mom?" asked Matt. "You don't look so good."

"I'm just tired," I replied. "I'm okay...really. I just think, though, it would be good if we all went through this together later this evening."

"Sure," Pete replied. "Whatever works."

Right now, I was so grateful for these young men who were my grown sons. I wished again that Chris, my oldest son, could be here. Susan's son, Will, was here though. He was very helpful and so different from his sister, Angie. All these men seemed to understand my hesitancy about the box and didn't push the issue. But I was curious, as well as apprehensive. After they returned to their cleanout jobs, I opened the top of the box and looked inside. Nothing there was that spectacular – only letters, photos, and telegrams. Yet, I knew when I examined them more closely, they would all be difficult for me.

It wasn't like I didn't know the story already. I knew about my real father since before I could remember. Each Saturday, Mother would place me up on the kitchen counter with my head hanging over the sink and begin to wash my hair. This was a Saturday ritual as sacred as mopping the floors before church on Sunday. In hindsight, it is now clear that she waited until this moment, when she had my full attention, to talk to me about sensitive subjects. This is where we had the 'Kotex talk' among others. But that was much later. When I was a small child, she used this time to tell me about my 'Angel Daddy' who was killed in the war before I was even born. I would look up at her prickly armpits, through the sudsy shampoo and see her lips quivering as she tried not to cry. I didn't understand much about what she tried to tell me, but I did know that I didn't like it when she would cry and that her crying seemed to be all about me being born after the war killed 'Angel Daddy.' Shampoo day made me very uncomfortable.

As I grew older, I gradually learned more of the story, yet there was always an overlay of something so sad about it, that I tried to avoid it altogether. Besides that, our shampoo day was the only time Mother ever brought up the subject, and I got the impression that something terrible would happen if I talked about it or asked questions at any other time. Both Mack and Susan seemed oblivious to this part of our mother's story. The subject never came up, and the only photos of my father were safely tucked away. Much later, I found out that my story was a rather common one, shared by many children who were born during the war years. And like many other families, it started with another war, three decades earlier.

After World War I, my grandfather, Conroy, married a young schoolteacher who lived on the next ranch over, Loona Elizabeth Pembley. We kids called her Noona. Soon, a baby girl was born. They hoped for more children, but after many years of marriage, several miscarriages, and a stillbirth, it was clear that there would only be my mother to carry on the family legacy.

Her diary and letters reveal that though she was raised a strict Southern Baptist not allowed to dance, drink, smoke, or play cards, she found a way to do all these things yet keep her parents from being any wiser about her escapades. But she was a good student, and after high school, her parents sent her off on the train to Baylor University, a good Southern Baptist college. After finding that she was queasy around blood, she gave up her dream of becoming a physician and focused on following in the steps of her mother, grandmother, and great-grandmother and becoming a teacher.

She graduated in 1942 when most of the young men she knew were signing up to fight against Hitler, and every able-bodied person was needed to keep things going on the home front. She easily secured a teaching job in a nearby town, living with another young teacher in a home that took in teachers.

It was there she met the man who would become my father. He was older and exempt from the first round of military enlistments because he had a family business to run – a gas-and-oil distributing business that he took over when his own father passed away several years before. Before his father's untimely death, he attended Texas Tech and earned his pilot's license. Trainer pilots were badly needed, and after asking my mother to marry him, he enlisted.

Mother told me later that he was the most eligible bachelor in town and swept her off her feet. They were married January 2, 1944, right before he reported for duty. After his basic training, he had a week's leave in March, and Mother joined him for some R-and-R before he was shipped to his first assignment. He told her not to worry because he would be posted stateside, not sent to the front. Pilots were trained on U.S. soil. He was assigned to a base in Nashville, and she returned home to live with her parents and help her father as a bookkeeper at the dealership. Soon it was apparent that a baby would be joining the family about Christmas time.

Each day brought news of the war effort in Europe. There was D-Day and the push toward the German front. But there were daily telegrams from the War Department too, notifying another local family that a beloved son or husband would not be coming home. During those months, my mother later told me, she felt she 'could count her lucky stars' that her husband was not posted overseas. Yet his letters to her tell of his own misgivings:

July 12
United State Army Air Forces
July 12, 1944
Stamford, Texas

My Dearest Sweetheart,

I had a bad misfortune to happen to me Monday afternoon – one of the cadets in my flight, Kissinger by name, from Milwaukee, Wis., was killed in a crackup. He was solo about 5:15 yesterday when the accident occurred. I had just passed him on a check ride which I gave him just before I left on Friday. This is just one of those things that we do not have control over, regardless of how hard we try…

In August 1944, on a hot afternoon as my mother sat, typing, a car pulled up next to the front door of the dealership, and a man walked solemnly into her office.

"Tula Malinda?" he asked.

"Yes?" replied my mother, turning toward her father's old friend, Harry Barlow, who now worked for Western Union. "Oh hi, Harry. Daddy's not here right now. Can I help you?"

Harry's voice trembled, "I have a telegram for you."

"Hmm, I'm not expecting anything…" she said, looking into the sad, compassionate face. Then it dawned on her. This was the kind of telegram women all over the country were receiving on a daily basis. But something must be wrong. This couldn't be for her. Her husband was in Nashville…

Her hands shook as she took the yellow paper from Harry.

"WE REGRET TO INFORM YOU STOP FLIGHT OFFICER H.D. STANLAN KILLED STOP PLANE CRASH ON TAKEOFF STOP 18 AUG. 1944 STOP DETAILS TO FOLLOW."

And with those few words, printed on the flimsy wartime paper, my mother's world came crashing down. My father would not be coming home.

The next day, another letter arrived, dated August 18, 1944:

Wednesday
August 17, 1944
Nashville

My Dearest Sweetheart,
   I was scheduled today for a training trip to Nassau, but it was called off at
the last minute due to weather, so we probably will go in a day or so. We are
not going to be stationed in Nashville but just a few days longer... We do not
have the slightest idea as to where we will be, but just as soon as I know, I'll
let you know...

Thursday:
   Tried to get this in the mail as I was out of envelopes yesterday. We learned
via the 'grapevine' today that our orders are now in the process, so by the time
you get this letter, I should be on my way to my final post...

The plane crashed on takeoff, killing both my father and the copilot. My mother just turned 24, and she was now a widow with a baby on the way in December. From now on, I would have an 'Angel-Daddy.'

Finally, the war ended, and those who made it through came home. Eligible men were at a premium, and after the shock of losing her first husband and giving birth to a fatherless child, Mother's stubborn determination came to her rescue. She needed to seize the day if she was going to provide me with a father and have more children. Her dreams of traveling the world with a handsome airplane pilot died with my father. Now she just wanted to be close to family, find a husband, and settle down.

About the time the rawness of her grief ran its course, an old friend from high school returned from his World War II posting in Alaska. He was eager to use his degree in agriculture to bring the latest farming techniques to the family farm and ranch which stretched over ten square miles. More than that, he could again enjoy his mother's excellent home cooking and perhaps look for a wife. While he was away, his brother became their father's right-hand man, using his degree from the University of Nebraska. The man who would become my father also had a degree, but his was from Iowa State. It was soon apparent that the differences between the two brothers ran much deeper than college rivalry. They would never see eye to eye when it came to managing their father's farm, or anything else, for that matter.

Not long after his return, he began courting Toogie, the very eligible young widow. He won her heart because among other reasons, he also doted on me, her young daughter. Then on February 14, 1948, Tula Malinda Conroy Stanlan and William Carlton Mihlbauer were married at the Little Chapel in the Woods in Denton, Texas. My mother wore a beaded, brown, silk suit, and my new daddy's niece and I were the flower girls. Nine months to the day after the wedding, my little sister, Susan Francis, was born. We moved into a remodeled hired-hand house on the farm, and a new life began for us all. Three years later, my brother, Mack, was born.

My sister and brother were full-siblings, I was a half. I wanted to be a 'whole,' but I was a 'half.' They didn't seem to notice the difference, but I did. First of all, my last name was different from theirs. Today, no one would blink an eye, but in my small town in the '50s, I felt I stood out like a kid with one eye. I was Stanlan. My sister and brother were Mihlbauers.

The year I turned ten, my mother took advantage of my vulnerable position as I lay on the kitchen counter, ready for her to apply the final vinegar rinse guaranteed to leave my hair shiny and sleek. "How would you like it if we changed your last name?" she asked. "Daddy wants to adopt you, but I thought I should let you decide."

I looked up under my mother's arm into the place directly in my line of vision and again saw the sprinkle of dark black hairs nested in her armpit, smelling of Mum deodorant. Throughout the rest of my life, anytime I got a whiff of Mum, I would always remember that day. The question my mother asked was not one I was prepared to answer. Even though I hated my last name, the idea of a name change seemed like another nail in the coffin of my social acceptance. What would the kids at school think? Wouldn't I have to answer all kinds of questions? Wouldn't the other girls stand in a corner and talk about me?

It didn't occur to me, until later, that this decision was a terrible one to lay at the feet of a ten-year-old child. My mother, who wouldn't even allow me to choose my own clothes or the food I wanted to eat, suddenly wanted me to make a decision with the potential to change my life. I see it now for what it was – she didn't want the responsibility of making that decision herself. Was this because she still felt a loyalty to her first husband, my dead father? Was it because the Stanlan family insisted I keep the name? For whatever reason, the decision was left to me, and due to my perceived fourth-grade peer pressure, I told my mother I wanted to keep the name I was given at birth. It never occurred to me, until much later, just how much this would hurt the man I called 'Daddy' all my life. In my mind, he was my father, and his parents my real and beloved grandparents. However, my paternal heritage was much more complicated. From an early age, I was told that 'my real Angel Daddy was killed in the war.' But the only Daddy I knew was the one who lived with me and was a regular daddy, not an angel at all.

Each summer, Granddaddy Conroy, driving the newest model Oldsmobile, would cart me off 50 miles south to another, little, dusty Panhandle town to visit my 'other grandmother' whom I called Mama Stanlan. According to my mother, the only authority I knew, this grandmother didn't want me to change my last name. That, plus the fact that I didn't really understand the concept of a name change at such an early age meant I was saddled with a last name different from my mother, my daddy, my sister, my brother, and also Grandpa, Mimi, and my cousins. When I went away in the summers, my brother and sister didn't get to come – a situation I felt was unfair. It wasn't because the week away was such an exciting prospect, but because I wanted someone to share the pain of a week with Ma Stone.

Ma Stone was Mama Stanlan's elderly mother, my great-grandmother. She wore black and lived in the backroom. She dipped snuff which she spit out into a disgusting coffee can beside her rocking chair. Each morning, Mama Stanlan (I always called her both names) would have to boil Ma Stone's bed sheets in a big iron kettle in the backyard and then hang them up to dry on the clothesline. Besides her strong odor, Ma Stone's eyes were red-rimmed and drippy, and she talked endlessly about skies full of birds, asking me to look up into the sky at birds that didn't exist. Mama Stanlan told me she 'was talking out of her head' and to ignore her. This was very hard to do, as she would scream at Mama Stanlan at odd times of the day and night, and her room was right across the hall from where I slept.

Despite all odds, Mama Stanlan herself was a cheerful woman who made the best cornbread and coffee of anyone. She didn't drive or have a car, so we walked to town under an umbrella to protect us from the hot July sun. We visited each little store around the square, collecting provisions for the week. I don't recall how we got everything home, but I suspect there was a delivery service for the town's elderly.

On Wednesday nights, she took me with her to prayer meeting where I was the only child present. I would wrap my short legs around the legs of the folding chair and try to stay awake as each of the good Baptist ladies asked for God's guidance and/or intervention. Usually some kind person would offer us a ride home, though the sun stayed up late on summer evenings.

By the time I was in fourth grade, the visits became easier because all of Mama Stanlan's remaining children went in together to purchase her a television for Christmas. This completely changed her life and my summer visits. Now we ate our milk and cornbread on T.V. trays in the living room so we could watch 'I Love Lucy.' Mama S turned it up loud to drown out the rambling talk coming from the backroom, and there we sat in the blue glow of the black-and-white screen until the T.V. station played The Star-Spangled Banner and signed off for the night.

Even though I was told over and over that I belonged to these people, where I really felt at home was not with Angel Daddy's relatives but with the man, I called Daddy, and Mimi, the grandmother who made luscious, lemon, meringue pies, canned hundreds of jars of black-eyed peas, the one who sang and played the piano when she wasn't reading racy novels or racing back and forth to town in her snappy Chevrolet.

Nobody I knew had two daddies, and I would have been perfectly fine with just one. But whenever I got up enough courage to ask my mother about it, she got all trembly. Her chin quivered and her voice shook. I did love my mother, and I didn't like seeing her fall to pieces, so I learned to just live with things as they were. This was my lot in life, and I would just have to make the most of it.

Looking back on it with the perspective of time, I now realize what a gift my mother gave me when she remarried. The family she married into was a different clan from either my mother's Scotch-Irish ancestors or Angel Daddy's who spent several generations in the Blue Ridge Mountains of Kentucky and Tennessee, developing an affinity for gospel music, loud going-to-hell preaching, and altar calls.

The Mihlbauer-Crowley families were from the upper Midwest and therefore had a more progressive, pragmatic stripe. They were religious but were far from the Bible-thumpers of both my mother's and birth-father's families. My mother's family were definitely readers, but their books of choice were the Bible and religious tracts, whereas Daddy's family loved literature and classical music and were pleased when a Black family moved into the house across the road from them. It wasn't long before Mimi invited the kids to come play and stay for lunch. By that time, I considered myself too old to play, but both my sister and brother developed lasting friendship with our new neighbors. In the meantime, Mother took us all aside and told us to please not mention this to Granddaddy and Noona. They just wouldn't understand.

I continued to visit Mama Stanlan each summer, accompanying her to Baptist tent-meeting revivals and attending the nine-year-old boys' Sunday school class that she taught. When I was 12 years old, Ma Stone finally died. She was 98 years old, and Mama Stanlan cared for her most of her adult life. My paternal grandfather, Mama Stanlan's husband, died in the '30s, prompting Angel-Daddy to drop out of college and come home to manage the gas station and supply store his father owned. When Angel Daddy died in the war, the business was sold. The money didn't last long though. Mama Stanlan was left practically destitute to care for her mother who slowly drifted into dementia.

Mother insisted we attend Ma Stone's funeral. It was the first time I saw a dead body in a casket, and I recoiled when I saw her lying there so still and waxy. Mama Stanlan vowed that now that she was free, she would travel to visit her children and grandchildren. She came to our house once for a very strained visit. Daddy did not like to be reminded about Angel Daddy and forgot his manners more than once, showing his resentment at her intrusion into his family. Two years later, Mama Stanlan herself died on the operating table of a brain tumor. Less than a year later, her daughter, my aunt, and her husband were killed by a drunken driver on their way home from settling her estate in Amarillo. My ties to Angel Daddy's family slowly disappeared. I was left with only the memory and the name.

Chapter Twenty-three
Contemplation and Confrontation

After more than an hour's walk through the pasture, reliving these childhood memories and nurturing my hurt and anger, I headed back to the house. It was time to quit feeling sorry for myself and move on. I promised Stu a decision by Wednesday and time was passing fast. The dogs beat me back, yipping and barking with delight as they recognized a familiar Oldsmobile and its owner, Carla. Her dog, Doc, jumped out of the car to greet them as soon as Carla opened the door. I was less enthusiastic about her visit. But knowing I was trapped, I trudged up to the front porch where my old friend greeted me with her hands on her hips.

"Well, there you are," she said. "I've been waitin' on you. Just gettin' ready to call the sheriff to look for you when I heard the dogs a barkin' down in the pasture. What the Sam Hill you doin' down there in the heat of the day?"

Before I could reply, Carla marched into the house and took a seat at the kitchen table. Sitting wide legged, she took off the sweaty Stetson that belonged to her late husband, Buzz, and looked at me with exasperation. She was dressed in her usual attire – baggy rolled-up Levi's and one of Buzz's ragged flannel shirts.

I followed her inside, like the naughty kid she thought I was. "I have a feeling you didn't come out to help me with the last of the cleanup, did you, Carla?"

She sniffed loudly and pulled her wadded Kleenex from her shirt pocket. "Well, you know me. I'm always glad to help, but no, I did not come out to help you. I came to ask you what in Sam Hill you're doing to that sister of yours? I must'a stopped by over there right after you left, and I never seen her so upset, and I've seen her in lots of situations. Now, I'm not sayin' she'd done everything right, tryin' to raise all those kids for that good-for-nothing daughter of hers...bless her heart. No, I'm not sayin' that. I'm a sayin' that you got no business thinkin' dividing up the farmland is a good idea. First of all, I'm not so sure she could even manage it by herself... Now, you know I love your sister and all, but bless her sweetheart, she just can't always get it together like she needs to... And second of all...well, I heard you might be thinking of selling out. Now how long have I known you and your mama and daddy, and before that Mimi and Jacob and the whole family? And I hear you're just about to sell that land??? My goodness, gal, what the hell's wrong with you? Well, now I know all about how your sister can say some pretty mean things – now I do know that. But you know good and well her heart. It's as good and pure as gold. And besides all that, I hate to see you girls here a fighin' like a couple of old alley cats."

Finally, she paused to take a breath. Carla was definitely not what I needed right now, but I had no choice. "Look, Carla," I began. "I know you mean well. No one could be a better friend to Susan than you, but this is really something the two of us have to work out."

"Lord have mercy, girl, when did ya'll ever sit down, and, as you say, 'work things out'? Now you listen to me. Susan needs you. You are the only one left with a lick of sense when it comes to that family. If you're not around to put a stop to it, she'll give Angie and those grandkids everything that's left, little by little. And then what'll she have? Now, I know what you're gonna say, 'nothing but a couple of run-down houses, a farm running out of water, a ton of bills, and taxes she can't pay.' But you know as well as I do there's your family's blood, sweat, and tears in that land and if you're around—"

"Carla!" I tried to break into her lecture.

"Now you just be quiet, you hear? I know what I'm a talkin' about, so you just be quiet now—"

"Carla... Carla! Carla, stop! There's one thing you don't understand. As much as you think she needs my help, she doesn't want it, understand? She doesn't want my help."

"Oh, for heaven's sake, you're not going to listen to that, are you?"

"I'm not doing her any good. All I do is provide something for her to bounce off of. First it was her husband, Hugh, then it was Mother, then Mack, and now me. As long as she has us to be the target of her anger and frustration, she won't turn it around and place the blame back where it belongs. As long as she's blaming somebody else, she doesn't have to take responsibility for her own decisions with the kids and money. How she looked the other way when Angie and Hilario were swindling our mother out of money right and left. It's not all her fault, I know that, but she has to quit blaming everybody and everything else."

Carla pushed herself up from the chair and clomped over to the sink to add water to her glass of ice cubes. Amazingly, she seemed to be considering what I just said, so I forged ahead. "Please understand. Don't think I haven't thought about everything you said. I have. But it's time for her to grow up and go it alone."

There. I said it.

Carla leveled her gaze at me, her blue eyes blazing. "And you know, missy, you know what's bound to happen?"

"I know we can't continue to play this game forever. I have to deal out and be done with it, for my own good and for my family's, as well as for my sister and her family."

Plopping down heavily into the creaking chair, she sighed loudly, puffing out her cheeks. "Well, all I can say is I hope you know what you're doin'. You do know, I hope, that land is a limited resource – just like Buzz and your daddy always preached about – once the land belongs to someone else, it's gone for good, and besides it's bound to be all used up one of these days if you're not here to see it's managed like your daddy used to do, and then I think you'll be sorry you walked away from it."

I didn't know what to say. As I collected my thoughts, I noticed Carla's face soften, and I could see tears welling up in her eyes. "Oh, damn it to hell," she moaned. "What I'm a really sayin' is I'll miss you. I already do. I mean, I miss everybody – all the Mihlbauers, your grandparents, Mimi, Jacob, your parents, Carl and Toogie, and Mack – the whole damn family, and my ornery ol' Buzz, plus all the other folks that raised us and loved us all, no matter whether we were family or not. I miss all the stories and cruising Dip Street and goin' to the drive-in at the Dairy Queen for Cokes. Oh hell, I even miss the party lines and everyone knowing everybody's business. Now all these kids have their heads buried in their cellphones and videogames. Lordy, what happened to us? Huh? What happened?"

She wiped her eyes on her shirt tail. I got up, leaned over, and gave her a hug. She smelled like Carla always smelled, a pungent combination of fried bacon and Vick's VapoRub.

226

"I know," I said. "I know. I miss them too. All of them."

She hugged me back, then pulled away as if embarrassed by her own emotions. She fumbled for the wadded Kleenex in her pocket and loudly blew her nose. Then, picking up her sweaty ol' Stetson, with the sides turned up, she whipped it on her head and pushed herself away from the table. "Well, I gotta be goin'. I said what I came to say. That's all I can do. I feel better for it. I'll be praying for you, even though I hardly go to church anymore, if you can believe that. I tried ever' one of 'em in town, and none of 'em seems to match what I believe, so now it's just between me and God. So, anyway, I'll be prayin' for both of you, just like Florie Barnes used to do. Remember that? She used to always say to folks, 'I'll just be praying that Jesus will just plain ol' bless the socks right off your feet.'"

No matter how much she scolded, Carla always made me smile. I gave her another quick hug. She was unique and I loved her for it. "Come on, Doc," she called to her goofy ol' retriever. "You and me gotta get to work. We done all we can do here."

Doc rose up on arthritic knees and followed Carla out to the rusty Olds. "So, when is it you're a takin' off from here? I'm askin' 'cause I could give you a ride up to the airport if that sister of yours is still hissin' and spittin' like a wet hen."

"Would you?" I asked. "Lyle has offered too, but I haven't spoken with him lately, so between the two of you, surely we can work out something. I'll be leaving Friday. By then, I should have done all I can do here. I'm anxious to get home. I've been gone over three weeks."

"Well, I'll be glad to help you out, but I still don't see why you prefer bein' up there with all those Yankees."

To Carla and others, the term 'Yankee' implied someone who looked down their noses at Texans. But this time, Carla had a twinkle in her eye, and I knew she was purposely trying to get under my skin. "Carla Crowder," I said, "You know good and well we're Cheeseheads in Wisconsin. You know, Midwesterners, who always take hot dishes to church suppers. You can't be too pretentious when you're carrying a tuna casserole to a potluck or driving in a blizzard up to Green Bay for a Packer game."

She gave me one of her crooked smiles. "Ya'll be good now." Doc jumped clumsily into the passenger seat, and he and Carla took off for town. As I watched them disappear in a cloud of dust, I glanced down at my phone. I had a message from Stu. The meeting was set for Wednesday morning at 9:00.

All of this was coming too fast. I knew we had to divide up the land. It just wasn't possible for Susan and me to work together. But selling my part to Skeeter? That seemed almost a betrayal of the unwritten family rules. One moment, I was convinced it was a good idea, and just when I thought my mind was made up, I second-guessed it. At least all we definitely had to decide on Wednesday was the land division, so I still had some time.

My strong desire to get back home was all I could think of right now. So, the following day, I arranged for a moving pod to transport a few items back to Wisconsin. There was a small oak table, my mother's wooden childhood highchair, a rocking chair that belonged to Noona's mother, my great-grandmother, plus my mother's hope chest containing embroidered linens and hats she wore in the 1950s. I opened the beautiful, old, steamer trunk and realized the family Bible was now lying at the bottom, wrapped in my grandmother's shawl. This was the Conroy bible and it needed to stay near where my great-grandparents settled the prairie so many years before. Maybe I could give it to a museum – an artifact representing the family history of the homesteaders. Gently, I laid it on the table of top of a few old photos I planned to save.

When the truck showed up and was loaded, I surveyed what was left. Carefully, I filed the paperwork for the trust in the large file cabinet, placing it above the drawer holding my great-grandmother's sterling silver. I would be returning in late September to sign the final papers to dissolve the trust, but for now, I had done all I could do. Before the meeting, I needed to talk to Susan again. Even though I told her about it during our confrontation in her backyard, she probably thought I would change my mind. I dreaded talking to her, but it wouldn't be right to spring it on her at the meeting.

Before I did that, I needed some moral support. I had to involve my sons, and I remembered my promise to call Emily who was spending the summer in Wyoming. I would tell her about the reunion she missed and hope she didn't mind listening to the next chapter of a long-time friend's family dilemma.

She didn't disappoint me. After hearing about her wildlife adventures in Yellowstone and catching her up on all the reunion news I could still remember, I asked for her input about the land.

"Emily," I began. "Can I ask for your opinion? I can't work with Susan any longer. She seems to resent anything I do to try and help her, and we disagree about every single decision that has to do with the farm or the trust. I'm thinking about bailing out…"

She was quiet for a minute, thoughtful as usual. "So, you're saying you want to divide everything up, or do you want to give it up completely?"

"Both, I guess. Oh, I don't know. I know I want to divide it, and I'm on the fence about selling my part to Skeeter even though he's willing to give me the appraisal price." I paused. "Carla thinks I'm crazy to even think about it."

"Of course she does," replied Emily, "but you're not Carla. The town and land around it are all she knows. You have a broader perspective. I think you have to do what you think is best and what is right for you both."

"Susan will never think selling the farm is best or right. To her, it is the Holy Grail – something beyond measure – something sacred…"

Emily paused again. "And what do you think?"

I sighed, considering her question. "I think I need to get out of Dodge and let her be the boss of her own property. That's the only way she will take responsibility. Otherwise, it's always my fault, no matter what happens. But selling the farm…that unearths so much more."

"Dally, you have the answer right there. This is what you've been moving toward for a long time – now the door is open, but you're afraid to walk through it. I say, go ahead, race for the exit, and don't look back."

"But I do have feelings for this place – strong feelings, since so much of it is wrapped up in family and childhood memories." I let out a deep sigh. "I would also feel some guilt about deciding to sell."

"Well," Emily continued, "you will for a while. It's part of the process. Just let yourself feel that. Lean into it." She paused. "I'll check on you in a couple of weeks and see how you are doing, okay?"

"So, you really think this is the right thing to do?" I asked.

"I think you just answered that for yourself, remember?"

"You know, though, I'm really not a Mihlbauer…"

"Look, living and loving together for a lifetime is what makes family, not our DNA. You know that." The uplift to her voice gave her away. I could almost see her smiling, granting her permission. I thanked her and promised to reconnect in a couple of weeks. As I pressed the red button on my cellphone, I offered up a small prayer for her advice. How blessed I was to have such friends. As she knew so well, decisions like this were never easy, especially when family and land was involved. She gave me a shot of strength. I now felt strong enough to call Susan. I was relieved, though, when the answering machine picked up the call and I could leave a message with the impersonal voice who answered on the other end of the line.

"Susan, it's me. I just want to remind you of our meeting tomorrow with Stu and Andy. It's at 9:00. Uh…and uh…well, like I said, I'm planning on following the trust and dividing up the land like Skeeter suggested. Okay? Anyway, see you in morning. Bye-bye."

Chapter Twenty-four

Home Again

Since I hadn't heard from her, I didn't know if Susan would show up for the meeting the next day or not. When I arrived, she wasn't there. Stu met me in the reception area and abruptly led me back to his office. "Okay," he said. "Let's get this done. Here are the papers for you to look over. I need to make a quick phone call and then we can talk about them." He set aside another stack of papers. "Now these here are for Susan. Same as yours. If she comes in before I get back, just have her look them over too. I'll be back as soon as I can get this client off the phone."

He seemed impatient today, and I didn't blame him. He and Andy both put in a lot of time just watching us quibble about what should have been fairly straightforward. I fervently hoped Susan wouldn't throw a wrench into things today.

I took a deep breath and looked up. On Stu's wall was a Carl Smith painting I only glanced at before. Now I looked more deeply. It was a western vista with a huge sky, typical of work of artists in the era when western landscapes were popular. The sky took up most of the canvas. Huge thunderheads gave off a purple glow so typical of the violent storms in this part of the country. There were distant mountains in the background, and in the foreground, appearing small and vulnerable, were two riders on horseback. Today, the painting spoke to me of the power and magnificence of nature and of the insignificance of humans in the total scheme of things. The land would survive just as it had in its many permutations. Humans would come and go, trying to control what they thought was theirs, but in the end...

I was deep into my reverie, the legal documents unread, when I heard Stu's secretary in the outer office greeting Susan who breezed in amid a flurry of apologies.

"Well, now, we're just glad you're here now," Tammy, the secretary, replied soothingly in her soft West Texas drawl, showing Susan in.

"Morning," I greeted her. "These papers are for you to look over. Stu had to take a call, but he'll be right back."

She didn't look at me or greet me but picked up the papers and pulled her glasses out of her purse. The long awkward silence that followed seemed louder than her complaints. Both of us read in silence. Finally, she sighed loudly, pushed back the chair, and threw her reading glasses across the table. "None of this makes any sense. Why doesn't Stu just get his butt in here and tell us what it says. I don't have time to figure it out."

I looked up from my own reading. "Yes," I said. "It's pretty dense... Stu oughta be back in a minute." I hesitated. "Do you want me to tell you what I think it says?"

"No. I do not want to hear about anything you think I need to know. I'm waiting five minutes, and then I'm leaving."

Please, God, help this be over soon, I prayed silently just as Stu burst into the room.

He didn't waste any time. "Good morning, Susan. Have you had a chance to look over those papers?"

"None of them make any sense to me, but I guess that doesn't matter."

He was at a loss for words as Susan glared at him across the table. "Let me see if I can explain things," he said, weary lines seeming to grow around his mouth. "Basically this is a draft of a legal document, required by law, dissolving the trust. The effective date is September 11, 2013. It divides up all your parents' property between you and your sister. You receive 45%, and she gets 55%. So that means you get your house in town, the farmhouse section with the farmhouse, and three-fourths of the Sutter section. You also get your percentage of the old duplex, and the lots in town. Dalinda gets the J.R. section, Section 12 which is actually two-thirds of a section, the McMurry half-section, and one-fourth of the Sutter section."

Susan stared blankly at Stu. "So, that's it?"

"Pretty much. Do you have questions?"

"No. What good would my questions do? It's been decided."

Clearing his throat, Stu looked directly at Susan and said evenly, "We followed the trust agreement, Susan, just like your folks wanted. But it is a draft. You could theoretically divide things differently, but this includes almost all the property you wanted. Dividing it in a different way would get mighty complicated."

I let out a long breath, not aware I'd been holding it. Stu's words seemed to vindicate me.

Susan looked down, staring at the table. Cradling her trembling chin in her hands, she replied in a broken voice, "Daddy would never have wanted this. Never. Not my daddy. He would never have done this to me."

I fumbled through my purse and found a Kleenex which I offered to her. Grabbing it out of my hand, she continued to sob softly. I knew what she was probably thinking. She was our father's favorite and as a little girl was able to charm him into giving her what she wanted. That little girl was still in the room, expecting to be rescued from the words of the trust. Even though she was getting the best farmland, plus the farmhouse, her portion was still less than mine. She was convinced this was unfair and all of us were against her.

Again, I looked up at the painting above Stu's desk. The sky appeared darker, a deep purple, creating a feeling of gloom. Stu looked on helplessly. When neither of us responded, he continued quietly, "Well then, if all this seems to be in order, I will add all the required legal descriptions. Then, Dalinda, when you come back in September, you and Susan can sign it and I'll get 'er put to bed for you."

I pulled my eyes away from the painting but avoided looking at my sister. "Okay," I said. "That works for me."

For several long minutes, we waited for Susan to reply. Instead, she sat still, her head buried in Kleenex. Stu and I exchanged glances. Finally, he snapped his folder shut decisively, stood up, and pulled off his glasses. "I think that should do it, ladies. Unless there are any other questions, I'll show you to the door. I think Tammy already left for lunch."

I rose unsteadily, realizing I was shaking. "We appreciate all your work on this, Stu, and also on Mack's estate," I managed to say.

"Glad to help you out. Now, you have a safe trip home and I'll see you in September."

I glanced over my shoulder as I left the office and saw Susan gathering up her papers and purse, stumbling after me into the outer room. Suddenly, we found ourselves out on the hot sidewalk, blinded by the sun.

I turned to her. "I have the key to the file cabinet to give you. I forgot all about it yesterday…" She walked away from me and got into her van.

"Here," I said, following her. "I'm putting this into your safekeeping. All the farm files are there, plus papers from both Mother and Daddy. I tried to organize them as best as I could…"

She took the key, looking at me with both sadness and deep resentment.

"I'll call you tomorrow before I leave," I said.

Without responding, she started the van and drove down the street.

It would be wrong to say I had no regrets or second thoughts. Severing this tie with my sister felt a bit like death. Had I made a mistake? Should I have divided it all 50/50, despite my parents' wishes? Should I have insisted we keep the whole thing and then moved down to manage it? None of these choices seemed right, either, but there was an unsettled feeling nagging at me too. I knew I would never let my sister, or her children and grandchildren, go completely down the drain, so to speak, yet on the other hand, I knew Susan needed to have the freedom to make her own choices and mistakes and deal with the consequences. But this was not easy. And I did wonder how Mack would have handled it if I had been the one to die.

As it turned out, Lyle drove me to the airport. At the last minute, Carla called to tell me she had a sick calf she needed to attend to. "Now, I'm so sorry I just can't make it, you know these little calves of mine, I just baby 'em like I'm their mama cow, and if I run off, no wonder what'll happened in this hot weather and all…but I tell you what, when you come back in September, I'll sure pick you up, so don't you go bothering anybody else, you hear me now? So, you take care now." *"Click."* With her usual abrupt ending to phone conversations, I found myself talking into a dead phone. With Carla, there was never the formalities of a goodbye. I was actually relieved Carla couldn't drive me. She was the opposite of Susan. She drove about ten miles over the speed limit, straddling the lanes on the expressway, talking nonstop. Lyle was a safer option.

Still haunted by finding my brother dead and alone that January night, Lyle wanted to talk about Mack on the way to Amarillo. "I figure maybe his blood pressure dropped suddenly, since there was a leak in his aorta. Then I think he just fell out of his chair and landed with his head on the trashcan. That's what I think… I don't imagine he felt a thing – he just went like that." Lyle snapped his fingers with his free hand. "I want to think, at least, that's just the way it was."

"I bet he did go like that," I replied, trying to help. "I know I'd rather go quickly than linger half-alive in a nursing home. I'm just so glad it was you, and not Susan, who found him." I paused, reflecting on that winter day. "I wonder, though, if the meeting we had that morning before it happened had anything to do with it. That's when we told him we wanted to manage the farm with him as equal partners. That was hard for him to hear. He worked long and hard to pull the farm from the brink after Angie almost sank the whole thing with what she did to Mother..."

"Oh, I don't know," Lyle replied. "I had lunch with him right after that meeting, remember? He seemed fine then. Of course, it probably was later that day, into the evening, when it happened. So, I guess we'll never know. There sure won't never be anyone like him, though, that's for sure."

I looked over at the man beside me who seemed to still be grieving. "I miss him too," I said. For a while, we drove along in silence, each thinking our own thoughts about Mack and his life and death.

After a while, Lyle spoke up, "So, what's going on with the farm now? Did you and your sister ever figure that out?"

"Yes. We're dividing it up. I'll take part, and she'll take part. It's best that way. It's gotten to the point that I really can't work with Susan."

"Oh," replied Lyle, "I get that. Mack felt just like that too toward the end."

"So, you think I'm doing the right thing?"

"All I know is that if there had been any way Mack could have avoided conflict with Susan, he would have tried it. And then he was bound by the trust, you know. He had to follow that. He'd tell her that, though, and she'd cry and scream and just flat lose it, and he was at a loss to know what to do. It sure did bother him. Ate at him every damn day."

I knew Mack had problems with Susan and her demands, but it must have been worse than I thought. Lyle saw him every day and was the one person Mack confided in. If Lyle said it was true, then it was true. I felt greater appreciation for my brother than I ever had while he was alive. Now it was too late to tell him.

As we neared the airport, our conversation turned to neutral topics again – mutual friends and the weather. It was as though the heavy stuff had to stay in the car rather than be exposed to the hot August sun. We drove up to the departure gates, and Lyle jumped out to help me with my bags. "I'll see you again in September," I began. "I have to come back to finish up a few things and sign the final papers for Mack's estate and the trust." For some reason, I couldn't bring myself to tell him I was thinking of selling my part to Skeeter.

Lyle enveloped me in a bear hug and then I was alone in the impersonal confines of an airport with its familiar electronic boards and bustling travelers all eager to be in a different place. This, to me, always seemed a holding area – a halfway point between comings and goings – neither here, nor there. It perfectly fitted my mood as I stood, staring out the wide windows into the blue sky hazy with August heat.

****

Within a few days, I was caught up in another life – one in stark contrast to the one I left behind in Texas. The young woman who was my pet sitter seemed reluctant to leave and return to her parents' basement, but I was in no mood for small talk and eager to reestablish my place in the household order. My dog ran around in circles, barking wildly, while my cat turned her back and completely ignored me for the first week. It was so good to look out at the green trees and grass and to have internet and T.V. Most of all, it was so nice to have a few peaceful days to do nothing but sort through the mail.

The contrast between my home now and the home of my childhood could not have been greater. Here, I felt cozy and protected by the tall green of the trees and serenity of my suburban neighborhood. When on the Tumbleweed farm, I felt more exposed but also more in touch with something eternal. The scope of the world in Texas was as far as the distant horizon. Here I could only see as far as my backyard. Here my world was under control; there it was unmanageable chaos.

I had a busy August ahead. Continuing a long tradition, I met 15 long-time friends at a lovely Northern Wisconsin lake cottage where we spent the week swimming, hiking, kayaking, sailing, and sharing laughter and heartaches with one another. Many of us were educators who first coalesced into a group when we attended a church circle many years before. Together we weathered death, divorce, cancer, caring for aging relatives, and raising children. Our lives were interwoven, stitched together with wit and wisdom, tears and laughter. Mostly we ate great food and enjoyed the water in a spirit of camaraderie.

After 23 years, we had the Up-North trip down to a science. Some of the group were already up at their summer homes. The rest of us crammed into someone's van or sedan with our coolers full of food, bags of clothes, books, swimsuits, sunblock, and memories of our previous trips. It was an early departure, and as usual, I was late and greeted with the inevitable scolding.

"Hurray! Dalinda is here! Now we can finally leave!"

"Very funny," I growled. "I never can figure out why we have to be here at 7:30. What difference does it make if we get to Mary's at 11:30 or 12:30? We're on vacation."

"She's expecting us at 11:30. If we leave right now," June looked down at her watch, "we should be there at 11:38, but we have to get going."

There was a flurry of repacking the trunks, complaints about uncooperative seatbelts, and then we were off.

"Excellent. We are leaving at 7:43. We should only arrive about five minutes late."

I sank down in my seat and glared out the window.

Sheryl spoke up, "We are going to stop for coffee, aren't we? I mean, we always do…"

"I'll need to use the bathroom before long, so we'd better," this was from Amy.

Now I spoke up, deciding to attempt congeniality, "So, who has dinner tonight?"

"Well," said Beth, "look at your schedule. June has it all written up for us. I sure hope whoever has it remembered that I can't eat nuts. Someone always forgets."

"Betty is allergic to gluten now," added Amy. "I hope everyone remembers that. And I think that Jackie is low salt. It used to be a lot easier when we could just pop any old thing in our mouths and not worry about it. I mean, I really try to eat low carb. I hope everyone knows that, and Becky doesn't eat onions."

We drove in silence for a few miles. Then June called to me from the front seat, "Dalinda, where have you been all summer? I've hardly seen you."

"Don't you remember? I was in Texas, closing out my brother's estate and trying to figure out what to do with all the things from four generations."

"Oh, that's right. That's where your sister is, right?"

"Uh huh."

Sheryl turned to me, her voice low and gentle, "So, what's going on there? Are things any better?"

I sighed deeply and shook my head. "It's one of those family situations that sounds like fiction, but it's very true and very complicated."

Now everyone was quiet, hoping I'd continue.

"Do you mind if we don't talk about it right now? I don't have the energy to go into it."

"Oh, no, no, of course not," said June, a bit too quickly and enthusiastically. "You need to get away from all that. But you know we are here for you if you want to vent."

Amy turned to look at me from the passenger seat. "After what you've already shared with us, I can't imagine it being worse."

There were murmurs of agreement. "I know. But it is." In the past, I shared much of the story with these long-time friends, but I was tired of thinking about it right now.

Sheryl, the peacemaker, picked up on my mood. "Okay, ladies, it's time to change the subject. I just hope we have great weather this year and can get in the lake and stay down on the dock. I think we all could use some sunshine and laughter—" Sometimes Sheryl was a bit too cheerful.

"Oh, I forgot to tell you," interrupted June. "My grandson made the varsity team for this fall. Isn't that super?"

Sheryl and I exchanged knowing looks that said, "Here we go again."

It always started out like this. After all, there was a 20-year age span between the oldest and the youngest. Maxine was 80 and Deb was 60. Our personalities ranged from sweet and quiet to loud and outspoken and everything in between. We each were opinionated in our own way and insisted on claiming our territory.

We ranged from active sports enthusiasts to content couch potatoes. We included the chronically tardy to the always punctual. Among us were progressive activists and conservative traditionalists; there were the neat-as-a-pin and then those of us who stuffed the extra clutter in the oven as the doorbell rang. We were artists, writers, quilters, creative seamstresses, volleyball players, pickle-ball players, gourmet cooks, kayakers, bikers, swimmers, sailors; one of us who knew all the movie actors and songs of the 1940s and '50s, another who could call up all the camp songs of our childhood. We included mostly educators but also a professional musician, a travel agent, a stay-at-home mom, and someone we could always count on to pray, and another who always had a slightly off-color joke and cracked witty remarks.

After we gathered at Mary's, all 16 of us talking at once as we greeted with hugs, we sang our 'Oh' song. This was a tradition dating back to the group's beginning when someone suggested reviving the Johnny Appleseed song from church and Girl Scout camp, which started with 'Oh, the Lord is good to me, and so I thank the Lord for giving me the things I need, the sun and the rain and the apple trees...'

As soon as we warbled the final note, Becky spoke up, "So, you'll never guess what Ron said to me this week."

"Okay, what?" Beth asked as we all lined up with our plates, awaiting our turn for a helping of Mary's famous chicken salad.

"Well, I was working in the garden and I bent over to pull out a weed and he gave me a slap on the butt and said, 'Your butt is the size of a big ol' Weber Grill.'"

"What?" All of us turned to look at Becky. "He actually said that?" Now she really had our attention.

"What did you do?"

"You didn't let him get away with that, did you?"

Becky was in no hurry to finish her story, "So, Mary, does the salad have any onion in it?"

"I'm not telling until you finish your story," Mary shot back, pouring water into our glasses.

"Well, that night after we got in bed, Ron began to get real frisky. So, I turned over and gave him my sweetest smile. 'Oh, honey, this big ol' Weber grill isn't about to get all fired up for one puny little teeny weenie.'"

There was a split second of silence before we all burst out laughing. Then sweet Maxine spoke up, "Did you really say that, Becky?"

There was usually at least one of us who didn't get the joke or fell for Becky's teasing.

But the Northwoods worked its magic, our laughter drowning even the sound of the loons on the lake. Through humor and the grace of God, we again became sisters, forgetting and forgiving each other's quirks and faults and appreciating the uniqueness of each individual.

Why didn't this work with my own sister?

Chapter Twenty-five
Second Guesses

After this week of retreat, I returned to real life. I paid the bills and attended to a much-neglected garden. While I pulled weeds, I had lots of time to think about the Texas decisions. I had not heard from Susan. And perhaps it was guilt, but after another week passed, I decided to call my sister. No one answered, which was not unusual. I left a message, doubting she would call me back. But later that day, she did.

Dispensing with formalities, she got right to the point, "When are you coming back here?"

"My reservation is for the tenth."

"So, are you staying at the farmhouse?"

"No. I cleaned out the refrigerator, so I'll just go to the Select Inn and stay there a couple of days. I can handle two days there, I think."

The Select Inn was at one time a shiny new Best Western, but that was 25 years ago when the expressway came through west of town. The present owner dispensed with any pretense of niceties. As a result, the pressure in the shower was either full force or a small trickle – take your pick. The soap was the size of a large postage stamp and crumbled in your hand when you removed the waxy wrapper. Sheets and towels were of questionable cleanliness. But it was either that or the Select Inn, build shortly after World War II, with accoutrements to match. I continued, "My plan is to rent a car in Amarillo this time and sell Mack's old pickup."

The pickup was still a painful subject between us, and I realized I should have probably left out telling her that part of my plan.

"So, you're even taking that away from me, huh?"

"No, Susan," I replied. "When I sell it, you get half of the money. Remember, this is from Mack's estate. We each get 50% of that and the new pickup."

"Oh. Well, right now I can use the money." Oddly, there was no mention of her grandson needing a car. As I argued before, she needed the money. "You know," she continued, "you left a lot of stuff still in the farmhouse. I hope you're planning to clean that out."

I bit my tongue. How many days did I try to persuade her to help me make decisions about the items still in the farmhouse? "Well," I replied. "I will have about three days. I'll do as much as I can. Remember, though, we have to meet with Stu to finalize things so he can prepare all the paperwork to end the trust."

This time, there was only silence on her end of the line. I waited for a minute or so, then said, "All right, so I guess I'll see you on the tenth."

"Yep," she replied breezily. "Then you'll be through with me, I guess. You'll sell to Skeeter, and then Mihlbauer Farms will be no more."

"No," I replied. "If I sell to Skeeter, it is because he will care for the farm like Daddy did. But I am not through with you. You will always be my sister."

The screen on my cellphone went dark. She hung up. Our connection was broken.

In the days that followed, I spent time with my book-club friend, Joyce, who was all ears to hear about my reunion and the latest update on the chaos in my family. We usually talked while walking in a nearby park.

"I can't figure out why your sister is so upset. Even if you sell your part of the farm, why does that matter? And why doesn't she just sell her part too? It's not like the land is that valuable or anything."

"Joyce, I've told you before. When there is water, the land is very rich agricultural land. It's not worthless by any means."

"What about selling it for subdivisions? Wouldn't that be better?" I turned my back and rolled my eyes. No one here understood about our farmland. It was so different from Wisconsin farmland, not the kind you just subdivided and sold for homesites. Joyce, and many others here, had no idea what the land looked like. In their own way, they were just as provincial as my Texas friends. There was no real comprehension about the land or culture in a different region, even though we were living in the same country.

"Joyce, no one wants to buy a lot that's seven miles out in the country on flat grassland. Or, at least, very few people want that. We are talking about a whole different climate and geographic area here. And as far as my sister goes, the farm represents the family itself – our history, our heritage. It is a tangible reminder of our parents and grandparents and our childhood. That's the part she can't let go of." I paused as Joyce considered this, then continued, "As for me, I let go of my childhood years ago after my own children came along, and especially after I was divorced. That's when I realized all my childhood assumptions were holding me back. I mean, the boys and I always went back there to visit, and I still appreciated the hard work of my grandparents and parents, but our life was elsewhere. Anyway, what I'm trying to say is that, for me, it's not as hard as it is for Susan."

We reached the top of a hill and Joyce stopped to take a sip from her water bottle. She shook her head. "Well, it seems pretty silly to me. I mean, is it really worth that much? Does it provide her an income?"

There was a bench nearby and I sat down to give my little dog a drink of water. From here, we could look down on a cluster of neat homes with professional-looking landscaping. So different from where I grew up... I thought about Joyce's question. "If it were just my sister, she could make it work, but it can't possibly support her plus 11 other people."

"Right," answered Joyce. "That's what I mean. It makes no sense to me. She could just sell the farm and then she could support all those kids and grandkids."

"Yes, Joyce, you're probably right, but don't you see? She is not coming from a rational place. This is all tied up with her emotions."

Joyce looked at me blankly. This was clearly not something she identified with. My friend made decisions based on facts. Emotions, for her, just cluttered up clear thinking.

I was tired of talking about all of this. "Let's turn around, okay? We can go back to my place and order a pizza or something. I want to hear about what's been going on here since I've been gone."

Chapter Twenty-six
Book Club and Carla

The next weeks went by much too fast. There was so much I neglected at home while I was gone, and still a bit of summer to enjoy. I was able to make Joyce happy and attend our August book-club meeting. Since all my book-club friends knew, or thought they knew, about the problems I was dealing with in Texas, they wanted to know what was decided and my rationale for dividing and selling the farm. Their responses and advice were as varied as my friends, and in the middle of a rather disinterested discussion of Mrs. Lincoln's Dressmaker, they were more than happy to offer their opinions.

As we sat around the coffee table, sipping wine, our hostess, Joan, spoke first, "Well, I just can't help feeling sorry for your sister. I can't imagine trying to raise all those kids. It seems like she needs all the help from you she can get."

"I really feel the same way," replied Louise. "Sounds to me like you are throwing her to the lions in her own backyard."

"Well, now, wait a minute," countered Kate. "Hasn't Susan taken all kinds of money and given it to that crazy daughter of hers? I'd think you'd have to put a stop to that sometime or other."

"Yes. That's what happened and what I'm trying to do," I replied rather defensively.

"Frankly, I think you should just sell that farm and take your sister on a long cruise. Bet she hasn't had a vacation in who knows how long. Aren't you getting all kinds of money from selling out?"

"It's not worth that much, is it? I always thought from what you said, it was just a little, old, dirt farm."

"Wait," I replied. "It's a pretty complicated situation. I will get a nice chunk of money, but I've already decided what I'll do with it."

I stared at the cracker dripping with cheese dip. Where had this definitive answer come from? Somewhere in my subconscious, my decision was made. Even though I considered the plan I now spoke of with such certainty, I didn't realize until now that selling the farm was really what I wanted to do. Time seemed to slow down. I looked around and saw all my book-club friends staring at me, waiting for my answer.

"I've decided to pay off all my sons' student loans and then let them pay me instead of the banks, or whatever. I'll charge them a low interest rate, and then I'll set up a trust with the money, and it will go toward my grandchildren's college education."

For one sweet moment, they were all quiet, carrot sticks in midair.

Then Joyce chimed in, "What the hell you want to do that for? Why don't you use it to enjoy the rest of your life? That's sure what I'd do."

"I'm going out to see my daughter in California and I believe in college. Did you know that my grandson is going to grad school to study Arabic? Can you imagine?" Connie always turned the conversation back toward whatever was at the top of her mind at the moment.

I pretended I hadn't heard Connie and answered Joyce, "It's important to me that I use the money to do something that my parents would have approved of. So, this is what I've decided."

"I plan to go to his graduation in May, though, no matter if he is going on to school."

Ignoring Connie's comment, Joyce grabbed a handful of nuts from the coffee-table bowl, took a long sip of her wine, and looked at me. "Well, suit yourself. I just always had the idea you just grew a little wheat and so forth. You think you can find someone who wants to buy it?"

I poured myself another glass of wine and turned to her. "I already have a buyer, Joyce. He's the man who rents our land already. He's anxious to get it. And, for your information, it's not exactly a 'little bit of wheat.' We're talking about two square miles of farmland."

Joyce's eyes got big and she set her glass on the table as she considered this. "Well, excuse me. I just had this idea…"

Connie continued to discuss her grandson as the rest of us focused on my farmland dilemma. "I think he'll have a B.S. degree by then, but I really need to ask him next time I talk to him. It is a little confusing."

"So, how does your sister feel about that?" asked Louise.

"Just about how you'd expect her to feel. She's really mad at me and also sad about it, I think."

"And you're still going ahead with it?" she asked.

"That's my plan. I think so," I said, suddenly feeling not at all sure I was doing the right thing.

"Well, far be it from me to interfere," continued Louise, "It just seems a mite unfair to me, considering that your sister has been there all this time…"

"Now, what do you know about it, Louise?" It was Joyce coming to my defense. "I don't think we know the half of it, and so I say we all just mind our own business."

Louise spoke up after swallowing a hefty bite of cheese and cracker, "You're a fine one to talk, Joyce. Nobody in town loves knowing everybody's business more than you, and you know it."

There was a twinkle in Louise's eye, but it was lost on Joyce. Red welts began appearing on her neck and she swallowed hard. She didn't like being caught at her own game. "Well, I meant…well, you know that I didn't mean anything by it… It's just that I thought—"

"Oh dear," said Joan, our hostess, interrupting Joyce. "Well, now I'm sorry I even brought it up. Let's just all take a deep breath and think about the business at hand, Mrs. Lincoln's Dressmaker, okay?"

"I think I'll probably wear that black-and-white dress I got last year at Macy's."

We all turned to look at Connie. "What are you talking about, Connie?" asked Louise.

"His graduation. My grandson's graduation. That's the dress I'm wearing. Weren't you all talking about dresses?"

So much for the advice of my book-club friends. A few days passed as I tried to be content with my decision, but I decided to get Sheryl's opinion, my long-time friend and part of the Up-North group. Her own family was sometimes challenging, and she knew the secrets of being a good listener. Besides that, she knew how to keep everyone else's business under her hat. It didn't hurt, either, that I knew more than almost anyone about her, since we had both been single-mother divorcees together a few decades before. Because she knew all about the background of the farm, including my niece's swindling that bilked my mother out of most of the farm's money, she didn't need a synopsis to weigh in on the guilty feelings I wanted to dump into her lap.

I slid into the booth at the little coffee shop and she greeted me with an understanding smile. "Well," I said. "Just about the time I thought I overcame all the baggage of my childhood, here comes another load. I'm in the middle of a guilt trip about my farm decision. The intellectual part of me knows I'm doing the best thing for everyone, but the emotional side is screaming at me to reconsider."

"So, you're questioning your decision-making?"

"Exactly."

"Well, I understand that. You're dealing with a lot…your brother's death, the disposition of the farm and the houses. All of that. I think something would be wrong with you if you didn't second-guess your choice."

We both ordered coffee and she continued, "Play it out in your head. What will happen if you just continue on the same path as before?"

"Oh, heavens. I guess I would be run ragged trying to deal with all the farm matters from home or traveling down to deal with them there. I don't think I have the stamina for that anymore."

"Okay, what else?"

"Angie will keep on grinding her mother down until she gets whatever she wants at the moment and then I'll have to step in and stop it, like Mack did, because if that continues to happen, we can't pay the bills much less have anything left over as profit for either of us to live on."

"Wait. Wait, wait, wait! You are telling me that if you divide the land, you would still feel responsible for your sister? Wouldn't she have her part and you have yours? Why is that your responsibility?"

"I know Susan. She would still lay on the guilt trip and I would have to constantly be fending off the requests for help."

"So, you are saying that you'd feel responsible and, in the end, Susan would be even worse off than she is now?"

"That's what it looks like to me."

"So, do you really think that's an option?"

"I don't know…"

"Sounds like you've decided to divide up the land but you're still trying to figure out whether to sell it or not, right? So, even if you each have your own land and the guy who rents it still does what he's doing now, you'd still feel like you were too close to it?"

"Well, yes, I guess. Mainly, I'd just still have the responsibility of dealing with it all. I don't know… I guess I'm just tired of it all. I am selfish enough to just want some time to myself."

"So, after teaching middle school for 30 years, plus teaching summer school and working at various other jobs to make ends meet, plus getting your master's and raising three sons alone, you think you need a rest?" Sheryl, more than most people, understood where I was coming from.

"Yes," I said sheepishly. "I do."

"Well, I can't imagine why."

"I know that I should just feel grateful for the way Mother and Daddy set up the trust, but Susan's life is so difficult compared to mine."

"Is that your fault or your responsibility?"

"Well, I don't know, is it? Am I my sister's keeper?"

"Do you think she wants you to be her keeper?"

For a minute, I considered this provocative question, then continued, "I know she doesn't want that. She let me know in no uncertain terms that my advice is awful, and she doesn't appreciate my help unless it is just exactly done the way she wants it done."

"So, she's put you in a double bind?"

"I guess so, if you put it like that."

"So, where does that leave you?" Sheryl asked, sipping her coffee.

"Back where I started, I guess. Still feeling guilty but knowing I'm probably doing the right thing."

Sheryl sat with her chin in her hand and looked up at me from across the table. "You know," she finally said, "our generation is one that was still raised with a heavy sense of duty, and I think we translate that into guilt."

Sheryl chuckled. "I still feel bad if I wear white shoes after Labor Day. That was an unwritten rule when I was growing up."

"Oh yes! We did have the rules, didn't we? Okay now, you've listened to me enough. What's going on with you and the grandsons?"

Our conversation turned to other things, and I left feeling better. But a few days later, my doubts returned. I always talked to myself, but in the past few years, this habit got worse. Fortunately, as long as I wasn't saying things like, 'walk,' 'outside,' or 'car,' my dog ignored me, and I went on chatting amiably with myself. When it became a problem was when I went to the grocery store. I began to notice other shoppers quickly steering their carts into other aisles before I realized that I was discussing whether I needed butter or yogurt. But today as I shopped, the argument went something like this: "I think she'll be fine after everything is over and she realizes that she has two houses and a big chunk of land that belongs to her. She can do anything she wants with it. Maybe she'll even decide to sell out to Skeeter and then have plenty of money."

I plucked a jar of applesauce off the shelf as I smiled at the lady looking at me suspiciously. "Of course, she may not have enough money to keep going. Then she might completely fall apart, and it would be all my fault."

By now, I was leaning over the frozen chicken breasts, trying to convince them I was doing the right thing. "Then what would happen to the kids? It's not the kids' fault. And I can see why Susan is mad at me. I don't blame her."

The large man with the two small children gave me an alarmed glance as I looked up from the dairy case where I was interspersing my argument with trying to remember if I needed milk. "But I have to get out of her way, don't I?"

I decided to move to a less-crowded aisle. "I don't know. I just don't know…" Now I was in an aisle where all the hair product was confusing me. I didn't need more confusion.

I pushed my cart toward frozen foods, pretending to care about the price of mixed vegetables. "Yes. That's what I decided. I'm sure that is for the best. I have to think of myself and my kids and grandkids, not just hers. Yes. That is the best decision."

Strolling toward the beverage aisle, I successfully avoided running into a harried-looking mom with three young children. I gave her one of my understanding smiles as I began to vacillate again. Of course, I could have split the land with her 50/50. I could have done that… But that wasn't what the trust says. That wasn't what my parents wanted. No. It wasn't…

I headed for checkout with the argument unresolved, with most items on my forgotten list still sitting on the shelves and with other shoppers now actively avoiding me. But when the friendly lady ringing up my purchases asked me about my day, I reverted back to semi-sane, paid for the groceries, and continued the argument in the car on the way home.

A few days later, Lyle called to ask if I needed a ride from the airport. By then, I decided that I really could not stomach the Choice Lodge for even three nights. Instead, I would rent a car at the airport and get a room at the Holiday Inn Express on the expressway, then drive back and forth. It was a 30-mile trip, but at this point, it was worth it. After explaining my plan to Lyle, I realized I left Carla thinking I needed to be picked up from the airport too. I would need to call her. Phone calls with Carla were not exactly my favorite thing, but I had no choice.

Since Carla always looked at her caller ID, she didn't even bother to say hello. "Well, I was wondering when I would hear from you. You better get back down here and talk to your sister; she's a mess and then all of those kids are actin' up, plus Angie's doing her usual pestering for money. It's just about more than a body can handle, I'll tell ya that, and I don't know what the truth is, but people 'round here sayin' you're a selling out to Skeeter, heaven knows, he's a good farmer, but that land's been in your family since before Moses was born, and I don't see as how you can just sell it like that."

"Carla? Carla? Wait a minute. Carla? Could you please just be quiet a minute? I have to tell you something, okay?"

"So, what 'cha talkin' about?" For a short second, Carla was silent.

"I'm talking about that I don't need a ride to the airport since I'm renting a car."

"Well, that'll cost you a bundle. You can always use the Billy Graham-mobile if you want. You know I always have it here for whoever needs it."

"Thanks, Carla. That's okay. I have so many things to do, and besides that, I've decided to stay in the Holiday Inn Express south of Amarillo."

"Why in the world are you stayin' there? Susan told me you were a stayin' at Select Inn, though why you'd do that instead of going over to Geneva's at Lariat Motel is beyond me."

"I know, Carla, but I really need some quiet time while I'm there. You know how noisy it is at the motels, with all those workers from the line for the wind turbines staying there."

"Well, honey, don't you live alone? I figure you get all the quiet time you need. But now, I'm not sayin' a word, it's not my business, now, is it? But I am tellin' you that you need to make up with your sister. I'm not sayin' anything about what might have happened, but I do know the gossip around town, and what everybody's sayin'."

"Well, thanks for letting me know. I tell you what, I'll give you a call soon as I get to town, and we can hash this whole thing out. Would that be okay?"

"Well, you know me, honey. I'm just glad to do whatever you say, but now don't forget about what I tol' you now."

In true Carla form, the phone went dead. She didn't bother with goodbyes either.

Before I knew it, my time at home was over. It was September and I was aboard my sixth flight to Amarillo in nine months. I settled into my seat and again began processing the farm decisions. After several conversations with Chris, Pete, and Matt, my scattered-to-four-corners sons, I felt more comfortable with my decisions. These young men of mine were each so unique. If my job as a mom was to raise independent sons, I deserved an A+. Not one of them thought like either of their brothers. In fact, they actively disagreed about most things, but in my decision about the farm, they were of one mind. "Mom, sell it. That's the best thing for everybody." They were disgusted with their cousin, Angie, and convinced that I would have a much more peaceful retirement without having to deal with fickle weather, the U.S.D.A., and my sister.

Yes, I thought. Yes. They are right. I will just sell it all to Skeeter and be done with it. But then…something held me back. Some strange, annoying, little voice in the back of my mind, or soul, that still wanted to keep a piece of that dry Texas prairie.

So, after several nights of tossing and turning in my sleep, I decided I would keep a quarter section of my family's land on the Sutter section.

Susan would have the other three-fourths, giving her 480 acres while my portion was 160. This percentage was already part of the division of property, it was just that now I would keep this part rather than selling it to Skeeter. The Sutter Section was farther away from the farmhouse than the other property, and also the land with the poorest water supply. Much of it was original grassland, which was never plowed, the roots of the short-stemmed prairie grass reaching down several feet to find the precious water. Some of the acreage was planted in either dry-land wheat or cotton, depending on the year. Of all the family farmland, this was the poorest quality. Skeeter knew this and was not interested in purchasing it. So, the best farmland would go to him and I would retain this humble quarter-section to remind me of the hard work and sacrifice of my parents and grandparents. And, if I was honest, keeping it would also alleviate my irrational sense that by selling the land I was somehow betraying my family.

I knew my sons would have a fit, because they made it clear it would be better for them if I just sold the whole thing. If they ended up with it, not only would Angie be breathing down their necks, there would be bills and taxes to pay yet very little guaranteed income. I understood that, for them, it would be much more trouble than it was worth. But I thought of that too. I might stipulate in my will that that part of my estate would go to my nephew, Will, Susan's son. Then it would be up to him to decide what to do with it.

I made my decision. Yet, a few lingering doubts nibbled at the edges of my conscience as the plane made a graceful landing on the tarmac. I breathed a sigh of relief as everything went smoothly as I picked up the rental and checked into the motel. I was relieved to have more freedom to come and go this time. Best of all, I had hot water showers, real soap, and decent coffee. All were necessary for my good mental health. The meeting to sign the final papers to divide the farm was two days away. A week before, Stu let me know that he could mail me the paperwork if I didn't want to make another trip. But I decided there were still too many loose ends to take care of, and that I needed to return.

Even though I originally decided to stay only three days, in the end, I decided to stay a few days longer. Maybe some of my guilt would be dissipated if I helped Susan do whatever she wanted to do with the items still in the farmhouse. The thing I was dreading the most was the anger I would face when I saw her. More than any other thing, I still wanted to be able to have a conversation with her.

We still had a few decisions to make. There was the old duplex in the trust. It was built by my great-grandmother in the '40s when all the soldiers came home and needed a place to live. Those were the days when farmers still needed hands to help plant, harvest, irrigate, and feed cattle. Now all that was primarily automated. The duplex had both a one-bedroom and two-bedroom unit and was rented out to hundreds of people through the years. We needed to decide whether to keep renting or sell it. Since there was less-sentimental value attached to this property than to the farm, I was hopeful Susan would agree to sell.

My relaxing time at the Holiday Inn Express was short-lived. After a good night's sleep, I drove to Tumbleweed. It was a perfect September morning. A few of the old wooden windmills could still be seen in the distance – a reminder of the days when cattle and cowboys were king. The peaceful grassland where cattle grazed gradually turned into miles and miles and rows upon rows of ripening cotton plants, the land of the cattlemen turning into farmland. The cerulean blue of the sky contrasting with the emerald green of the neat rows of little plants. At times I saw no other vehicles. It was just me with the land and sky. I was lulled into a feeling of tranquility despite what was to come.

As the sign welcoming me to Herschel County appeared on the horizon, my peaceful mood turned into one of apprehension. I decided to get it over with and visit my sister before I did anything else. Susan's old van was not in the driveway, but I knocked on the door. When no one answered, I pushed it open. Since it was September, the kids that usually lounged around the T.V. were at school. All was quiet, and the house smelled of bleach and cat litter. I called out, but when no one answered me, I walked through the house and pushed open the backdoor. No one but the dogs were in the backyard. Making my way back through the house, I quietly pushed open the spare-room door and saw someone sleeping soundly under the bedspread – probably Marty, the oldest grandson. I decided to leave him alone, and since no one else seemed to be at home, I decided to write Susan a note to let her know I was in town. I would come back later. Just as I was searching for pencil and paper, the front door flew open. My niece, Angie, stood looking at me. I stared back at her. This was the confrontation both of us had been avoiding for far too long.

Chapter Twenty-seven
The Road Home

We stared at each other a moment, neither of us prepared for this unexpected meeting. Then Angie slammed the screen door behind her and demanded, "Where's Mom? She said she would be here."

"I don't know," I replied. "I just got here."

My niece marched past me and slapped down a large Slushy on the overflowing dining table. She loomed over me, tall and angular. No one would suspect by looking at her that she gave birth to nine children. She was all sharp edges, with a drooping eyelid and glasses that looked ready to fall off her nose. I watched as she dumped out the paper bag she carried, scattering French fries across the table, then tore open the thin paper containing what looked like a large burrito. She sat down and bit into the food. Then she looked up at me and asked, "What are you doing here?"

I still stood by the front door with my arms crossed in defiance. "I might ask you the same thing."

"Well, this is my mom's house. It doesn't belong to you, and you have no right even being here."

"As a matter of fact, until the final papers are signed, this house still belongs to the trust, and since I'm the trustee, I do have a legal right to be here."

"Fuck you," she said between bites of burrito. "That stupid trust is something you and Mack dreamed up to screw me out of the inheritance Tutu wanted me to have. She wanted me and my kids to have whatever we needed and now you're taking it all away."

I walked toward her, shaking my head in disbelief. "Angie, you stole Tutu's identity – her social-security number – and convinced someone to open up a credit card in her name. Then you maxed it out, charging frivolous stuff, and never paid the bills with her name on them because they were being delivered to the house she was letting you and your family live in for free!"

"Tutu wanted me to have that house. I have papers to prove it."

"Oh, you mean the one signed by both you and Hilario, saying you agree to pay rent which would then be used to cover the mortgage she took out?" I asked, my voice rising.

My niece stood up, confronting me directly, spitting food out her mouth as she spoke, "She gave the house to me, and Mack took it away!"

I moved toward her, narrowing my eyes. "You signed a contract, promising to pay, and you never paid a red cent. All the money to cover the mortgage payments came from the trust, and on top of that, you went every day to see your grandmother and harassed her for money, and then you and Hilario went home and sat on your rear ends, watching T.V. or playing videogames."

With one swift swipe of her arm, she sent the remainder of her lunch, plus dishes, utensils, pens, and paper flying off the table. "You're a damned liar! A liar! Tutu loved me."

I backed away from her fury. "Yes, she did love you, and you took advantage of her love and swindled a loving, fragile woman who was also your grandmother." With that, I grabbed my purse and started for the door, my heart pounding in my ears.

As I opened the door, she called after me, "Mom said she left me a check here. What did you do with it?"

Without answering, I slammed the door behind me and headed toward my rental car. Parked beside it was Angie's red Mustang – newly washed and gleaming in the bright sunlight.

There was a time when Angie was a little girl that I felt close to her. My sons and I came to visit my parents and sister's family at least once a year, and it always seemed to me that my boys, plus Susan's son, Will, ganged up on Angie. After all, she was the only girl. She would come sobbing to me that the boys were picking on her and doing awful things to her. I would usually offer my sympathetic arms and call the boys over for their punishment. However, the boys became furious when this happened.

"No, Mom!" they protested. "NO! We didn't put the dead mouse in her bed. She found it dead and put it there herself! She just wants your sympathy. We didn't do it!" I faced four pairs of determined, angry eyes more than once when things like this happened. Eventually, I began to see Angie's game for what it was. She was a master manipulator. I was slow to learn what they knew all along. Now, years later, the last thing any of them wanted was to have to share land or anything else with her. They knew that would never work.

I drove around town for a few minutes, letting the air conditioning help cool me off, before I looked for Susan. I tried calling her cellphone but got no answer, so I decided to look for her in all the likely places, starting with the farmhouse. The highway before me shimmered with an early September mirage, giving the feeling that I was headed toward a large lake. But, like many things here on the Great Plains, it beckoned you ahead, then disappeared into disappointment and dust. Farm-to-Market Road 119 heading east was a paved two-lane road. It continued several more miles, but my turnoff came at the three-mile marker. I turned north onto a county road paved only as far as the 'country club,' a low-slung building that sat on the top of a draw. At one time, it was a bustling place, for this area at least, but now the vivid green circles scattered among the dusty, gray, prairie grass were incongruous – strange alien circles created by some outer space beings seemed as likely as the truth. A lone golfer stood on the green next to the clubhouse, lobbing balls down into the draw.

The pavement ended, but not the road. I continued to the bottom of the draw onto a gravel road over a large culvert. The old creek bed was now dry, but should we have an unlikely gully washer, it would quickly fill with water and run over the road, leaving heavy clay and debris as it receded. Opposite the golf course on the other side of the dry creek bed at the top of the draw was a wide prairie. Here were six square miles of grassland never touched by a plow. This was known as the Powell Land. It was fenced-in prairie, peppered with soapweed, yucca, and mesquite. Cattle grazed it but were seldom seen from the road. There was also an ancient three-story house smack-dab in the middle that always reminded me of the house in the Elizabeth Taylor, Rock Hudson, James Dean movie, Giant. Ever since I was a young girl, I wanted to climb over the barbed wire, avoiding the entrapped tumbleweeds, walk through the grassland until I arrived at the grand and mysterious house in the center. I never did this, though, since trespassing was strictly forbidden and, according to my mother, there wasn't anything the least bit mysterious or interesting about the man who lived there. He was old and kept to himself. People respected that. Still, even today, I yearned to park the car, climb over the fence, and lose myself in the prairie grass.

On the other side, the road was bordered by cultivated cropland. Mostly green cotton planted in straight rows, while in other fields old wheat stubble was still visible. The roadbed itself was dry-packed soil, similar to clay, with deep ditches on each side. My father called these 'bar ditches.' They were created by the county road graders' deep blades which cut sharply into the edges, bringing up dirt and trash to build up the driving surface after a sudden thunderstorm. Driving the dusty summer roads, this is where our Chevys got nails in their tires and in the winters and spring where our vehicles bogged down in snow and mud.

One more mile north and the row of houses in Finchville appeared on the horizon. This was where Skeeter lived and also his uncle, Jerry Bob, and two of Jerry Bob's sisters. All the sprawling houses were set in a row. Several, smaller, employee houses completed what looked like a little village. But I didn't continue to this compound. Instead I turned east before getting to Finchville road, took a right turn on a nameless one-lane road, drove another mile, then a left turn into the farmhouse yard. Sure enough, Susan's van was there. My car was quickly surrounded by barking dogs as I stepped out into the September sun. Susan or Skeeter fed them now, but since I was with them almost a month, we seemed to have bonded. One real concern was what would happen to them. I hoped Susan would continue to feed and look out for them since she would own the farmhouse.

The explosive meeting with Angie rattled me, but the slow drive helped to quiet my nerves. I walked up to the house. Hearing the dogs, Susan came out of the house, curious about seeing an unfamiliar car.

"Oh. Where did you come from?" she asked without preliminaries.

"Just blew in from Wisconsin, via the Holiday Inn Express south of Amarillo."

It seemed no time passed since I was last there. She picked up on the conversation just as before but without referring to the pending farmland division and sale, "Good. You can help me with all this stuff you left here. I thought you said you got everything cleaned out?"

"What I said was that I either took or got rid of everything I didn't think you'd want. I didn't want to throw away anything I thought you might use. Most of what's left is the furniture you said you wanted to keep."

"So, when did you get here?"

"Last night. I drove down this morning and stopped at your house."

"So, was Angie there?"

"She came in right after I did," I said. "She was looking for you and a check she said you had for her."

"Yeah. That's why I'm here. I'm tired of her pestering me for money."

I sank down into the rusty, old, lawn chair and stared at her in disbelief. This attitude was a change for my sister. She seldom criticized her daughter, no matter whom she took advantage of. Maybe her anger at Angie diffused some of her anger toward me, because she seemed more amenable to me than usual.

I didn't reply. I didn't want to tell her that Angie and I tangled. She probably suspected that already. I changed the subject, "So, thanks for feeding the dogs."

"It costs a lot to feed four big dogs. I can't keep doing it."

"Okay," I said. "I'll pay for their food until we figure out what to do."

"What to do?"

"With Mack's dogs."

"Oh."

"They're attached to this place, but we need to do something," I said.

"Well, I can't take them to my house. I have four already, and half the time Angie or the kids leave their dogs with me, so I can't take them."

"Okay," I said. "Maybe Lyle?"

"Nope. Asked him already. I guess I'll get whoever rents this place to take care of them."

"So, you've decided to rent it out? I thought you were thinking about moving out here. But if you don't rent, we'll have to find someone who would like a pack of dogs or find someone to take care of them here. I suppose you could have whoever rents the house care for them in return for lower rent."

Susan shrugged. "I guess. I'm not sure I want to rent the house out."

"You just said you were going to rent it out, so what's the deal?"

"Well, I don't make quick decisions like you do; I care about Mack's dogs and I really want to find someone to take care of them."

It seemed that no matter what I said, I seemed to be on the wrong side of Susan. I took a deep breath and slowly blew it out before I answered, "Have you asked Skeeter?"

"They don't want any more dogs, and besides that, Jerry Bob doesn't like other people's dogs, even said he'd shoot 'em if he sees them messin' with his cattle."

"He'd do that?"

"Yep. He would."

"Well, Shane and Patch are both pretty old. I don't know about Fiz. Jack, though, he's probably pretty young." With the mention of his name, Jack nuzzled my hand. "Surely, we can find homes for them," I continued.

"I can't keep taking care of them. I have my hands full," Susan replied. "I'll see if whoever rents this place will take them, but if that doesn't work, it's your problem."

I didn't argue. It was my problem. I was executrix of Mack's estate, therefore responsible for deposing of all his property – even his beloved dogs.

Susan continued, "Do you realize what a mess you've left me?"

"Wait a minute," I said. "You thought you might want to live here, remember? You didn't want me to throw anything away. I did as much as I could."

"I can't live here. There are too many memories. I just need you to help me with all of this. It's so overwhelming."

Only now did she realize what I was trying to tell her. I bit my tongue. "Well, I'm here now. What can I help with?"

Her face registered surprise. She obviously did not expect me to offer my help. "I'm working back here," she replied as she led me toward the bathroom at the back of the house. This was the part Mack never used, preferring to heat and air-condition only his living area. While we were growing up, this was our only bathroom, resulting in screaming fights over time spent in front of the mirror, versus necessities. The room gave off the musty smell of something long neglected. As I followed my sister, I noticed the doors to a tall, high cabinet were open and the former contents spread out in the bathtub. There were vials of various shampoos, lotions, hair sprays, medicated creams, bandages, hair pins, and rollers.

"You sure didn't do any cleaning out in here." Susan sniffed. "So, what do we do with all this?"

"I didn't throw the entire contents of the cabinet in the bathtub! Who did this?"

"I don't know. Probably Angie."

"Why don't we get her to clean it up, otherwise, just toss it all. And what is she doing in here anyway?" I replied.

"Well, you weren't here, and I needed help. You want to throw it all away?"

"Do you want any of it?"

"I don't know," my sister replied, indecisive as usual.

I sighed. "Well, I don't want it. What else is in there?"

Susan continued pulling small containers from what was left in the cabinet – old Coty bath and face powder, rouges, smelly old lipsticks and hair products decades old – our mother's collection of a lifetime. Finally she pulled out a small square box and handed it to me. I took off the top and looked at what was inside. "Oh, my God!" I exclaimed.

"What is it?" asked my sister.

Tangled together were several narrow stretched-out elastic belts with claw-like hooks dangling from the middle of each. "Look! Mother kept our old Kotex belts!"

"Oh, yuck!" Susan gingerly poked at the tangle of pale-pink elastic belts and held them at the end of her fingers.

"They smell like old rubber," I offered. "Do these ever bring back memories!!!"

"Oh, they were awful! Remember when that awful fastener would get tangled up in...well, you know..."

"Oh yeah, the pubic hair. That hurt so bad, and it always happened in a class where the teacher had a policy about going to the bathroom. You could only go if it was an emergency."

"Yeah, and I had lots of emergencies. Can you believe she saved these?" Susan asked.

"Yes," I replied. "Sadly, yes, I can believe it."

"Just think," Susan added, "my daughter or granddaughters have no idea what these are for."

"They don't know how good they have it, do they?" It felt good to agree about something for a change.

We were almost finished with the cabinet when Susan pulled out one last box. Like some of the others we found, this one was labeled with my mother's neat magic-marker writing. In clear black letters, it was identified as 'STRING TOO SHORT TO TIE.'

We looked at each other, thoroughly baffled. Susan took off the top, and there, inside, were hundreds of little strings definitely 'too short to tie.'

I put my hands over my face and shook my head, laughing with amazement.

"She kept this!" Susan said. "She kept string too short to tie! Why would she do that? Why? What would you use that for? What in the world?"

"Oh, our dear mother!" I exclaimed. "Remember, she always said she never threw anything away that she didn't need the next day?"

"But little pieces of string?" asked my sister, incredulous.

"Looks like," I said.

"And what do we do with this?" Susan asked.

"This?" I asked. "This, we keep. Otherwise no one will believe us."

"After that, I need a break," said Susan. "Let's go sit outside." For the first time in a very long time, we were briefly sisters, giggling like teenagers at our mother's idiosyncrasies.

We just settled down on the front porch in the squeaky, old, metal, lawn chairs when the dogs rose up and we heard someone barreling down the road toward the driveway. There was a squeal of brakes and spray of dust as the red Mustang came into view.

Chapter Twenty-eight
September Reckoning

Angie squealed the car to a stop, jumped out, and stormed up onto the porch.

"Where is my check?" she demanded, confronting my sister. "They're getting ready to repossess my car and I need it now! Otherwise, you're going to be driving me everywhere or I'll just take your car. I need the check now!"

One by one, the dogs slunk down off the porch and away from Angie. Susan continued smoking, but I could see her body tense, her breathing coming hard and fast. "Calm down," she said to her daughter. "You know how this affects my blood pressure. I already told you I don't have any money to give you."

"You did not!" Angie screamed. "You said you'd help pay for it."

Susan looked at her daughter and shook her head. "I helped by buying you a van. It was your choice to trade it for the Mustang and a loan."

"You lie! That is not what you said. You are such a liar."

My sister was shaking and shrinking into herself. With defeat in her voice, she gestured toward me. "You will have to ask her for money. She's the one who is controlling everything."

My niece circled her mother, eyes blazing, then pointed at me. "She won't give me anything. She doesn't care about my kids or me. She's just like Mack. They don't give a damn, never have, neither one of them. I've paid all this money and now I'll lose it – your money – it will be gone, and the car will be gone, and I won't have a way to get food for my kids, and it is all your fault!" She was shrieking with fury. None of her usual strategies was working. "So, I'll just tell the kids that their grandmother doesn't care about them. She doesn't care if they can't get to school. She doesn't give a damn."

So far, I kept quiet, but now I jumped in, "Your kids live with their grandmother about 95% of the time. She is the one who buys them food and takes them to school, not you."

"You have no idea what I do. You stay away, up there in your big house with all your perfect kids and grandkids with their fancy college degrees that Tutu paid for with all my money. And you think I'm the problem?" My niece was ruthless and sadly believed the lies she invented herself.

Susan stumbled to her feet, practically in tears. "Don't say that to the kids. Don't tell them I don't care. Don't say that. They believe what you tell them. I'll get the money. Somehow, I'll get the money. Just leave right now, okay? I'll have to go to the bank and all…"

I looked at my sister with disbelief. She was giving in to her daughter when she didn't even have enough to live on herself. Angie looked at me with a triumphant smile on her face, spun around, and headed toward her car. Susan grabbed her purse and headed out to her van. I was close behind.

"Are you really going to give her the payment for the car?"

Susan turned around to look at me. "Just stay out of this, okay? This is just what I have to do, and I will need some money from the trust. Just add it to what I already owe, okay? You can at least do that for me, can't you?"

And with that, I was left holding the box of 'Strings Too Short to Tie' and feeling helpless to change this strange, alternative universe I found myself inhabiting. The dogs slowly returned to their chosen places on the porch, and I gave each of them a pat on the head. As I entered the house, Taylor Swift was letting me know that she was never going to make-up with me again.

How appropriate, I thought. *How appropriate.* I gathered up my purse and closed up the house as much as I could, considering there was an always-open doggy-door that could accommodate a German shepherd.

I was relieved to get back to the Holiday Inn Express and find a place to have a glass of wine with my dinner. As I ate, I thought about my day and the days to follow. After all the papers were signed, I would just have to let the chips fall as they may, even if it meant leaving Susan to deal with this intractable problem. Anything I tried to do, short of signing over the farm and all its assets to Susan and, thus, to Angie, would never be enough to fill this bottomless pit.

I did worry about the children. What would happen to them? Their lives had already been so disrupted by their father's alcoholism and abuse, plus their mother's neglect and lack of moral center. It was my sister who was the only stability in their lives. Perhaps, to some degree, Mack had also been that for them, because he stood as an example of a healthy contributing member of society, yet my brother had no experience relating to children and was always at a loss with what to even say to them. Susan's former husband, their grandfather, seemed to care about the oldest boy but was much too busy with work and golf to even remember the names of the others. The kids barely noticed when he left town after the divorce and remarried, washing his hands of the entire situation many years before. Susan was truly alone in her determination to be a guiding light for all these young kids. It was overwhelming and totally unfair.

But the thing I had to remember was that this was truly what she wanted to do – what she felt called to do. I certainly disagreed with how she indulged Angie and let the resources disappear, but I couldn't fault her for her commitment to these children who needed her. She made her choices, and it was now up to me to respect those choices and get out of the way. That was the only way I could play it out.

The following day, I returned to the farmhouse after taking money out of the trust for the last time, then writing a check to Susan who paid the required 'quiet money' to Angie. Maybe for a few days, Susan would have peace. And now that I was letting Susan take the lead, she seemed to be more willing to work together on finishing the work at the farmhouse. We seemed to have reached an unspoken agreement to not speak of the impending division and sale of the farm while we cleaned and cleared out the remainder of these many lives. Consequently we finally opened suitcases hidden deep in a basement closet. They were full of family photos, boxes of small reels of 16mm family home-movies, and even the circa 1940 Kodak projector.

"Do you mind if I take the movies?" I asked. "I'll have them converted into DVDs so we can both have copies."

"Well, I don't care," she replied. "I have too much to do to worry about without worrying about old home-movies. They are probably all films of you as a baby, anyway. Most of them are addressed to Mrs. D.H. Stanlan. So, that was before Mother and Daddy got married. Besides, Daddy had more important things to do than worry about movies."

I must have touched on a sensitive subject, but I continued, "Okay, I'll box them up and get them shipped home. I do think, though, there are films of you and Mack on these too. Don't you remember seeing these when we were kids? Mother would plug in the old projector and put bed sheets up over the windows, and we would sit cross-legged on the floor, waiting for the movie to begin. But then she would have trouble threading the projector and we'd get antsy and start teasing each other. Finally, she'd get it threaded right and we'd watch these jumpy black-and-white movies of us running around in the yard with the dogs."

"Oh yeah, I do remember that," she replied. "Then she'd always give a little gasp and turn on the lights, and all the film would be on the floor because she forgot to thread the film through the other reel. It seems like those movies lasted about three minutes, but she was always so excited to show us what we looked like as little kids."

"And what the farm looked like, remember?"

For a moment, we remembered, as only siblings can. Then we moved onto some boxes of old farm financial records. Even though she didn't like doing the paperwork, Susan was attached to anything with the letterhead 'Mihlbauer Farms.' I was all for throwing them away, but I kept quiet. After several minutes of looking through them, she reluctantly decided they belonged in the recycling crate. Her stamina for this emotionally draining job was limited, and soon she collapsed onto a heavy carton. "I have to go. I have too many things to do at home. I can't do this very long, you know."

I looked around the house that was my childhood home. Most of the furniture was pushed up against the walls, awaiting Susan's decision to either keep it or find another place for it. One old couch sat in the middle of the room next to the leftover boxes crammed with the remainders of our parents' lives. They were waiting here for her too. Everything else, I either gave away, shipped home, or threw out. The only areas left to go through were the cabinets in the laundry room and a couple of small closets. A month ago, I would have stayed and continued the job without her, but now, I deferred to her wishes.

"Okay," I said, "I think I'll head back to the motel and stop at the Panhandle Plains Museum on my way. I haven't been there for many years and I want to check it out. Besides that, we need to find a resting place for the family Bible. I think they would be interested, since one of the Conroy brothers was a city founder. If we don't put it in a safe place, I'm afraid it will get lost and eventually tossed. I don't want that to happen."

"Are you saying I don't take care of the things that belong to our family?"

"No, I'm not saying that. I'm saying that we need to preserve the history in a place where others can see it."

Susan looked down at the heavy Bible precariously balanced on top of an assortment of photos and papers and leafed through it, not making eye contact. "I don't think that's what you mean at all."

"What?" I demanded, my pent-up anger breaking through. "That is exactly what I mean. Why are you always so angry? I'm sick of this. You're acting like a two-year-old. Grow up!"

Susan looked at me with daggers in her eyes, then turned and, with one swift swipe, shoved the Bible off the table. It hit the floor with a loud thud as she stood up and turned to escape the room.

Before I had time to think, I grabbed her arm and yanked. "Stop! Just stop! Quit running away!" I was furious that she would treat this family heirloom with such a lack of reverence. It was held records of our family going back almost 200 years. I gripped her arm tighter.

With fire in her eyes, she turned to me. "You let me go! Let me go!" She tried to jerk her arm away, but my nails dug into her skin.

"No! Not this time."

We stared at each other, the family Bible on the floor between us. Finally, I looked away and let her go. This was a hopeless situation. Then, instead of racing out the door, she sank down hard onto the tattered couch, sobbing quietly.

Her sobs disgusted me. I was so tired of her hysterics and was about to make a nasty remark and walk out the door when she stopped crying long enough to look up at me.

"You don't understand. You've never understood. This is grief. Grief. I am so, so sad..." Sobbing quietly, she continued, "I've lost my marriage, my father, my mother, and my brother. My son is thousands of miles away and now I've lost the farm... It's grief. Don't you see? It's grief." Now feeling a bit guilty, I sank down beside her, suddenly at a loss for words as she continued, "I don't understand you. I don't. Why aren't you grieving? You really don't have any feelings, do you? I don't think you even cried when Mack died. You're like a cold stone wall."

For minutes, I sat there – anger, guilt, compassion each taking stage. The tension in the room was palpable, and I was glad that none of the kids were around. Finally, I found my voice, choosing compassion. "Susan," I began, "everyone grieves in their own way. Most of the time, I've been hundreds of miles away, out of your sight. Just because you didn't see me crying doesn't mean I didn't grieve."

She blew her nose and wiped at her eyes. "It's loss. I have lost so much. So much... You could at least wait. Everybody says you should wait a year after a death to make a decision, but you are always in such a yank – Hurry up! Hurry up! You could at least wait until I can think straight before you do anything with the farm."

I wanted to run out of the room and away from all of this, but I stayed rooted to my place on the couch. I couldn't deny her loss, or at least the acknowledgment that things in her life were changed for good. As a child, she was adored and protected. She grew up in a Cinderella world where Prince Charming swept you off your feet and you lived happily ever after with a sweet little baby sleeping quietly in the freshly decorated nursery. Maybe that was once my dream too, but that illusion was shattered early in my adult life when I was thrown back on my own resources. It seemed to me that Susan always looked for that strength outside herself – that is, until recently. Now she felt all alone out at the end of her rope with her daughter's family pulling the strings.

Finally, she looked up at me. "Is it the money? Is that what you want? You're mad at me about all the money Angie spent, so, to get even, you are planning on taking Skeeter's money in exchange for Daddy's farm, aren't you?"

For a minute, I questioned myself and my motivation. Up until now, the question of selling to Skeeter was not final, at least not in my mind, despite the fact that I'd already told him I would accept his offer. In the deepest recesses of my mind, I rationalized that I could still change my mine. But somehow, Susan figured out what I had not even admitted to myself. There was no doubt any money from the sale of my part of the farm would help me, but that wasn't really it. For all I knew, that hard, dry farmland might someday be worth a bundle. Who knew? Maybe they would strike oil or gas or lease the acreage for a huge wind farm. I had no way of knowing. "No," I began, "it's not the money. I guess I just want to focus on other things beside the farm. Skeeter knows so much about it, and he loves it. A person like that should have it, someone who will live here and care about it as much as Daddy did."

Susan looked at me, not seeming to comprehend. "I didn't tell you, but last week, we had an emergency."

Why are you changing the subject? I wanted to scream. Then, so, what else is new? But instead, I frowned at her. "What happened now?"

"It was Treenie. She had an abscessed tooth. They called me from school because she was in so much pain. Angie couldn't find the Medicaid card, so I just gave her Tylenol, but then a few days later, she couldn't even open her mouth. Finally, the Medicaid card showed up and I called around to get her an appointment, but no one would see her. No dentist around here takes Medicaid. Angie said she knew that, but she never bothered to tell me."

"Oh, that poor child." By now, I was sympathetic. "What did you do?"

"I finally got an appointment with my dentist, but only after I paid for the whole thing myself. I couldn't leave her in that kind of pain."

"No," I said. "No, you couldn't." Again, I was realizing what a dilemma she faced daily. "Did you have enough money?"

"Ha, what a question. I never have enough money. I'll just have to delay the electric bill this month. My friend, Julie, works there, and she usually lets me pay it out."

One part of me felt my sister's pain. Another part wondered if this was a clever ploy to play on my sympathies. I did not want to feel any sympathy right now. This conversation was smothering my resolve.

I rose, intending to go outside for a breath of fresh air, when Susan blew her nose, this time more loudly. "So, that's the kind of thing I spend money on. I need to help those kids."

I knew what my line was supposed to be. I was supposed to be the rescuer, swooping in to save the day. Instead, I took a deep breath and said, "What about their parents? Wouldn't it be better if they got jobs so they could be the ones worried about money for the dentist?"

Susan gave me a cold look. "Yeah. I knew that's what you'd say. You really just don't understand at all."

"It's not that I don't understand," I said, my voice whining upward. "I get that you want to take care of your grandkids. But what you don't get is that not all the crop money in the world would be enough to fill their bottomless needs. You're trying to accomplish the impossible and when your friends and family try to tell you that, you take it out on us and lay on the guilt. You know, if you sold part of the land you're going to get, you could at least meet some of the need."

"I will not sell Daddy's land. I told you that before."

With a sudden feeling of resolve, I grabbed my purse and sunglasses. For once, she simply stared at me, and I was the one who walked out the door. This time, I would do what I wanted to do and check out the museum instead of letting her guilt me into playing by her rules.

The Panhandle Plains Museum was a testament to the hard scrabble life of the pioneers who carved out a living from what was then known as The Great American Desert. It was a repository for leftover dreams. Local people worked very hard to preserve and protect the artifacts of a bygone era, and many of the documents and letters attested to this. For a few hours, I lost myself among the trappings of an age gone by. There was even a reproduction of a dugout where you could sit and look out the window until what looked and sounded like a thunderstorm blew in, creating the effect of the kind of fear and loneliness the people must have felt living such isolated lives deep in the prairie. The curator I needed to talk to wasn't available, so I made an appointment to come back, bringing the family Bible and maybe my sister. Something of the struggle and triumph of our great-grandparents needed to be preserved here.

I was due at Stu's office the next day. It was my job as the trustee to sign off on dissolving the trust. There were also papers to divide the land, and papers to accept Skeeter's offer to purchase my share of the farm. Insisting that she didn't have the stomach to sit through any more humiliating meetings, Susan already signed the document dividing the land. That meant it wasn't necessary for her to be here… So, I alone met Stu in his office. I glanced up at the Carl Smith painting one more time. Today, the golden edges of sunlight behind clouds over the distant mountains seemed to glow. I hoped this was a good omen.

Stu burst in a few minutes later, full of apologies for keeping me waiting. He was obviously glad to get this behind him but also seemed to want to chat a few minutes.

"So," he asked, "do you think Susan will be able to manage with the money she will be earning from her share of the farm?"

"I don't know," I replied. "I tried to explore that with her, but she does not want any advice or help from me, so I gave up. I think if she just had herself to take care of, she'd be fine, but unfortunately, she is trying to care for ten other people. I don't know how she's going to do it. She was not able to do it when Mother and Mack were giving her money. She ended up spending down so much of the trust that now she gets less of the land and property."

Stu looked thoughtful. "You know, I wondered why she just didn't consider selling at least part of her farmland to Skeeter. I asked her about that, and she gave me an unusual answer."

"What was that?" I asked.

"Well, she said that if she got a chunk of money, Angie would just end up getting it, because she's so good at nagging Susan until she gets her way. Then Susan told me she was saving the farm for her son, Will, since he had not gotten anything close to the all the money Angie had." Stu pushed against his desk and leaned back in his chair, chewing on the temples of his bifocals. "I don't think she has any faith in her ability to say no to Angie."

I considered this. "Nope. She has never been able to say no to her daughter, but her son is such a completely different person. He's proud and frugal and not about to pester his mom for money."

"Well, there you have it. Her decision is based on that as much as the desire to preserve the land for sentimental reasons – not that that is not still a part of her reasoning. Anyway, I'm just worried about her ability to pay her bills and take care of all those kids."

"So am I, Stu," I replied. "But at this point, there's nothing either of us can do except warn her of what she may face."

Aware that time was passing, Stu was suddenly all business again. "Okie-dokie, well, let's get these papers signed and get you out a' here. I had Tammy get 'em all put together so all you have to do is put your John Hancock on the bottom line and we are done."

I pulled the papers toward me, putting on my reading glasses. The first two were fairly straightforward. I signed off to dissolve the trust and then to divide the land. I took a deep breath when I looked at the last one. It was Skeeter's offer to purchase my share of the farm. Even up until this final moment, I was unsure I wouldn't change my mind.

I took a deep breath, smiled up at Stu, and signed my name.

"So, what happens next?" I asked.

"Well, it will take a bit to get all the land retitled and all the loose ends tied up. Besides all that, Skeeter has a crop to harvest that will still be divided between you and your sister. I figure it'll be toward the end of the year before you get 'er all wrapped up."

"Okay. Is that it then?"

"Yep, it is, and here's wishing you and Susan both good luck," Stu said, standing up. "It's been a pleasure working with you."

It was time for me to go. "Thank you, Stu. Your help has been invaluable. I so appreciate all you've done to help me since Mack died. I won't forget it."

We shook hands and he squeezed my arm as I went out the door. I breathed a sigh of relief as I walked up the street to my rental car. I was almost finished with the work here. Hurrah!

I felt about 20 pounds lighter as I drove to the post office to mail a few packages home. After that, I decided to visit Susan and see if we could at least agree about what to do with the family Bible. That was one last thing I wanted to get taken care of before I left.

As I walked up to the door, I heard angry voices coming from the house. With a stream of obscenities, Angie burst through the front door, almost knocking me down, as she screamed at her mother, "Go to hell! Go to hell! I'm going to take my kids away and you'll never see them again. Never. They hate you for what you have done to them. I hope you burn in hell!" She jumped in her car and laid rubber on the street as the Mustang sped away.

Tentatively I went to the door, afraid of what I'd find. "Susan? Is everything okay?" No one answered me and I made my way to the backyard where I found my sister, her hands shaking, and tears streaming down her face.

"What happened?" I asked.

Her lips quivered as she sobbed out her story, "She took it. I know she did. She always takes what she wants, and now she says she's taking the kids away. She won't take care of them. I know she won't. She never does."

"What?" I asked. "What did she take?"

"I don't think I can tell you," she moaned between sobs as she paced back and forth in her tramped-down backyard.

I stood by the backdoor, waiting for the pacing to stop. "Look, Angie isn't going to take the kids away. She has no money unless you give it to her. And where would she go?"

"She will. She will take them. You don't know her like I do. She says she will."

I watched quietly until she finally sat down hard into a dilapidated lawn chair. "She wants to hurt me and so she will take them away. She has enough money now."

"Now? How did she get money? You mean the money for the Mustang?"

My sister looked at me helplessly. "She took things from the farmhouse and sold them."

"What did she take? How did she get in?" I demanded.

Now it was my sister's turn to be quiet. Finally she spoke, her voice almost a whisper, "She took the silver – Noona's sterling silver – and she took other stuff too."

"How? When? What else?"

"The films and projector. She said she took them and threw them away when nobody wanted to buy them at a resale shop. They did want to buy the silver though. She took the silver to Amarillo and sold it. It's gone. There's probably other stuff too. I just don't know about it."

"But how did that happen? How did she get into the filing cabinet? And why would she even want to take the films and projector?" I stood above my sister, hand on my hips.

"I don't want to tell you. You blame me for everything." Now Susan's tears of frustration turned to anger directed at me.

"I'm not blaming you. I just want to know why and how this happened. How did she get in the house and into the file cabinet with the silver?"

"It's not my fault! It's not! If you finished cleaning out the house, it would never have happened!"

"So, she must have gotten hold of the keys, right?" I replied, resigned to the fact. Susan didn't answer me. Instead, she lit another of her Mobile Mart cigarettes and stared at the ground as her dogs huddled around her.

I continued, "But why the projector and films?"

After a long silence, she looked up. "Yesterday, I mentioned that we found the projector and films and you wanted them. I guess she thought that meant they were worth something – I mean, worth money. She tried to pawn them off, but that didn't work. I got really mad at her just now. She stole the films. And then…and then she threw them in a dumpster. She ruined all I had left of our memories. I mean, I know what I said about all the films being of you…but I remember now. There were lots of us at the farm when we were little – you and me and Mack."

My voice softened and I placed a hand on her shoulder. "I am so sorry," I said, feeling the loss and despair myself. The uselessness of my niece's actions smacked of a cruel mean-spiritedness that was never a part of our family. My niece was given nothing but love, yet she rewarded the mother who loved her by treating her this way.

I pulled up a large popcorn can, turned it over, and sat down. "You know," I began, "she's only threatening to take away the kids because she knows how much that bothers you. I can almost guarantee she will not do that. Mainly because she becomes overwhelmed just being with them for one day. That's why she leaves them with you. Susan," I continued, "She uses the kids as pawns. I know that is hard to hear, but that is how I see it."

"But you don't have an adopted child. You don't understand. You have no idea, so just stop trying to tell me how to feel, okay? I know what I know."

Sighing deeply, I realized my time here was over. I had to realize there really was nothing I could do. "Okay," I said. "I'm leaving in the morning, and I came to tell you that the papers are signed, so now the farmhouse, homeplace, and three-fourths of the Sutter section is officially yours. I'll call you when I get back home. My flight leaves early in the morning."

I stood up and waited for some response, but when it didn't come, I made my way through the house. The older boys, 18 and 19, were just getting out of bed. Dressed only in underwear, they poured cereal into large mixing bowls and greeted me sleepily. "Good afternoon," I said. "Just getting up?"

They nodded, walked into the dining room, and shoved papers and leftover food aside to make room for their breakfast. "Hey," I said to them. "Could you two guys do me a favor and clean up this house for your grandmother? And then, when that's done, how about going out and looking for a job? You can't keep sponging off your grandmother. She's done more than enough. It's time for you to be standing on your own two feet."

The oldest gave me a weak smile, got up from the table, and turned on a videogame. "So, are you gonna help Gramma with the farmhouse?" he asked.

I resisted my need to strangle him. Instead I took a deep breath and looked him in the eye. "Not today," I said. "Today I get ready to go home. You and your brothers could help her though. How about that?"

There was no response. I was beyond angry.

The violent sound of the game followed me out of the house to the rental car. For a few minutes, I just sat there. All this was almost too much to take in. I fumbled around in my purse for my keys and pulled out a set with my grandfather's faded car-dealership keychain.

These weren't the keys for my rental. They were the keys to the old pickup!

I completely forgot about dropping Trusty Rusty off at Irv's Used Car Lot. Susan was supposed to help drive me to the farm to pick it up, and in all the commotion, it never got done. Eugene promised $2000.00 for it, money divided equally between Susan and me, since it had belonged to Mack.

For several minutes, I sat there, thinking. I knew what I needed to do. Marching back up to the front porch, I pushed open the door, nodded to the boys in their underwear, and located Susan talking on the phone, still in the backyard.

"Here," I blurted out. "These belong to you." I thrust the keys toward her.

"What?" Susan looked at me as though I were a ghost. "I'll call you back," she said into the phone, then, "I thought you left. What are you doing back? What are you talking about?"

"These are for the old pickup. We forgot to take it to Irv's and get the money. So, now it's yours. You do with it whatever you want."

She looked at me with stunned surprise. "Are you sure?"

"Yes," I said. "I am sure. It's yours to do as you want."

She stumbled to her feet and, with one arm, reached out almost like she meant to give me an awkward hug. Then she stopped, looking down at the keys I thrust into her hands. "Okay. Thanks. Thanks a lot."

"No problem," I replied, "You may need it." I practically raced through the house back to the car. God help me, I couldn't wait to get out of there.

Chapter Twenty-nine
Takings and Leavings

I didn't know what I expected as I drove out of town, but right now, I felt numb – not relief, not anger, not anything. The past few weeks and months were just too much. It would take me a while to sort it all out. Then, just as I was about to leave the old Farm-to-Market road and go onto the Interstate entrance ramp, I remembered the family Bible.

"Oh shit!" I said aloud. "I can't leave it there! If Angie took the film projector, she might also decide, out of spite, to do away with that." I made a quick turn east, down the nearest dirt road which would lead to the farm.

Even though Susan had the key, the farmhouse itself was not secure. There was a doggy door that provided access to the house for the dogs. The dogs themselves were our only burglar alarm. I thought the file cabinet was securely locked, but I hadn't counted on my niece's criminal ingenuity.

Without much difficulty, I was able to squeeze enough of my body into the house through the doggy door to turn the lock on the doorknob and get inside. The dogs thought this unusual performance was all for their benefit and whined and licked my face as I lay sprawled out on the back porch. Already, the house smelled of vacancy – an odd combination of mold, mice, and, faintly, natural gas. I wasn't sure if the dogs were fed, so after feeding them, I went downstairs to where the film and projector had been stored. Sure enough, the projector was nowhere to be found but, amazingly, there were three films lying outside the closet on the floor. They must have fallen out of the box as the culprit made off with the others. Angry and heartbroken, I picked them up as though they were precious jewels and went upstairs to retrieve the Bible.

Surely, I thought, Susan moved it back on the table after dropping it to the floor the day before. But no. There it lay, right where she left it.

It was large and heavy, probably weighing over ten pounds. It dated to the early 19th century and had a thick leather cover. Because the bindings were coming away from the pages, I lifted it gently and turned to the list of births and deaths. There, in someone's scratchy writing, were listed the family members of my great-grandparents – the Conroy clan. Here, I found the death records for three small boys, my great-grandfather's little brothers, all dead of unknown causes before they were ten years old. His mother, Mary Ann, my great-great grandmother who died soon after her young sons. His sister, Hattie, whose dress we found in a trunk earlier, was listed too. She lived long enough to attend Normal school, then died at 22 of meningitis. The only survivors were my great-grandfather, his older brother, and their father.

The handwriting changed soon after that. Instead of something that looked like it came from the U.S. constitution, now it was penmanship in the Palmer method. It was this generation who moved to Texas and became the first settlers in my hometown. Still, in these generations there were also childhood deaths and sudden disappearances of relatives who appeared briefly in the last generation. Recorded was the death of my grandfather's brother, his partner in their fledgling car dealership, murdered by a hitchhiker while delivering a car to the next town. His widow was listed too, along with their daughter and the deaths of her next two husbands. For some reason, it also mentions that she was hired as a census taker. A job for a woman was unusual in those days, but with a daughter to raise and after losing three husbands, the city fathers must have decided she needed a means of support.

My imagination always began to work overtime when I examined all these pieces of past lives, trying to piece them together with all I'd been told as a child. Truly it was an intriguing story. But, today, I needed to move ahead.

Wrapping the Bible in an old tablecloth, I carried it out to the car. I couldn't leave it here, no matter what my sister's wishes were. It needed to be safe.

I went in to take one last look around at the house. This time, I could not afford to forget anything else, but that wasn't the real reason I went back in. I needed to say goodbye to the dogs and all the memories. As I stood in the middle of what had been my family's living room, I thought of all the family gatherings that were a part of it. One end served as our dining room when we had company, and the other end was where my father proudly placed our first T.V. It was where I became an unlikely fan of the Brooklyn Dodgers in 1955, since we only got one channel. This was where, as a small child, I watched my parents read and also watched them argue passionately over politics. Now, stripped of all but a sagging armchair, boxes, and trunks, it looked sad and desolate. After taking one last look at the bedrooms and kitchen, I picked up the precious little films and said a silent prayer. This house was no longer mine. I could only hope and pray that my sister would choose wisely and use this house and all the other precious resources in a healthy and responsible way, though that was an unlikely prospect.

The dogs' tails drooped as I let myself out of the house. They knew I was leaving, and they were lonely. They needed a pack leader and were confused by all the changes. I bent down and petted each one. "Susan will take good care of you," I promised hopefully. And, with that, I got in the car and drove away, tears stinging my eyes.

I made four right-angled turns onto dirt roads, passing fields with straight rows of green cotton plants interspersed by pastureland, dust following the car like some kind of phantom spirit. Finally I pulled onto the interstate. Tumbleweed, with her water tower and grain elevators, receded in the rearview mirror. From a distance, those tall structures looked like the skyline of an impressive city rising up over the plains. Many travelers, including my great-grandparents, were fooled by the optical illusions of the mirages and almost imperceptible curve of the earth. Looked at from a distance, small playa lakes became grand inland seas, and tiny hills appeared as mountains.

They came here with big dreams, younger sons and daughters searching for greener pastures. They left farms behind in Missouri, Illinois, Michigan, Tennessee, Kentucky, Virginia, Ireland, Pomerania, Scotland, and other places. They purchased inexpensive land for pennies on the acre and dug shallow wells powered by windmills to bring up water from the overflowing aquifer. They founded cities, towns, farms, ranches, businesses. They worked hard and saw much of their dream realized, especially after Europe was devastated by World War II and the world depended on the bounty of the Great Plains for food.

I thought about them as the miles stretched ahead like a straight blue ribbon. Now, on either side, pastures and straight rows of grain sorghum reached to the horizon. A few miles more and the terrain grew more rugged, cactus and mesquite replacing the row crops. Now there were small dips in the level road as the colors of the canyon chasm came into view. For hundreds of years, this was home to the native American plains tribes, like the Apache and

Comanche, who followed the great herds of buffalo from the Dakotas south. They were people of the land and sky who worshipped the sun and danced for days to bring rain to the parched prairie. Here and there, barbed wire appeared, fencing in herds of grazing cattle that would eventually become T-bones and hamburgers for chain restaurants.

After a few miles, the empty spaces gave way to a scattering of homes and businesses, set back from the road, followed by subdivisions with names like Canyon Creek Crossing Estates. Only a few more miles, and the car dealerships appeared with their acres and acres of shiny new vehicles. These soon disappeared, and the landscape filled with Dunkin' Donuts, McDonald's, Hobby Lobby, Starbucks, Exxon stations, and Holiday Inn Express, all looking the same whether they were on the outskirts of Amarillo, Des Moines, Cleveland, or Milwaukee.

My reverie over, I realized I was in the parking lot of my motel. As if waking from a dream, I lugged my overnight bag into the motel and hurried to the museum, hoping someone would be there to help me. Fortunately, the person I needed to talk to was there. He was a thin, balding man whose accent indicated he was definitely not from West Texas. One of those people with no facial affect, he introduced himself as Jordan Van Nuys, director of research, greeting me with the right words, just not the kind of friendly expression I was expecting. He ushered me up the stairs into his work area.

"I have a family Bible I thought the museum might be interested in," I explained. "My great-grandfather was the first settler of Tumbleweed, and his brother, Uncle Link and his wife, Aunt Vi, were some of the earliest settlers here. We are trying to find a home for this family history, and I thought it might fit in nicely in the museum."

Mr. Van Nuys didn't respond but put on a pair of white cotton gloves and began carefully turning the pages. Finally, he stood up and looked at me. "This seems authentic. We try to archive family stories here, as well as artifacts, and I think this would interest our curator of interpretation. However," he continued, "it's in pretty bad shape. Some of the pages are loose, so I doubt it will be put on display. Is that okay with your family?"

"Yes," I said. "But I was wondering if it would be possible to have copies made of the front pages with all the family information. It's important that we preserve the records."

Mr. Van Nuys opened the Bible and examined the pages intended for recording information about the family. After what seemed like endless minutes, he took off his glasses and looked down at me. "I think we could do that, but we don't have time today. If you can leave me all your contact information, I will send it to you."

"Okay," I agreed reluctantly, despite I was hoping to take the copies with me. "It's hard to give it up, but it should be here rather than miles away with me." When the librarian didn't respond, I continued, "We just want a safe place for it, and also we want to be able to visit here and see it whenever we want. Is that possible?"

"Everyone needs an appointment," he said, turning back to the large book on the table.

"Our family has donated to the museum before," I explained. "About three years ago, we gave you a side saddle and saddle bags that belonged to my grandfather's first cousin, Dr. Jessie Gibbens? She was quite an interesting lady. Her mother was the sister of the two Conroy brothers. Her name was Elizabeth, and she and Jessie are both listed in the Bible."

The taciturn museum man nodded thoughtfully. "Okay. We'll do some research. Can we keep it now?"

"Would you please? I have a plane to catch in the morning. My sister and I are clearing out our parents' farmhouse and…"

Before I could continue with my explanation, we were interrupted by a young woman with a question about the microfiche. Mr. Van Nuys turned his attention to her, seeming to forget I was there. After waiting a few minutes for him to return to our conversation, I wandered away to look within the stacks. Suddenly, seeming to notice I wasn't beside him anymore, he appeared at my elbow. "I'm sorry, but no one is allowed in the stacks without permission. You can return at another time. It is best to make an appointment, you know."

"Oh. Well, I didn't mean any harm. You see, I live in Wisconsin, and I don't know when I'll get back here…sorry."

"If you'll just fill out some paperwork, you can leave the Bible here, and we'll contact you."

I was taken aback by his dismissal. For some reason, I thought the museum would be as excited about the family history recorded in the Bible as I was. But I signed the paperwork, wandered around the visitor-approved section of the museum for a while, and then drove back to the motel.

I should have felt a sense of relief – the Bible was in a safe place, and I was going home. But Mr. van Nuys's reception left me cold. What was this I was feeling? Sorrow? Anger? Guilt? Maybe just a sense of letdown, like after the birth of a baby? As usual, I tried to put a name to it when it should have been obvious: my brother was dead, my parents gone, and my sister estranged from me. All the romance of the stories I'd been told about my recent ancestors seemed ragged, with pages torn away. Did it all just come down to this? Why did I feel so responsible for carrying on their story?

As I drove, I remembered reading about an old Welsh word '*hiraeth.*' The writer said it didn't translate well into English but denotes a homesickness for a home you cannot return to, a home that maybe never was, or the yearning, nostalgia, and grief for lost places. As rich as our English language was, sometimes it failed to capture a feeling like '*hiraeth*' which seemed what I was now feeling. Then, laid on top of this was a layer of guilt – a sense that I was a deserter. It was almost like survivor guilt. My rational side knew I was doing what I needed to do to help my sister take responsibility, but there was the emotional side that nagged at my conscience.

Back at my motel, the evening loomed, and I was afraid even more than one glass of wine at dinner would do little to assuage my gloom. I also worried about what was to happen to all the stories and the richness of the lives listed in the bible. I was sure that the stodgy ol' museum guy wasn't going to keep those stories alive. The names in the front of the bible were just names until they were brought to life.

The more I thought about it, the more I remembered. There were their letters and old photos. There was Hattie's pre-Civil War dress from Missouri. There were the fine china and crystal brought from Mississippi that my Conroy grandmother used when she entertained the First Baptist Church Missionary Society, and there was her well-used Bible with its soft, onion-thin pages.

Mimi, my Mihlbauer grandmother, left delicious recipes written in her own swirly handwriting. Most important, she bequeathed her zest for life. I thought of Grandpa Mihlbauer's coffee mug and his many beloved books on horticulture. My Conroy granddaddy left his cigarette holder and ledgers from 40 years of his Chevrolet-Oldsmobile dealership, plus an old pack of Lucky Strikes. My great-grandmothers left lovely, handmade lace doilies and carefully sewn underwear, skirts, and blouses. My father left the rusting farm equipment and hundreds of books on history, animal husbandry, and politics, plus his love for the land and for the cattle he cared for. Mother left her Christmas bows from 1952-1989, her fierce independence, and her String-Too-Short-to-Tie.

But I also took things with me besides the few, rescued, film reels. I took the wisdom instilled by my parents and grandparents, the strong faith of their commitment to God's grace, and the lessons learned as I was taught to work beside them. I took from my mother and grandmothers their legacy of standing up for others as well as standing up for myself as a strong woman. From my grandfathers, I took the importance of hard work, and the dignity of always doing your best, and never ever giving up. My father taught me to trust my own judgment and believe in myself.

And my sister taught me too. From her, I took an important lesson – one that occurred to me as I drove with the straight roads and flat prairie spread in front of me. It was something she first heard from one of her preschool pupils many years ago. For some unknown reason, it now rose to consciousness. The story went like this:

Two little girls were arguing about what game to play. Each tried to talk the other into playing her game. After a few minutes of this back-and-forth disagreement, one of them finally turned to the other and said, "I know! Why don't you be you, and I'll be me?" Then each child went off happily to play her own game.

It was time to let my sister be herself no matter where that led. I knew that the old comfortable camaraderie would never really be there for us again, and that, I mourned. Yet I was hopeful that, with time, she could speak to me without bitterness and that I could come to see her choices through a different lens, feeling more compassion than anger.

The Tumbleweed of my childhood was no more. The world of today is light years removed from that time and place. And it was my generation who needed to take responsibility. We left the little farming communities in the dust, trading them for the busy, frantic lives of metropolitan living with its work and activities. We could look back longingly and yearn for homegrown black-eyed peas and send our grandchildren to Farm Camps where we paid for them to experience the chores, we would have given our lives to avoid, but we could never truly return.

The next morning, I checked out and headed to the airport. The interstate clover-leafed into a circle as I saw the airport exit in front of me. Suddenly and unexpectedly, I felt giddy with relief. The closing of the farm sale to Skeeter wasn't until after this year's crops were harvested, but I would not have to return. Stu assured me I could sign the paperwork digitally by using a notary public as witness. My work here was over!

I returned the rental car and checked in for my flight. While I waited for the plane that would return me to sanity and normalcy, I decided to call Susan. I wanted to tell her about the film reels I found and what I remembered about the wisdom of her preschoolers. She answered right away, sounding more defeated and weary than usual.

"So, you're leaving this morning?" she asked.

"Yes, I'm waiting for my flight right now."

She was quiet for a moment. "Well, have a safe flight. I guess I won't be seeing you anymore."

"What do you mean?" I asked.

"Well, you won't be coming back here. You don't like it here and there's really no reason for you to come back now that you've sold most of the farm, and Mother, Daddy, and Mack are gone."

Even though it shouldn't have surprised me, I was stunned by her answer. "No," I replied. "I mean, I will be coming back. You are still my sister, and this is where I grew up. I will come back, just not as often as in the past few years."

"There won't be room here for you, you know. I just don't have room for you to stay here."

I swallowed hard, then said, "I know. I know that. I will need to stay someplace else. But I will do that. You are still my family…"

She didn't reply, so I continued, "Look, one reason I called was because I remembered something I wanted to share with you."

"What's that?" she asked.

"Remember when you had the preschool? I remember you telling me about these two little girls who each wanted her own way. Is that ringing a bell?"

"No. How do you expect me to remember what happened in my preschool class 40 years ago?"

"Well, wait until I tell you about it. It just popped into my mind yesterday, out of the blue. Anyway, these two little girls were trying to figure out which one of them was the Queen Bee of the preschool. One of them finally turned to the other and said, 'I'll tell you what. Why don't you be you, and I'll be me?'"

My sister was quiet on the other end of the line. "So, why are telling me this?"

"Don't you see?" I said. "We are like those little girls. I want you to be like me, and you want me to be like you."

"But I always thought before that we were alike."

"Yeah. Me too. But we were wrong. And that isn't the worst thing in the world."

I heard Susan sigh, and after a long silence, she said, "It makes me sad. I mean, it makes me sad that we aren't alike anymore."

"Yeah, but this means that we can get to know a whole new person who is nothing but herself, not pretending to be what she is not."

"Okay, now you're getting way too philosophical for me," there was just the slightest uplift in her voice. I thought she was ready to hang up, but then she said, "Sure, Sister, I get it." Then, "I thought you had to get on a plane?"

"Yeah. Yeah, I do. I just thought...well, I thought that nugget of preschool wisdom was worth remembering."

"Sounds like you're just making all that up."

Now it was my turn to be quiet. What could I say? Everything that ran through my mind sounded defensive. I wanted to leave on a more positive note, but it looked like that was not to be.

Then she said softly, "Call me when you're home safe, okay?"

"Yes. Yes, I will," I replied.

Her phone clicked off and I looked up to see passengers getting in line for boarding. Since I purchased an early-bird boarding pass, I was one of the first to settle into my seat. Before putting my phone into airplane mode, I checked email and messages. There was a voicemail message from a number I did not recognize, but it didn't take me long to recognize the voice of the caller:

"Well, you got off without telling me goodbye, didn't you? 'Course I don't blame you for wantin' to pull out of town, I guess. You know I'm not one bit happy with you, but Lyle and me decided what we'd do was set up a big ol' blockade out by the interstate and stop ya before you could make your getaway. We figured maybe the two of us together could talk some sense into you. Hang on to you a while. It's like with you gone, all those good memories of Mack and your daddy and Tutu are goin' along with you. Well, but then we got to

282

thinkin' that nothin' would make our sheriff, J.D. Hawkins, happier than to throw two old reprobates like me and Lyle in the hoosegow and we didn't want to give him the satisfaction, but what I called to say is that Susan, that sister of yours, has more gumption and grit than she knows, and she'll be just fine, so don't worry your head about it. Besides that, me and Lyle and bunch of other folks are here for her and all those kids. You gotta go on and be yourself and do whatever it is you do up there in all that cold country, so that's all I called to say."

I took a deep breath for Carla as the phone went dead. I sat looking at it a minute. One thing was for sure, if Susan had a friend like Carla, it was a good as a whole community beside her. I heaved a sigh of relief, pulled on my seatbelt, and put my head back, smiling to myself. I was going home to find a place for my mother's 'Strings Too Short to Tie.' Carla was right, the tales and memories should be preserved. Somehow, I needed to find a way to tell the stories and preserve the relationships. As difficult as it might be, I needed to find a way to tie all the loose ends together into something both strong and stretchy – something that kept us all connected but allowed each the freedom to grow in our own unique and crazy way.

The plane taxied down the tarmac, roaring as it accelerated.

Then, with a lift of the wings, I was airborne into the blue Panhandle sky.

The End

CPSIA information can be obtained
at www.ICGtesting.com
Printed in the USA
LVHW080508230821
695875LV00003B/37

9 781649 791023